Supermarket Shoppology

The science of supermarket shopping

And a strategy to spend less and get more

©Phillip Adcock 2011

SUPERMARKET SHOPPOLOGY

by

Copyright © 2011 by Phillip Adcock

ISBN: 978-0-9569564-0-8

Published by Shopping Behaviour Xplained Limited in conjunction with Writersworld Limited

Copy edited by Ian Large

Cover design by Charles Leveroni

Printed and bound by www.printondemand-worldwide.com

www.writersworld.co.uk

WRITERSWORLD
2 Bear Close
Woodstock
Oxfordshire
OX20 1JX
England

The text pages of this book are produced via an independent certification process that ensures the trees from which the paper is produced come from well managed sources that exclude the risk of using illegally logged timber while leaving options to use post-consumer recycled paper as well.

Acknowledgements

As I began to think about all the people whom I should thank for their input and support to make this book possible, the list just grew and grew. So, first I would like to thank my wife, Kay, and daughter, Amy, for continuing to inspire me to work on this project day and night, month after month.

Next, I would like to thank my auntie Sylvia Jones, who many years ago gave me one of those 'get anything you want' self-help books. This book introduced me to the subject of the human brain, for which I remain deeply indebted.

I would also like to thank the great and the good in academia for their continual advancements in the understanding of how human beings operate, in particular, Robert Plutchik, Steven Pinker and Antonio Damasio. I am also grateful that their work is so accessible.

Special thanks must go to the team at Shopping Behaviour Xplained Ltd who continually push the boundaries of human understanding by converting shopper research insights into tactics and strategies that drive sales and increase customer satisfaction.

It would be remiss of me not to mention the gratitude I owe to Paul Maplesden of Freelance Editing Services Ltd. His editing and approach helped me make this book insightful, entertaining and enjoyably readable.

The illustrations were provided by freelance 3D artist, Mr Dave Davidson, for which I must say a personal thank you.

Finally, to all those science teachers who make this fascinating subject so boring and irrelevant to teenagers: Change. Change the way you teach, spice it up. There is nothing more exciting and inspiring than understanding how we as a species developed, how we function and why we are what we are.

Table of Contents

Introduction 9

Some interesting facts about shopping 10

How this book works 12

Section 1 How the brain, mind and body shop 17

An overview 18

An introduction to the brain 22

Evolution 28

Instinct 35

How the brain works 38

Short and long term memory 46

Single scripted behaviour and chunking 56

What is emotion? 61

What emotions do 73

Primary and social emotions 77

Emotions through cognition to feeling 81

Advancing Maslow's hierarchy of needs 87

The central six fitness indicators 92

Priming 105

Human physiology 108

Autonomic responses 112

The five senses – How the eyes work 115

The five senses – Looking or seeing 120

The five senses – Smell, hearing, touch and taste 123

Men and women 128

How the brain, mind and body shop, a summary 131

Section 2 How shoppers are targeted 137

Introduction 138

What is a supermarket? 140

What is a brand? 144

First impressions inside the supermarket 148

The psychology of crowds 151

Category management 155

Packaging unwrapped 159

Price – Fact, fiction, reality and perception 165

Value 171

Why we don't all shop at Aldi, Netto or Lidl? 174

In-store communications 177

Adjacencies 182

Targeting the shopper, conclusion and summary 185

Section 3 How to become a smarter shopper 189

Introduction 190

The five modes of shopping 190

Inexperienced shopping 192

Experiential shopping 196

Considered shopping 200

Grab & go shopping 205

Impulse shopping 209

Understanding your own mode of shopping 212

Creating a strategy to shop more effectively 213

Technique One – Focussing on Outcomes and Benefits 214

Technique Two – Leverage and Anchoring 217

Prepare yourself properly for shopping 227

Understand that you will be swayed 231

Be aware of your surroundings in the supermarket 240

Create more reasoned motives for your shopping behaviour 247

Make conscious decisions about the way that you shop 252

Add structure to your shopping experience (shopping lists etc.) 257

Shop differently to change your perspective 260

Review purchasing to make better decisions in future 262

Final thoughts 269

Glossary 273

Selected reading list 279

About the author 284

Introduction

Everybody shops. It is estimated that the average adult in the developed world spends more than 200 days of his or her life shopping for food – a considerable amount of time.

In this book, you'll learn not just how and why you shop, but also what causes you to buy what you do and behave as you do when you walk into a supermarket. If you're a retailer, you'll learn new insights into the minds of shoppers and what attracts people to specific shops, aisles, brands and individual products.

For retailers and shoppers, this book will illustrate how purchasing decisions are made, what lies behind the needs for different products and how to become a smarter shopper or retailer. If you follow and apply the practical steps in this book, you'll be able to recognise your own approach to shopping and become a more efficient and practical shopper.

In addition to providing a thorough explanation of the science of shopping, this book also offers many insights into how people function as part of the human race, and how the evolution of our society and culture affects the way we behave. You can apply this knowledge in many areas of society and interactions, with other people and even inanimate objects. I'll explain the basis on which we make many of our life choices, and how the brain and mind could be either a help or a hindrance.

Overall, this book demonstrates how we can all be more masterful of our actions, through showing how we make decisions to act in a particular way. Although the book refers to shoppers, shopping and related activity, you are invited to consider the information in a much broader context as many of the topics refer not only to shopping, but also to most of modern day society.

Some interesting facts about shopping

There's been a great deal of research to understand and identify how we shop, and I've included a few of the more interesting facts below to help illustrate just why shopping is so important, both to our society and to us.

Have you ever stopped to think how integral the subject of shopping is throughout the modern world? Every year, approaching 500 billion dollars (ZenithOptimedia) are spent on advertising and promotions, aimed at encouraging us to consume certain brands. As part of this investment, the big retailers and brands spend millions of dollars every year researching every aspect of consumer behaviours and backgrounds including lifestyles, attitudes, demographics, and opinions.

But before we can interact/consume almost any brand (whether we eat, use, drive or do something else with it), it has to be bought, and this leads to the first important point in the context of modern day consumerism: For a consumer society to exist as it does today, a shopping activity precedes the use of almost any new product. In other words, consumer society is based on the activity of shopping. It follows that shopping is as, if not more, important than consumption/interaction, simply because the latter cannot happen without the former. Of course, it is very possible for shopping not to lead to consuming; we've all bought clothes with good intentions and never worn them, or purchased food that stays in the cupboard until long after the sell by date.

Here's a sobering thought: If we assume that our largest single purchase is a house, with an average price of £200,000 and a typical monthly mortgage payment of between £1,000 and £1,500, then for most of us, the second largest expenditure isn't the car, savings, holidays, investments, school fees or insurances, but supermarket shopping.

According to Verdict Research, on average, each family spends some £500 every month on groceries, around £150,000 over a 25 year period! That's enough for a second small house, a £7,500 per year pension or a top of the range sports car.

According to a 2006 survey of 3,000 women by GE Money, the average woman makes around 300 shopping trips a year, taking a total of around 400 hours. That's around 25,000 hours over a period of 63 years, or eight years in total, keeping their families fed and clothed and indulging in a little retail therapy.

Further information from the survey showed that food shopping alone can take more than an hour to complete each time; the average of 84 food shopping trips a year takes around 95 hours in the supermarket, equal to 12 working days. Over 90 trips are spent shopping for clothes, shoes, accessories and toiletries, taking around 170 hours in total.

Even shopping for more mundane items like toiletries takes around 17 hours over one year and 36 hours a year is spent buying gifts for friends and family. That's just the time people spend inside shops, with another 50 hours 'window shopping' and investigating the next purchase.

Stewart Macphail, of GE Money, said: 'Women clearly dedicate a lot of time to making sure they find the best deals and the most suitable items for their needs.' That's a common perception, and a theme that runs through this book is that perception and reality are very different things when it comes to supermarket shopping.

Shopping isn't just related to products that we can pick up and use though, and there's been an increased focus on intangible services and finances, with advice being offered from every perceivable corner of the library, High Street, bank, building society and, of course, supermarket.

Despite all of this, there isn't a great deal of practical and accessible advice available to us as shoppers. We'll address that issue by providing a plain English explanation of how our shopping brains, minds and bodies operate and the tricks and tools retailers use to influence how we shop and what we buy. We'll also explore what is known about how shoppers behave and function in-store and what the store does to influence us.

As a result, you'll be armed with the tools you need to be able to shop smarter and make sure you get value for money, whenever and wherever you shop.

How this book works

We'll begin by detailing, in everyday language, how evolution has helped to shape all of our shopper decision-making processes. For example, we human beings used to walk on all fours. Then some 6,000,000 years ago, having eaten all the good food in the trees, our ancestors came down from the trees. Upon landing on terra firma, it became apparent that the pampas grass on the plains was taller than we were making it impossible to see any threats or lunch opportunities. The result of this evolutionary challenge was that man decided to stand up on his hind legs. We could now see any oncoming threats, but we now had the challenge of balancing on two legs instead of four. Moreover, our eyes were so much further from things we may inadvertently tread upon. To address this issue, early man tended to walk looking down to avoid tripping over or stepping on the wrong things. Originally, this evolutionary compromise served a specific purpose, but even today we still respond more to things that are below eye level than we do to anything above. In the retail environment, messages on the supermarket floor have proved to be significantly more influential compared with any messages hanging from the ceiling. But, although overhead signs rarely influence us by way of any direct messaging, they do act as triggers to emotions through our peripheral vision.

A colleague of mine relates a good analogy of this sharp awareness of what is below us. He tells the tale of rabbits, who tend to hop along knowing that most of the dangers to them tend to come from above, such as birds of prey. As rabbits have evolved to look skywards, it follows that in the supermarket, they would respond well to hanging signs that promote special offers for carrots, lettuce and the like. Conversely, humans are evolutionarily hard wired to expect most dangers to come from below; for example tripping over rabbits, which leads to us to be significantly more likely to notice messages placed lower down on store shelves and even on the floor.

After illustrating how we function in terms of mental processing and physical behaviour, the book will detail how brands and retailers directly and indirectly influence our shopping behaviour and how they strive to optimise our propensity to purchase. A good example of 'creative' merchandising (by the way, retail merchandising is often referred to by professionals as 'manipulation with integrity') can be seen in most modern supermarkets. In the entrance area of the supermarket will be a larger than life stack of a product complete with impactful graphics (usually in red and white or red and yellow). These reception deals serve a number of purposes. First, they indicate to arriving shoppers that this store offers special deals and added value, and that the product on promotion must be exceptional value because of the size of the display and the promotional signage. This is a good example of perception being more persuasive than reality; it may be simply that the store has a surplus of that product.

Here's a specific example of perception outweighing reality in the minds of some shoppers. Recently, an independent greengrocer in the Midlands town of Rugeley in the UK had a special offer for fresh pears. The offer was 500 grams of pears for just £1. Right next door was a much larger branch of a leading supermarket chain. At the entrance to their fruit and vegetable section was a large display of fresh pears. The promotional fixture was adorned with a metre-high message that shouted 'fresh pears only 50p each'. Guess what? The supermarket sold far more pears than the smaller greengrocer. Lesson one from this book? When it comes to supermarket shopping, we tend to leave reality at home and let perception guide our decision making.

The final section of the book arms you with a strategy for much more cost effective and objective supermarket shopping. Many of the techniques and principles are just as effective whether in a Walmart store in the USA or a neighbourhood outlet in a market town in central England. For example, consider the use of lighting in supermarket clothing departments. The mannequins are exquisitely lit to show the clothes at their best. Powerful white bulbs highlight the colours, cut and detail of the garments in what is, visually, a very artificial situation. How many shoppers will be wearing the items in this type of lighting where whites look whiter and colours look more colourful? Combined with being modelled on a stick thin mannequin, they become irresistible. To help combat this, when trying on clothes in the store, try to stand in an area where there is as much natural light as possible to determine how the clothes really look on you.

You may well ask why retailers and brands go to such lengths to sell their wares. The answer largely lies in the structure of many retail businesses. Today's world of retail commerce is hamstrung by shareholders who demand better results (more profit) every trading period. This filters down to the retail and brand head offices that reward staff for their sales and profitability. As a result, there is a 'working towards the next bonus' culture. Martin Hayward wrote a great book entitled *Customers Are For Life, Not Just Your Next Bonus*, in which he writes: 'There is a creeping malaise in today's marketing world; a sickness that is spreading not just through business but across many areas in life – Politics, education, health, broadcasting... the list goes on. The condition is short-termism in all its expedient, lazy, self-serving and inefficient manifestations.' Unfortunately, at the time of writing this book, Martin's words are for the most part still being ignored.

Short-termism manifests itself in the ways larger retailers are structured and in the ways people shop. Deals such as 'buy now pay later' and '24 months interest free credit' offer us the opportunity to satisfy our short term wants and needs, with little or no consideration for any long term affordability or consequences.

One of the core strategies presented in this book involves helping you become less emotional and more objective as you travel along any particular 'path to purchase'. To become such a rational and sense-based shopping machine, you should first understand what drives your own decision-making processes in-store. Why do we make so many impulsive and irrational purchases that we often later regret? This will be covered in detail in Section One of the book, 'How the brain, mind and body shop'. It is a subject that surprisingly little has been written about and it is argued that shoppers and shopping are generally ignored by academia. There are university courses on clinical psychology, motivational psychology and neuroscience, but nothing on evolutionary shopper psychology or even evolutionary consumer psychology. Herein lies another fundamental problem: Most retailers and brands don't fully recognise the difference between shoppers and consumers.

So, the dictionary definition of a consumer is one who consumes goods or services, but often, consuming gets mistaken for purchasing. Who is the consumer of tinned dog food? It's the dog, not the purchaser. The shopper can indeed be the consumer, for example when buying a cup of coffee to drink on the way to work. But importantly, the definition of a shopper is one who visits stores in search of merchandise or bargains. A shopper can be a user (the coffee), chooser (Mummy, I want Coco Pops, please) or a payer (buying the bread for the family's sandwiches). A shopper can also be any combination of user, chooser and payer, even a combination of all three. Consumer research has been an established business aid for a number of decades with an entire research industry sector built on understanding consumers. Unfortunately, shoppers have only been recognised much more recently and subsequently there are only a handful of specialist agencies with the relevant expertise to deliver genuine shopper insight.

As this book will illustrate, because of the way our human brains shop, a number of the most established means of understanding them are based on consumer research tools. The result is that more often than not, key business strategies are based on what is thought to be shopper insight, but is in fact consumer post-rationalisation. Only when we fully understand what drives shoppers to shop the way they do and how the brain and mind make purchase decisions, can shopping behaviour really be explained properly.

Throughout the next chapters, you are invited on a journey through your own brain, mind and body. You'll be made aware of how you function, be alerted to some considerable flaws in mankind and be given the tools to empower you to shop more wisely. Some of the topics covered may surprise you, while others may well leave you feeling saddened and even depressed. Whatever the case, this book is aimed at consumers, shoppers, retailers, brand owners and students of retail. If you are involved with shopping, then I implore you to read on.

Section 1

How the brain, mind and body shop

An overview

From the stall in a Spanish market to the British High Street teeming with specialty shops, there are thousands of different types of store all over the world. Despite this, in the Western world, most shopping takes place in the supermarket, with their market share growing year after year. Many countries have large malls on the outskirts of towns and in the United States, many stores and shopping estates are designed as drive-to outlets.

Even with the development of the Internet, most consumer goods are still purchased from bricks-and-mortar stores, all of which have one thing in common: they offer the public in the developed world (which for brevity I will now refer to as shoppers) goods in return for money or credit.

Most of us shop, for clothes, food, luxuries, gifts and everything in between. For some, shopping is an enjoyable pastime, for a minority it's a compulsion and for still others shopping is just a chore. On the whole, we shop to meet our needs, which include: survival, socialising, self-expression, sex appeal, prestige and status. To meet these needs, and for a host of other reasons, almost all of us go to large buildings and hand over money. Behind these apparently innocuous motives are a number of deeper, meaningful root causes that drive our need to acquire new things, and it is these that we'll explore in this section.

If you've ever wondered how you ended up spending so much in the supermarket or what on earth drove you to buy that terrible beige cardigan from the clothing department, then you'll find the coming pages interesting and perhaps even enlightening. You'll find examples of why retailers lay out stores in the ways they do and what causes some brands to be so much more popular than others. Despite this, some questions will remain unanswered, such as why men can't help juggling a single lettuce before putting into the supermarket shopping trolley!

Before any meaningful discussion about shoppers and shopping can take place, we have to take a step back and to look at what we as shoppers are: Primarily, we are people, human beings, exhibiting behaviours that have evolved and developed over tens of thousands of years. There is a vast wealth of available knowledge on the subject of general human behaviour and recently there have been dramatic advancements in the understanding of people, particularly in terms of the inner workings of the brain and mind.

Although we understand much more about the functioning of the brain and mind now than we did a few decades ago, there is still much to learn. Technologies such as functional magnetic resonance imaging (fMRI) are teaching us a great deal, faster than ever before. Researchers are also using electroencephalography (EEG) to measure activity in specific areas of the brain to uncover which sections or groups of sections become active when reacting to different forms of stimuli. This can be applied to learn why we make the decisions we do, and what part or parts of our brains are telling us to do it.

Here's a thought-provoking example that demonstrates the greater level of understanding fMRI is helping to deliver. In a 2009 research study, Professor John-Dylan Haynes of the Bernstein Centre for Computational Neuroscience hooked people up to a scanner and then gave them a seemingly simple task. They were given a button to hold in each hand, and all they had to do was decide which button to press on a random basis. Their choice was simply the button in the left hand or the button in the right hand.

The results of this and similar studies are very interesting. After just a few goes pressing the button, the professor was able to predict accurately which button each participant would press next, simply by watching the output of their brain activity. In fact, he was able to foretell their choice as early as a full six seconds before the research participants had consciously decided which button to press. That means that the human brain has come to a decision several seconds before we are aware of having consciously made said choice.

In other words, some of our choices are clearly outside our conscious control, and, like other animals, we act instinctively (although we will often concoct a reason that we've behaved in a particular way).

fMRI, EEG and other relatively new technologies and research are at the foundation of what's termed neuro-marketing. This is a new field of marketing that studies consumers' sensorimotor, cognitive and affective responses to marketing stimuli, something that viewers of the film *Minority Report* might recognise.

A vast amount of very well-funded research into human brain and psychological activity is currently taking place and it's no coincidence that both science and commercial interests believe this investment will deliver profitable returns. Universities around the world are home to some of the foremost experts in the fields of psychology including neuroscience, biological psychology, clinical psychology and emotions, with constant breakthroughs and insights into how people function mentally. However, these academics tend to operate in highly intellectual silos, which means that a neuroscience professor from Harvard has little or no reason to have meaningful dialogue with a motivational sports psychologist from Cambridge.

Fortunately, the professors in academia do have something in common that most commercial researchers find very useful: They all tend to publish academic papers and write books that detail their findings to anyone willing to invest the time needed to read them.

What can be lacking in the arena of psychology is an area I term commercial psychology, a discipline involved with understanding the human brain and mind and how it reacts in commercial situations and environments.

Much of the content of this first section of the book is an easy to understand summary of some of the key research that can be found hidden in the pages of more than two thousand such publications that I've identified, validated, summarised, and described in plain English wherever possible. This research helps us to understand why we think as we do and explores the inescapable fact that our human brains are hard wired in particular ways as a result of millions of years of evolution.

I'll then provide a more detailed explanation of the workings of the brain and explore the short term and long term memory; your short term memory is that part of the mind that is responsible for habitual repeat purchases, often made using what are known as 'single scripted behaviours' (described later). Our long term memories are responsible for the purchases that are driven more by life choices and *emotion*, the most powerful decision determinant in the human brain. Quite simply, every decision, each and every one of us makes every single day of our lives is influenced to some extent by emotion. We'll explore the subject of emotion in considerable detail because it is fundamental to so much of our shopping and shopping behaviour.

We'll then discuss why we prioritise some purchases over others and introduce the concept of Maslow's hierarchy of needs. We'll examine a more refined version of what we as humans and shoppers need most, from physiological, psychological and evolutionary perspectives. You'll be introduced to an alternative set of needs based on what Geoffrey Miller, in his book *Must-Have*, refers to as 'The Central Six', a list of six personality aspects.

The role of the human body is also very important in shopping, including how we react autonomically, that is with no conscious involvement or control; examples of autonomic behaviour include sweating or getting goose bumps. In addition, each of the five senses will be covered from a shopper's and shopping perspective.

Finally in this section, no book on the subject of shoppers and shopping would be complete without exploring the differences in the ways men and women shop. You'll understand how women often seem to have eyes in the backs of their heads and why it is that men can stare into a supermarket chiller and be unable to see much of what is right in front of their noses!

An introduction to the brain

At the centre of almost all of our shopping activity is our brain. We need to know what it is, how it functions and find out what we really know about its core strengths and weaknesses. For the purposes of this book, when I talk about the human brain, I am referring to active and healthy brains although much of what has been learnt about human psychology and neuroscience comes from the studies of dysfunctional brains.

To begin with, based on evolution theory, the human brain has been evolving for hundreds of millions of years. The consensus of opinion estimates that the first vertebrates appeared on Earth some 600,000,000 years ago. Around 300,000,000 years later, reptiles evolved and crawled out of the swamps. Then, 100,000,000 years later, the first warm blooded mammals appeared. Humans, as we would understand them, have only been around for 100,000 years. For the record, money was only developed 65,000 years ago and the shopping cart or trolley is a very modern invention, being less than 100 years old.

For 98% of the time we have been evolving, we've only been concerned with fight or flight, eat or be eaten and opportunities to procreate and reproduce. According to Gary Marcus in his highly entertaining book *Kluge*, the ancestral brain system has been evolving for hundreds of millions of years, but cognitive reasoning is a very modern invention, having evolved as recently as 1,500,000 years ago.

The brain is the most complex and remarkable organ in nature and despite every species of mammal, bird, reptile, fish or amphibian having a brain, the human one is unique. In addition to controlling our autonomous nervous system (such as body temperature, blood pressure, heart rate and breathing), it accepts and processes a flood of information from the various senses, handles physical motion when walking, standing or sitting and gives us the ability and power to think, dream, reason, communicate and experience emotions.

So, what is the physical make up of your incredible human brain? The weight of a new born baby's brain is around 300 to 400 grams and it will grow to weigh around 1,300 to 1,400 grams by the time a person reaches adulthood. Our brains are made up of around 78% water, 11% lipids (naturally occurring molecules, which include fats, waxes, sterols and vitamins) plus some other stuff. Comparatively, our brain is slightly larger than that of a walrus and smaller than that found in the bottle-nosed dolphin.

Between 15 and 20% of blood pumped from the heart heads straight to the brain to supply it with the energy it needs. Our brains account for only 2% of our total body weight, but consume 20% of all the energy each of us burns up. Our brains consist of around 100 billion neurons, which are the basic information processing structures in the brain. They are connected to each other by synapses through which information flows from one neuron to another. Information passes between neurons by way of tiny chemical reactions in each cell that then send an impulse (electrical or chemical) along the synapse to the next neuron. The process of a neuron sending an impulse out is referred to as firing. So in summary, the human brain functions by way of neurons sending signals to other neurons (millions and millions of them) using synapses as connectors.

A route along lots of neurons is what is called a 'neural pathway' that connects one part of the brain to another. It is commonly believed that the more often a person uses the same neural pathway (carries out the same task for example), then the stronger and more embedded that behaviour becomes. This might explain why it is hard to break habits such as nail biting and even how that behaviour became a habit in the first place.

While there are as many as 10,000 specific *types* of neurons in the human brain, generally speaking, there are just three different *kinds*: motor neurons (that convey motor information), sensory neurons (that convey sensory information) and inter-neurons (these act as middlemen between other neurons, receiving information from the body's outside or inside environment and passing it along to the brain for further processing).

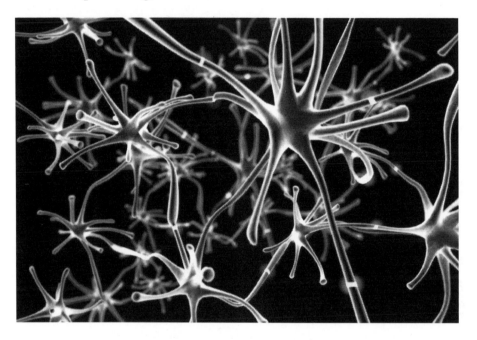

Figure 1 - Neurons in the brain

There's a particular type of neuron that's only recently been discovered known as a 'mirror neuron'. A mirror neuron is one that fires (sends or receives impulses) both when an animal or person acts and when that being observes the same action being performed by another. Thus, the neuron 'mirrors' the behaviour of the other, as though the observer were itself acting. In other words, we learn and hardwire our brains partly by copying the actions of others, and by doing so develop and embed neural pathways. This same action can often be the cause of such bad habits as nail biting and hair chewing. So in the case of nail biting, for example, it can become a habit as a result of seeing others do it and then copying them. Over time it becomes hard wired by creating its own established neural pathway and the longer it continues to be a habit, the more established and harder it is to break. However, it is possible to break habits and once you know the theory, the practice becomes somewhat easier.

If you want to break a habit, it is necessary to 'rewire' or break an established and embedded neural pathway, by wiring in a new set of activities. A good analogy is that of a vinyl record. Imagine the needle or stylus repeatedly staying in the same continuous groove and playing the music in the same order time after time – that's the habit. Now if a large scratch is made across the surface of the record, the stylus will jump out of its groove and play some parts of the tune in a different order – that's the habit broken.

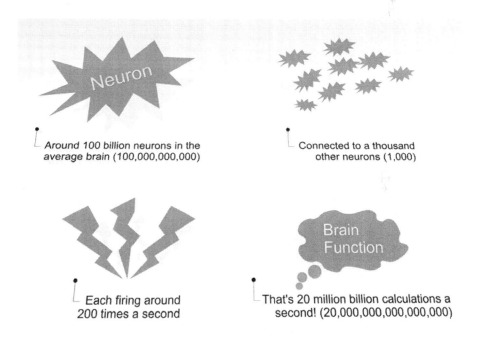

Around 100 billion neurons in the average brain (100,000,000,000)

Connected to a thousand other neurons (1,000)

Each firing around 200 times a second

That's 20 million billion calculations a second! (20,000,000,000,000,000)

Figure 2 - Neuron and brain processing speeds

In terms of how our brains operate, they are capable of carrying out incredible numbers of calculations in a remarkably short time. For example, a neuron can fire about once every 5 milliseconds, or about 200 times a second. The number of cells each neuron is connected to also varies, but as a rough estimate it is reasonable to say that each neuron is connected to 1,000 other neurons; so every time a neuron fires, about 1,000 other neurons get information about that firing. If this is then multiplied out, the result is 100 billion neurons X 200 firings per second X 1,000 connections per firing = 20 million billion calculations per second. That's fast! To put it into context, a typical 2GHz computer processor can handle a mere 2 billion calculations per second. However, as we'll discover, despite their amazing abilities, our brains still aren't all that well equipped to deal with 21st century shopping in the supermarket.

This remarkable organ between our ears is capable of almost unfathomable numbers of calculations in a single second; despite this, it isn't as wonderfully advanced as we'd like to believe. The oldest part of the brain, known as the brain stem, or reptilian brain, controls functions as critical to prehistoric animals as they are to humans. It's physically located at the bottom of the brain, regulates the central nervous system and is pivotal in maintaining consciousness and regulating the sleep cycle. It is an extremely important part of the brain because all information to and from our body passes through the brain stem on the way to or from our brain.

Above the brain stem are the parts of the brain that control the more refined processes such as eye movement, auditory reflexes and emotional responses: the midbrain and limbic system, also known as the mammalian brain. Finally, close to the surface of the brain are the components responsible for such things as decision making and language, collectively known as the cerebral cortex. In summary, our reptilian brains developed while we were still wallowing in the swamps, after we emerged onto dry land, we adapted and developed our mammalian brains, then finally and most recently (in evolutionary terms), we developed our 'higher' brains that gifted us with the powers of thought and reasoning.

Unfortunately our brains have been somewhat haphazardly cobbled together based on evolutionary needs, when ideally it would have been more advantageous to stop developing the old one and to start again and design something new. This constant adapting and developing of the original brain has led to other operational inefficiencies. For example, the right side of your brain controls muscles and receives sensory information from the left side of your body and vice versa. Similarly, within the eyes, light from the left strikes the right of the retina so any image people 'see' is actually reversed and the brain has to turn it round the right way again. With so much crossing over of stimuli and information, it's no wonder we struggle to shop efficiently in the modern supermarket. In fact it's quite astonishing that we can even walk and talk without getting all tangled up.

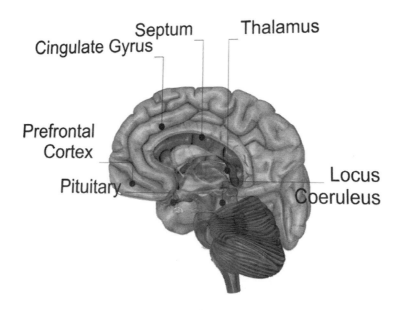

Figure 3 – The human brain

So what *has* evolution done for us as shoppers? Stimuli entering our brain via four of our five senses (sight, taste, touch and hearing) are filtered as they pass through a part of the brain known as the amygdala. This part of the brain is the first port of call for incoming stimuli, a type of passport control. The amygdala then sends impulses further into the brain to stimulate the sympathetic nervous system to enhance our reflexes. In other words, even before a person jumps with fright, the brain has begun processing the situation.

As previously stated, stimuli from only four of the senses goes through the amygdala. The unique sense is that of smell, which the brain processes without its assistance; this means that we process scents, smells and aromas at face value. One hypothesis as to why this is the case is linked to the somewhat haphazard way in which the brain evolved. Essentially, we tended to develop the senses most beneficial to our survival. Because we aren't able to cope with all five senses being advanced and providing continuous stimuli, something had to give and in the case of humans, smell was the least vital. You'll find more detailed information about each of the five senses later in the book.

This introduction to the brain has provided a basic working knowledge of how it's made up and a high level view of how it functions. Next, we'll look at a number of aspects of the human brain in more detail; to begin with, we'll explore evolution and how it is responsible for much of what we are and how we act.

Evolution

Evolution is at the foundation of why we shoppers behave as we do, so it's useful to understand exactly what we mean when we talk about evolution. In terms of a dictionary definition, it is the change or mutation of inherited traits of a population of organisms (animals or plant life) through successive generations. When a population splits into smaller groups, these groups evolve independently and develop into new species.

The website *All About Science* describes evolution very well by saying: 'Evolution is a gradual process in which something changes into a different and usually more complex or better form. Evolution is the process by which an organism becomes more sophisticated over time and in response to its environment.' Evolution as a biological mechanism is driven by natural selection and is the theory most favoured by scientists to explain phenomena in nature, so much so that it is generally assumed nowadays (and certainly for the purpose of this book) as fact.

The leading proponent of evolutionary theory was Charles Darwin, a 19th century English naturalist and author of *On the Origin of Species*. Darwin's Theory of Evolution states that all life is related and has descended from a common ancestor through a purely naturalistic, undirected 'descent with modification'. That is to say, complex creatures evolved from more simplistic ancestors naturally, over time.

In summary, as random genetic mutations occur within an organism's genetic code, the beneficial mutations are preserved because they aid survival. This beneficial mutation process is known as 'natural selection', or survival of the fittest, and these beneficial mutations are passed on to the next generation. Over time, the beneficial mutations accumulate and the result is an entirely different organism – not just a variation of the original, but an entirely different creature.

Evolution is how man advanced from ape, and it's fascinating to consider how we'll advance to be better equipped to shop in supermarkets many thousands of years in the future.

Darwin and many evolutionary scientists since concur that animals evolve the senses that most ensure their survival as a species. Dogs, for example, have highly acute senses of smell. Birds of prey have evolved with terrific eyesight. Other animals have developed very keen senses of hearing so they can escape approaching threats. Unusually, human beings haven't developed any particular sense over and above the others. It would appear that our sense of smell is the least beneficial to our survival and so has been metaphorically side-lined by the amygdala.

The aspects that drive changes and mutations in human evolution are predominately environmental fluctuations and population growth. As the number of people on Earth increases, so do the number of mutations generated by random chance. Our genetic inheritance is also affected by the diverse terrains, climates and social structures that we've inhabited since the last ice age.

Another important evolutionary aspect is that humans have evolved differently from other animals because of our ability to use cognition to evaluate situations. We are able to choose between alternative responses to situations, much more so than other members of the animal kingdom. However, whether we actively choose or simply rationalise and justify our own instinctive reaction is still open to debate and is being investigated partly through the work of Professor John-Dylan Haynes at the Bernstein Centre for Computational Neuroscience, as described earlier.

With apologies to evolutionary purists, I'd like to offer a very brief summary and hypothesis of human evolution and provide a context for how this affects us as shoppers. It begins with the Catarrhini (narrow nosed, tree primates who are probably our ancestors) some 30,000,000 years ago. More recently, some 6,000,000 years ago, our ancestors descended from the trees onto the savannahs of Africa.

Unfortunately, upon doing so it must have become apparent that the view wasn't anywhere near as good or advantageous. At this time, it is believed that our ancestors were still quadrupedal (literally meaning four feet) and moved about on all fours. Being this close to the ground, our ancestors were no longer able to look down on their surroundings or look over the tall pampas grass all around them. Over time, they evolved to stand up on their hind legs and were then able to see over the grasses. Now, they were able to see any threats approaching and spot potential meals. Because of these benefits, standing on hind legs quickly became an evolutionary advantage and man discovered that he could also see potential mates standing head and shoulders above the grass. In fact, standing on hind legs was so effective it was universally adopted and became a permanent evolutionary development in humankind.

There was however, and remains to this day, a small issue with balance. Unlike all other primates, we humans ordinarily walk upright. This posture makes particular demands on the vestibular apparatus, components located in the ears that, together with the brain, are responsible for maintaining balance. As humans, we balance a large body mass on very small areas of support and although we walk upright, our balance systems were originally designed for walking on all fours.

The balance-related stabilising organs in our brains (known as utricles or statoliths) were evolutionarily designed to balance us when we are on all fours, not moving about on just two feet, and our upright head position is actually tilted 30 degrees back from where these balance organs are most effective. Therefore, when you are walking amongst such underfoot distractions as floor graphics on a supermarket floor or any uneven surface, you'll often find yourself tipping your head 30 degrees forwards to get your statoliths into their most effective position; this is one of the reasons why we're more aware of things below our eye lines as we walk up and down the aisles of the supermarket.

Enough about walking, what about talking? This key evolutionary development happened much more recently. Our ancestors first learnt how to talk using a form of human speech in the Upper Palaeolithic period, about 50,000 years ago. In other words, speech has only been part of human communication for a fraction of our evolutionary development. As such, our brains aren't naturally wired to think in words, sentences, tonality and the like. We still imagine things as visual representations and when we see or hear a word or words, our brains need to convert them into a meaningful mental image. So, from an evolutionary point of view, shoppers are yet to evolve a natural ability to work with this new-fangled communication contraption known as language (spoken or written). This then supports the famous saying that a picture speaks a thousand words.

Even more recent was the creation of numbers, which were also first used by Palaeolithic peoples around 30,000 BCE (Before the Common Era). In terms of currency, R Buckminster Fuller writes in *Critical Path* that the Phoenicians graduated to money as an alternative to the labour intensive process of taking cattle along for trading around 1,500 BCE. The Phoenician money was formed into iron half-rings that looked like a pair of bull's horns. Whatever the precise timeline, money is a comparatively modern invention when viewed along an evolutionary timescale; in many ways it's much too modern for the brain to have evolved genuine, effective management strategies.

Evidence suggests that visual images have been processed by human brains and their evolutionary predecessors for around 10,000 times as long as language and words have been around. Is it any wonder then that so many advertising messages rely on graphic images to get their full message across? But why is it that, in light of this evolutionary limitation, so much in-store communication relies on words to communicate? Could it be that humankind needs to invent a pictorial illustration of BOGOF (buy one get one free)?

I expectantly wait for the marketers to create a picture of a sale, which will presumably be red and white on colour. You may wonder why red and white are used so predominantly in marketing and signage. The reason is that they are the two colours that most strongly contrast with each other and which we are evolutionarily predisposed to notice. When you are faced with a visually jarring message that is the same colour as fire, blood or the womb (all three of which are quite meaningful if trying to avoid extinction) displayed on a strongly contrasting background, you are very likely to look actively at the potential threat, meal or mate. This is a basic example of triggering a 'limbic system based reflex' by using the simple red and white special offer of sale signage seen the world over.

Before moving away from the subject of evolution, it's worth addressing the speed at which evolution takes place. Bruce J MacFadden, when working at the Department of Geology and Geophysics at Yale University, offers a scientific theorem that calculates the rate of evolution by working with horse teeth of all things. Suffice to say, human evolution happens very, very slowly. According to Stephen Jay Gould's assertion, civilization was built with essentially the same body and brain that Homo Sapiens has had for 40,000 years. However, recent research by anthropologist John Hawks of the University of Wisconsin, suggests that people today are genetically more different from people living 5,000 years ago than those predecessors were different from the Neanderthals who vanished 30,000 years before.

Many of the recent evolutionary genetic changes reflect differences in the human diet brought on by agriculture, as well as resistance to epidemic diseases that became mass killers following the growth of human civilizations. For example, some Africans have new genes providing resistance to malaria. In Europeans, there is a gene that makes them better able to digest milk as adults.

The changes have been driven by the colossal growth in the human population; from a few million to 6.5 billion in the past 10,000 years alone, with people moving into new environments, to which they needed to adapt, so says Henry Harpending, a University of Utah anthropologist. The latest findings suggest that human evolution is currently happening faster than scientists previously thought. John Hawks points out that most of the acceleration in evolution is over the last 10,000 years, which corresponds to population growth after agriculture was invented.

So, what does this have to do with shoppers and shopping? From an evolutionary perspective, we as shoppers haven't evolved at all as shops simply haven't been around for long enough. What this means is that as shoppers, we shop from an evolutionary standpoint stemming from a time before shops existed.

In other words, the human race has yet to become fully accustomed to the grocery store or any other retail outlet. The modern housewife behaves like an ancient, matriarchal gatherer when ambling down the aisles, collecting seeds, vegetables and berries for her family group, and the male behaves as an ancient mammoth hunter, darting around the shop purposefully, his mission clear and his goals precise. You might think, with modern intelligence that these 21st century tribal beings would be well equipped for the weekly shop, but alas, in reality, we still rely predominately on the results of hard wired evolution. Based on the science, the most effective way to get our attention is to cause us to evaluate a stimulus or situation from a fight, flight or fornicate perspective.

Retailers and brands are well aware of the primitive desires driving us shoppers and have themselves evolved and designed their produce to take advantage of these 'primitive' urges to grab our attention in-store. Once our attention has been grabbed, the brand or retailer then 'works with the moment' to manage our reflex reaction, influence our cognitive processes and take advantage of our resultant overall feeling at that time.

It is somewhat alarming that technological developments and retail advances are happening so much faster than humans can keep up with evolutionarily. How many times has the phrase 'that's obsolete' or 'they no longer make that model' been uttered to shoppers enquiring about their preferred product (particularly electrical, mobile phone or PC related)? This is, in my opinion, a fictitious argument, based on constantly advancing technological breakthroughs combined with marketers convincing us that these breakthroughs are the latest 'must haves'.

Although our bodies and brains have yet to evolve into being more efficient when it comes to shopping, is there any evidence that we've adapted in any way to life in the supermarket? To help answer that, the next sections explore how our brains function; in particular, what aspects of human brain functionality are relevant to the activity of supermarket shopping? How do we make decisions as shoppers, both from an evolutionary hunter–gatherer perspective and from the standpoint of being a 21st century inhabitant of planet Earth? In this next chapter we'll look at the most basic of our decision-making processes, something we share with most of the animal kingdom, instinct.

Instinct

At the most rudimentary level, an organism's survival depends on a collection of processes that maintains the integrity of cells and tissues throughout its structure, so says Antonio Damasio in his book, *Descartes' Error*. He explains that biological processes need a proper supply of oxygen and nutrients, fundamentally based on breathing and feeding. Some of the most basic biological regulatory mechanisms are conducted at a completely autonomic level; the individual in whom they operate is seldom consciously aware of them. For example, if you had to remember to breathe constantly, the chances are that you might not remember for very long!

At a marginally more complex level, there are those behaviours that let us know of their existence and impel us to perform in a particular way. These are called 'instincts' and once again, Antonio Damasio offers a good explanation of this type of instinctual process by way of example. He states that several hours after a meal, a person's blood sugar level drops and neurons within the hypothalamus (connected to many parts of the brain including the reptilian brain and the limbic system) detect the change. Activation of the correct circuitry causes the brain to alter the state of the body; in this case, the person feels hungry. As a consequence, he or she will take actions to satiate that hunger and the ingestion of food results in a correction of blood sugar levels. Finally, the hypothalamus detects another change in blood sugar, but this time an increase, and now the brain circuitry places the body in a state that results in a feeling of satiety or being full.

The aim of this entire instinctual process is to preserve life and health and these very same instincts are triggered in the aisles of the supermarket. We see people in supermarkets who are nervous, sweating, tired, confused, anxious and weak – all symptoms of hypoglycaemia (low blood sugar). A simple way to treat this condition is to eat, and when these people feel these symptoms in a supermarket, they have the instant remedy all around them. If we feel hungry, then instinctively we are driven to seek out and consume food. So doesn't it follow that if a retailer or brand can induce a state of hunger in us, as shoppers, then our instincts will force us to buy food? This is why so many authorities on shopping say that you should never go to the supermarket to do a big shop on an empty stomach.

An instinctive need for food doesn't just come from making shoppers feel hungry. Our brains are also equipped with a survival mode that will stock up on nutrients if we think that there may be a food shortage ahead. In the original hunter–gatherer days, humans were much less sure of when their next meal would come along. As a result, they would gorge themselves when food was plentiful and would be able to go for much longer between meals. In the 21st century supermarkets of the developed world, food shortages are almost unheard of. Despite this, the shoppers are still wired to feast before a probable famine that is very unlikely to occur.

In recent years, there have been isolated examples of food shortages such as of grains and sugar due to industrial action or problems in some part of the supply chain. As a direct result, what do most of us do when we hear of a shortage coming along? We stock up. To give another example, notice how much food we tend to buy in the days

just before Christmas, often far more than we and o[...]
possibly eat. We know that the supermarket will b[...]
Christmas Day and even Boxing Day too, which in[...]
us to stock up for the long (well, two day) period[...]
that is coming along.

This type of instinctive behaviour provides opportunities for retailers and brands to be able to communicate to us the possibility of limited availability, a typical example being a 'when it's gone it's gone' promotion (WIGIG). Our own research examined another technique of presenting shoppers with a messy and half empty bulk stack of product. When we researched different types of promotional displays, we found that these untidy and stock depleted sorts of promotions were shopped more and performed much better than pristine, fully stocked variants of the same special offer. It should be noted that this was only the case when researching instinctive responses to special offers. Similar research of an entire food-to-go fixture that contained no reduced pricing or special offers, identified an entirely opposite relationship between stock levels and the percentage of visitors who made a purchase. When the display was full, more than 90% of visitors made a purchase. When it was half empty, the number of purchasing visitors dropped to below 70%.

The inescapable truth is that we shoppers are, for the most part, at the mercy of our own instincts.

The Food Doctor, Ian Marber, provides a practical recommendation in his book *The Food Doctor Everyday Diet*, that says we should eat the right foods, in small amounts and often, as a vital part of his eating plan. This gives the body and brain a constant supply of energy throughout the day and avoids the blood sugar roller coaster, which in turn minimises things like tiredness and hunger. To help you survive your trip to the supermarket, try eating a piece of fruit or other healthy snack to avoid hunger before beginning your assault on the aisles.

summarise instincts, they are the most basic and rudimentary means by which we survive. Evolving from the most distant times in history, they help us to regulate bodily processes and tell our bodies when and how to address imbalances. Although we have little control over our instinctive actions, we are aware that the body is doing something. Therefore, we are able to make choices as to whether a better solution exists. Alternatively, we have the ability to 'head the instincts off at the pass' by pre-empting them and eating an apple as we walk across the supermarket car park towards the entrance to the store.

Instincts are the human brain's most basic way of functioning; although we exist instinctively, it's very useful to understand how the shopper's brain works, which we'll cover in the next chapter.

How the brain works

Our current understanding of the human brain is still far from complete and involves numerous hypotheses and best guesses. Within human beings, mental aspects such as consciousness, memory, intelligence, learning and imagination are all a long way from being fully understood. But, as Emerson M Pugh (author and professor emeritus of physics at Carnegie-Mellon University) famously said: 'If the human brain were so simple that we could understand it, we would be so simple that we couldn't.'

Many books have been written to help further our knowledge of how the brain works and in the following chapters I'll summarise and explore some of the key points while keeping the jargon to a minimum.

Let's begin by reminding ourselves of the brain's three main sections: The old or reptilian brain, the mammalian brain or limbic system, and the cerebral cortex or higher brain. The reptilian brain is basically the original 'straight out of the swamp' mental processing unit. It is the most ancient of the brains and consists of the upper part of the spinal cord and the basal ganglia, the diencephalon and parts of the midbrain, all of which sits on top of the spinal column. It represents a fundamental core of the nervous system and derives from a form of mammal-like reptile that once ranged widely over the world but disappeared during the Triassic period, having provided the evolutionary link between dinosaurs and mammals.

Around the reptilian brain is the second brain, collectively known as the limbic system or mammalian brain; a set of evolutionarily primitive brain structures located on top of the brainstem and buried under the cortex. Limbic system structures are involved in human emotions and motivations, particularly those that are related to survival including primal emotions like fear and anger. The limbic system is also involved in feelings of pleasure that are related to survival, such as those experienced from eating and sex.

The limbic system contains the thalamus, hippocampus and several other sub-sections. Whereas the role of the reptilian brain is to keep its owner alive, the limbic system is concerned with trying to ensure that the next generation will come to pass. It is this part of the brain that acts first, in response to any sensory stimulus we receive. A key function of the limbic system is to prepare the body for a course of action as a direct result of an incoming stimulus. For example, when someone is sitting in the cinema watching a horror movie and suddenly jumps during a particularly frightening scene, that jump was the fault of the limbic system. It arranged for sweaty palms, increased blood flow to certain parts of the body, hairs on the back of the neck to stand up and a number of other involuntary bodily reactions.

Sometime later (fractions of a second), the third part of the brain, the cerebral cortex or higher brain, gets involved and it takes a more thoughtful look at the situation. At this very moment, the owner of the brain is sitting motionless, sweaty and wide eyed, ready to fight or fly, but the higher brain comes to the conclusion that this cinematic experience is supposed to be entertaining and any way, good money was parted with for the pleasure of it. So instead of running screaming out of the cinema, the viewer relaxes and continues to watch the film. In summary, and as succinctly expressed by Joseph LeDoux, professor at the Centre for Neural Science at New York University, the job of the cortex (higher brain) is to prevent the inappropriate response to a situation as opposed to just producing the right one.

A wealth of information is available on the make up and working of the human brain, from the internal chemicals and neurotransmitters that manage thoughts and mechanical process, through to how and why other stimulants such as alcohol and drugs work.

As we are focussing on shoppers and shopping, let's look at the parts that help to explain shoppology, the science of shopping.

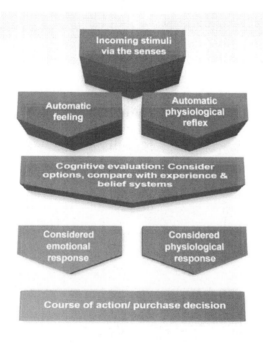

Figure 4 - Stimuli and responses

Bringing our human brains into the retail environment, particularly the supermarket, presents a number of issues. As we've been evolving as hunter–gatherers for 98% of the evolutionary timeline, our brains developed a means of effectively regulating hunger. In essence, our ancestors could go for long periods of time with little to no food and then feast at the end of a successful hunt or gather. These feasting instincts haven't gone away, and far from having to go for days without eating, modern day hunter–gatherers like us are faced with mountains of excess food in supermarkets.

Even when the poor consumer decides that dieting is needed, the brain takes over and kicks into 'survival mode'. What this means is that far from helping its owner to avoid food, it actively rebels. Knowing that less food is forthcoming, it basically sends out messages to eat as much now as possible, completely against any rational diet. According to Paul McKenna in *I Can Make You Thin*, dieting and starving yourself can actually make you fatter. He explains that when someone starves themselves by dieting, their body goes into what he refers to as fat storage mode. Because their body is made to think there is a famine, it concentrates on extracting all the fat out of whatever that person eats and then storing it so that they can survive said famine. In addition, the process of dieting and constantly overriding the body's natural requests for food actually alters a person's metabolism. He also goes on to say that when somebody desists from eating when they are hungry, their metabolism slows down so that the body can conserve energy.

Within the supermarket environment, you – as the poor owner of the brain – are being managed by this ravenous beast intent on hunting and gathering everything possible to avoid starvation and the possibility of extinction.

The three parts of your brain have evolved an efficient means of operating alongside one another through two different methods of processing information and controlling bodily functions. First, there is consciousness, which allows us to experience, understand and process conscious events, such as reading a newspaper. Then there is the unconscious, which is responsible for much 'innate' processing such as the habitual movements and reactions used in driving a car.

Unconscious mental processing accounts for 95% of our decision making and importantly, the only way you can be aware of, and be able to influence, your own decision making is if you have to conduct a certain amount of conscious processing. Gerald Zaltman, Harvard professor and author of *How Customers Think*, refers readers to an excellent explanation of the 95%/5% split between unconscious and conscious activity. The explanation comes from John Haugeland, who was a professor of philosophy at the University of Chicago and reads: 'Thus, compared to unconscious processing, conscious thinking is conspicuously slow and laborious – Not a lot faster than talking in fact. What's more, it is about as difficult to consciously entertain two distinct trains of thought at the same times as it is to engage in two distinct and different conversations at once; consciousness is in some sense a linear or serial process in contrast to the many simultaneous cognitions that are manifest in unconscious action.'

The unconscious aspects of our mental activity such as motor and cognitive routines and functions play a fundamental role in shaping and directing our conscious experiences. Consciousness itself evolved in humankind to help people review their past actions, give reason and explanation for them, and to help plan future choices and decisions.

When we are shopping, our brains assign different tasks to different parts of our mental processing systems: The conscious processes some aspects of our activities and the unconscious others. For example, the task of buying a daily pint of milk can actually be conducted with little or no conscious involvement. Conversely, purchasing a birthday card for the love of one's life will involve both conscious and unconscious processing as part of the process and the human brain is particularly adept at sharing its activities between the two different processing centres for optimal efficiency. Another example of our brain's ability to work-share is that information (i.e. memories) can also be stored in either the short term or long term memory, a subject covered in more detail later in the book.

Retailers and brands communicate intentionally and unintentionally with both our conscious and unconscious mental processing centres all the time. Anything that we as shoppers are aware of is being managed by the conscious part of our brain. But, there's also a whole lot of stuff happening in a busy store that simply isn't 'on our radar'. For example, stop in the aisle and listen to all the sounds around. Suddenly, you'll become aware of many sounds that you weren't previously 'conscious' of. Take a deep intake of breath and consider what ambient smells and aromas are present. Within the supermarket, there will often be a lingering smell of fresh bread. This is no accident, it is widely reported that supermarkets pump an artificial smell of baking bread into stores to get shopper's taste buds going by creating an instinctive tummy rumbling 'must have carbohydrates' effect.

What follows is an example of just how inefficiently the average shopper mentally behaves and processes information in a typical supermarket. Imagine a big shopping trip on a Saturday to the supermarket with an average shopper – we'll call her Sue. Sue is a woman in her mid thirties, very busy, somewhat short of time, with a household to feed and a limited budget. Just like every other Saturday, the moment she enters the shop she is greeted by an overwhelming multi-sensory onslaught! All around her, other shoppers are 'hunting' and 'gathering' for all they are worth, the checkouts bleep as the staff scan item after item before they relieve the shoppers of their hard earned money. Shelf packers continually replenish the stocks in the aisles, making sure that all the products 'face the front' and that there are no unsightly gaps between items. The smell of fresh bread mingles with the scent of fruit and vegetables and wafts through the air.

Almost as soon as Sue has realised she's in the supermarket, she finds herself in the fruit and vegetable section; this is no coincidence and is the same in most Western countries, but not in France, for some reason. Store designers want shoppers to be presented with fresh, bright and multi-sensorially appealing produce from around the world as quickly as possible. This communicates a number of subtle messages to Sue, including freshness, bright colours and health.

She is conscientious about making sure she attempts to meet her 'five-a-day' supply of fruit and vegetables, for the sake of her health and that of her children so she makes sure to stock up well, even though they are often priced somewhat cheaper at the local market or farm shop. She thinks she's making random choices, but they have been carefully influenced by those in charge of this particular supermarket. When she is faced with a positive wall of fresh tomatoes, ranging from the cheap, everyday tomatoes, each exquisitely lit and presented as perfect red balls of promise and bulging with gustatory temptation. Next to them are the big beef tomatoes, more expensive, but the colour, smell and perceived added health benefits of a bigger 'five-a-day' component is just too good to resist. She picks those larger, costlier beef tomatoes, chemically modified and delivered just in time for her Saturday morning visit to that store. Little does she know that this wonderful looking bulbous delight is little more than a coloured bag of tasteless water? But never mind; add plenty of salad dressing (sugar) and seasoning (salt) and they'll taste just great.

Now she moves on to the vegetables for the Sunday roast; starting with the potatoes, Sue buys the best quality Jersey new potatoes, recently imported and already scrubbed and ready to cook. Although they are more expensive, she is unable to resist the promise of the newest new potatoes fresh from the fields of Jersey. Now for some fruit. She approaches the large, yellow display of bananas, appreciating the feel and aroma of the fruit. Moments later, she is unable to resist and into the trolley go the bunch of bananas with little or no thought of how much they cost. Next, she approaches a pallet of succulent looking melons; she feels their shape and smells for their ripeness. They find their way into the trolley before she leaves the fruit and vegetables and heads off towards other aisles.

Several minutes later and with a few other items in her trolley, she wanders into the meat aisle. Here, there are numerous cuts of meat from all around the world. Steak from Scotland, best Argentinean beef fillet, chicken from numerous farms across the country but branded to indicate it all comes from a single small town or village, and succulent lamb, all the way from New Zealand. It's all she can do to stop herself buying a different joint of meat for every day of the week, let alone just for the Sunday roast.

After restricting herself to a single prime cut of topside of beef, the corn fed chicken breasts leap off the shelf towards her with their yellow hue and after a brief and barely critical investigation of the merits of corn feeding, into the trolley they go, even though they are much more expensive than the other, much plainer value-pack chicken breasts. Sue continues to amble aimlessly around the supermarket and more and more items not on any shopping list get added to the trolley, all appearing to be 'good ideas at the time'. A pack of luxury chocolate biscuits all the way from Belgium, some South African red and white wine, a tub of that luxury ice cream she'd seen advertised last night on TV and the irresistible cream cakes all bypass reasoning and logic and go straight into the trolley

After a long while that seemed like no time at all, Sue finds herself only halfway round the store, but with a trolley that is close to overflowing. Even after rearranging the contents, she resigns herself to the fact that everything else will have to wait. She trudges, exhausted, towards the front of the store and the long line of checkouts. Sue dutifully places each of her items onto the conveyor belt and then watches as her goods are scanned by the checkout girl. Shock, horror: The bill is over £200, which is more than her weekly income; regretfully, she hands over her credit card and vows to be more restrained next week before finishing her trip and heading back to the car.

This typical scenario illustrates just how easy it is for us to spend so much money in the supermarkets, because the cold, hard truth is that most of us make lousy supermarket shoppers. It's no good blaming the corporate giants of multi-sensory temptation, as we've simply not been trained how to shop and our brains have been wired with other priorities.

When it comes to understanding how our brains function when shopping, the fact is that despite their amazing complexity and sophistication, they hardly manage at all. We cannot rely on our brains to reach prudent, wise or even practical shopping decisions as they have yet to evolve sufficiently to perform the function of 21st century supermarket shopping. Instead, they operate well out of any comfort zone, relying on instincts and triggers that were developed a very long time ago.

What we need is to rewire our thought processes to better align evolutionary, needs-based triggers with modern day temptations in-store. To create this blueprint for future shopping, we need to understand not only how the brain processes information and functions, but also the causes that lie behind our functions, behaviour and decision making.

Many of our purchase decisions are based on previous experiences either real, perceived or reported by friends and peers. Simply put, we often buy items because of what we remember about the item after buying it previously. This brings us to the subject of the next chapter, memory.

Short and long term memory

Humans have developed two fundamentally different types of memory: Short term working memory and long term memory. Once again, the 'rule of two' is an attempt by evolution to make the brain more fit for purpose. As our brains struggle to cope with all that 21st century life has to throw at them, they have to adapt and compromise, often somewhat crudely and inefficiently.

Many thousands of years ago, either up in the trees or balancing on hind legs somewhere in the savannahs of Africa, life was much simpler. Kill or be killed, find a mate and procreate, gather nuts and berries. As a consequence, early man had much less to remember; as time has passed, however, language, numbers and many other abstract concepts have developed, all actively contributing to human advancement.

Each of these processes, functions and activities take up some space in the brain, and although something of an over-simplification, all the stuff that people need to remember must be accessible by way of some form of filing system to optimise memory efficiency. To paraphrase Homer Simpson, 'Every time I learn a new stupid thing, something important has to go to make way for it.'

Faced with a life threatening decision to be made in the blink of an eye, we don't want to root around the archives of our minds for the answers on what course of action to take. Conversely, the words to 'Good Ship Lollipop', by Shirley Temple shouldn't be at the forefront of our thoughts every waking hour of our life.

In essence, memory within the human brain can be compared to the different sorts of memory contained in any modern day computer. The basic functions are handled by a human's short term memory, which is similar to how computers use RAM (random access memory), which is very limited in size (comparatively) and is restricted by how much information it can hold at any one time. The long term memory is more like the much larger capacity hard drives that users fill with music, photos, data, and all their learnt and other created things.

In the case of the computer, RAM is supported by what is called 'virtual memory'. This is actually 'borrowed' from the main hard drive to help with software and some hardware functionality. Most of us have at some time or other experienced a computer crash when suddenly the thing locks up and is unable to do anything. Based on my own experience, this typically happens either when scanning the machine for viruses or just moments before a scheduled auto-save was due to occur!

Another analogy to illustrate how our brains function is to think of them as being like a social networking site with each member of the network representing a neuron. When a member sends a message to another member, a connection is made (this is the synapse between different neurons). The more connections a member has, the more connections they can make simultaneously. So, a well connected member of the social network can communicate to all their connections in a split second.

In essence, this is how the brain does it. What's more, the more often the brain makes the same connection between certain neurons (members), then the more 'hardwired' that connection becomes; in a similar way some social network connections are auto-completed as favourites or friends. What we might see as favourites on social network sites relate to habits when it comes to human brains and these are managed by the brain with little or no conscious awareness or cognitive input.

We can combine the personal computer/human memory analogy with that of the thought process and social networking to explain why we have two memories and how they interlink. We each store all of our social network contact details within our long term memories. In there are all the details about all the people we know. As long as these contacts are online, then the neural pathways are available to make contact with them. When we decide to make contact with an acquaintance in the social network, the short term memory retrieves the minimum amount of detail from the long term memory to enable contact to be made. It then assists in the actual connection, which once made, it can leave alone.

Although this isn't a perfect analogy, it does summarise the two types of human memory function working together. In the case of our shopping brains, both short term and long term memories have responsibilities. For example, imagine you are in the supermarket looking to buy your regular brand of filter coffee. Typically, the long term memory is responsible for your brand preference by way of emotional connections with particular products. Once you've located your preferred brand on the shelf, the short term memory, may well check the price and compare any offers for competing brands. Then coffee is then selected and dropped into your trolley.

Crucially, as soon as your short term working memory has finished with its involvement in the coffee buying process, it erases all the data it used while conducting the evaluation and moves on to the next immediate task that you need it to undertake. Should a market research interviewer now walk up to you and ask about your coffee purchasing process and experience, it is more than likely that you'll be unable to relate the physical aspects of the process.

In a shopper study by Shopping Behaviour Xplained, hot beverage shoppers in the UK were asked the costs of the items they had dropped into their trolleys just seconds earlier. An astonishing 56% admitted that they didn't know. A further 20% guessed, but guessed incorrectly. Observation of the same shoppers on CCTV confirmed that many did study prices and evaluate special offers and promotions but because they did so with their short term working memories, they erased the information immediately they'd selected their chosen tea or coffee.

In summary, remembering that the red berries are sweet but the green ones are bitter is straightforward and is what our brains are wired to do. Conversely, evaluating whether Carte Noire coffee in a refill pack is better value at so much money per 100 grams, compared with Nescafé, which is slightly more expensive per 100 grams, but is on a '3 for the price of 2' deal starts to scramble our limited brain power.

To simplify things, as shoppers, we'll often develop specific shopping habits. For example, if you know that you always buy a box of Kellogg's cornflakes during your weekly big shop, then you needn't worry your brain about the detail, all you need to do is remember a trigger and then let habit make the purchase for you. The trigger may be just the sight of the breakfast cereals aisle, the Kellogg's logo or the rooster that adorns the front of every box of Kellogg's cornflakes.

The fact is that conditioned, uncontrollable and potentially damaging shopping habits definitely exist, and they're responsible for more regular repeat purchases than most of us would care to know. Typically, during a weekly supermarket shop, an average of 60% of the purchases are made by way of a habitual managed process, triggered by a single stimulus and then completed automatically. Many of these mundane, regular repeat purchases take place with no consideration or mental evaluative input. We see a cue or receive a trigger from another sense and that initiates a set of behaviours that in turn leads to the repeat purchase. This process is known as a single scripted behaviour, a subject that we'll cover in more detail later on.

These groups of behaviours have evolved to allow our brains to cope more efficiently with all the tasks expected of them. Despite this, our short term working memory struggles to handle all the aspects of the 21st century. As a workaround, human brains have developed a process known as 'chunking' which helps spread the mental workload. Before we explore single scripted behaviour and chunking, we'll examine the functions of the two different types of memory and what their predominate responsibilities are.

Our short term memories handle all the mundane, minute to minute decisions. However, they tend to be notoriously limited in how much they can cope with. Common consensus estimates that our short term memories can only process seven plus or minus two pieces of information at any one time. A piece of information could be any stimulus that needs some degree of conscious processing and that reaches our awareness from any of the five senses (visual, auditory, kinaesthetic, olfactory or gustatory).

This special number of seven plus or minus two items was first identified by George Miller in 1956. Based on subsequent research, a growing body of experts has developed and refined the seven plus or minus two theory into a set of teaching principles known as Cognitive Load Theory. In their book *Efficiency in Learning*, Ruth Clark, Frank Nguyen and John Sweller define Cognitive Load Theory as a universal set of learning principles resulting in an efficient instructional environment as a consequence of leveraging human cognitive learning processes. Or to put it so you can cognitively understand the last sentence: Cognitive Load Theory explains how to make complex things easy to understand. It is based on understanding how those trying to learn actually process incoming information to retain it for future use (remember it). The incoming new information is then broken down into manageable sized 'packets' that can be processed and embedded into the brain. In other words, we aren't able to learn a new dance routine instantly, but we can learn two or three dance steps at a time. The number of steps we can learn depends on a number of factors including intelligence, interest in the subject matter and learning environment (in a dance studio or on a bus). The learning ability of a particular person or group of people to a particular subject is known as their cognitive load threshold.

Cognitive load thresholds vary by individual and by familiarity with the subject matter; a good example of how the cognitive load threshold changes can be illustrated by thinking back to when we first learnt to drive a car. When you're first behind the wheel the process is very alien. For a beginner, driving a car is a mentally draining series of conscious evaluations and adjustments. As a new driver we constantly have to evaluate any number of situations and soon become cognitively 'full'. However as time passes, driving appears to become easier and even second nature. This is because groups of behaviours have been chunked together which reduces the input needed from the short term working memory. What we find so mentally taxing and stressful as a new driver can be handled with ease once we've been driving for a while. As more experienced motorists, we can not only drive with much less mental effort, but can also hold a conversation, listen to the radio, take a drink from a bottle of water and more. Some people are so comfortable that they even think they could shave, put on make-up or even change their clothes, which is needless to say, highly illegal and dangerous!

Regarding the behaviour of the short term working memory in the context of supermarket shopping, price is often cited as being a key factor in store and product choice and is often given as the reason why a particular item was selected or rejected. Yet, when studies of price awareness have been carried out in supermarkets, typically, around 50% of respondents don't know how much items cost just minutes after selecting them from the shelf because the short term memory doesn't need to hold that information anymore. This means that the memory of those prices is simply erased before the researchers began speaking with the shoppers. Further evidence of this part of the mind's limited functionality can be found in *The Private Life of The Brain*, an excellent book by an Oxford professor, Susan Greenfield. In it she explains and quantifies, with evidenced examples, that the human short term working memory can store information for no longer than eighteen seconds.

This explains why shoppers, when asked about shopping aspects such as prices, normally resort to rationalised responses and guesses. However, observing the same shoppers at the shelves clearly shows that at the moment of truth, many actively compare prices and offers. From a shopping perspective, prices are important at the moment of truth and weigh into our decisions; it's just that as shoppers we forget that importance in just a few seconds.

Fortunately, we aren't solely reliant on our short term working memories; we also possess a long term memory, which is a much more powerful processing and storage unit. Our long term memories store all the things that we've experienced. To give phenomenal power, the sound of a familiar song memory of a particular holiday from years prev where we were, what we ate or drank, the weath with, and an incredible amount of additional detail.

Back in the store, the innocuous sight of a famous brand name or logo can trigger all types of associations with positive product experiences, aspirations or pain avoidance from the long term memory. The sight of a certain brand of soap could remind us of our childhoods in great detail or the smell of a particular perfume might trigger memories of happiness, love or other emotions.

To complicate matters further, although the long term memory can be thought of as a single entity, it actually operates through the coming together of three different mental processes.

The first type of long term memory is that of procedural memory. We need this for learned skills, such as playing a musical instrument. To embed something into the procedural long term memory, we have to learn the procedure, often from many hours of frustrating experience. It often takes many repeated attempts at a new procedure before the final coordinated execution involving brain, senses and motor skills. This form of manual hardwiring of the brain is further hindered because we tend to forget things until they are learnt and embedded. As a result, we have to keep re-learning parts of a procedure until the entire procedure is wired in.

The next long term memory type is known as declarative memory and is explicit in that people are aware that they are actually learning something. For example, declarative memory is what is most active when at school, learning a foreign language or mathematical formulae.

The third type of long term memory, which many consider to be similar to declarative memory, is called episodic memory. Episodic

...ory is responsible for storing episodes from life, such as remembering a trip to the coast or an evening out and can be thought of as reliving a past event. Incidentally, episodic memory retains information relating to episodes much more easily than is the case with either procedural or declarative memory. According to Trygg Engen who wrote in an article that appeared in *American Scientist*: 'memories triggered by episodic odours (smells) only fade by 3% over a 12 month period', which might help to explain why so many of us prefer to use the washing powder our mums used.

To summarise these three types of memory in relation to shopping in the supermarket: We may learn about the benefits of eating plenty of fruit and vegetables (declarative). Many of us know how to buy fresh fruit and vegetables from our local supermarket (procedural) and we might recall having a particularly nice fresh fruit salad on a picnic last Sunday (episodic).

The long term memory has a clever way of indexing so much information; it stores things as little components, which can then form part of something meaningful when associated with the right criteria and within the appropriate context. For example, directly in front of a person is a tin box with rounded edges, it is white and made of metal and has lights on the front. As more details are received, the long term memory filters down the options. So far, the thing being described could be a number of things but by adding more contexts, it becomes clearer. It has glass in the door and it is possible to see inside. The white tin box is in the launderette, which means it's a washing machine or tumble drier.

In principal, this is how the long term memory operates and it's something of which retailers and marketers are well aware. By using this technique, the brain is able to use stored components as part of different overall memories, which in turn aids storage efficiency and recall.

An important (some say the only) means of embedding things into any of our long term memories, particularly episodic, is to attach emotions and feelings to them. This is what advertisers often do; they take an everyday product, such as a bottle of disinfectant, then attach an emotional association such as a mother caring for her beloved toddler. Suddenly the disinfectant goes into the 'caring' section of the long term memory.

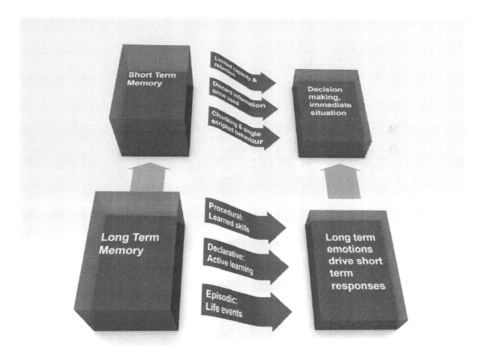

Figure 5 - Short and long term memory behaviour

As shoppers, we continually train and adapt ourselves to shop, particularly for those mundane, regular, repeat purchases. We learn procedurally how to shop the supermarket every week. Additionally, we are constantly being educated about the benefits of both the products we use and the products we should use. Finally, often under the influence of advertisers and marketers, we shop the store with an ever-increasing head full of emotional product associations and usage episodes.

With so much going on mentally, it's no surprise that our brains leave some of the more basic purchases to our short term working memories. Because of their extremely limited mental processing power, the short term memory becomes more efficient through single scripted behaviour and chunking, which we'll now explore in more detail.

Single scripted behaviour and chunking

Two important techniques that our brains use to cope with living in the 21st century are single scripted behaviours and chunking. We've previously mentioned that we use these techniques when shopping to help minimise the mental effort involved in the process of buying things from supermarkets, and many other activities too. So, just what are single scripted behaviours and what exactly is chunking?

First, looking at single scripted behaviours, these scripts are a sequence of expected behaviours in response to a given situation. Single scripts can be learnt and once known and practiced can become parts of larger scripts. An example of a learnt set of scripts would be seen when we enter a restaurant: The first part of the script normally involves us choosing a table. The script continues with us reading the menu and choosing that we want to eat. Next, we'll normally order, then after waiting a while, eat. Finally, after a good meal we would typically pay the bill and leave. This restaurant episode is quite a long script, but even so, as consumers we learn it and use it. As a restaurant goer you are unlikely to enter a restaurant and go straight to the head waiter to try and pay for the meal you have yet to choose.

People continually follow established scripts and also learn new ones. Typically, new scripts are acquired through habit, practice and simple routine. Following scripts is a useful practice because it saves the time and mental effort of figuring out an appropriate behaviour each time a situation is encountered.

These scripted behaviours can be negative as well as positive. For example, after giving up smoking, some regular pub goers find that they are drinking more. One reason is that they replace the scripted behaviour of using their hands every 20 minutes or so to smoke a cigarette, with another use for their hands. In the pub environment, a simple and frequent answer is just to have another sip of whatever their chosen libation is.

Using behavioural scripts involves us learning a group of behaviours or actions that can be carried out below any conscious level and that can be triggered by a single stimulus. Another everyday example of such behaviour is the act of shaking hands. We don't have to go through a complicated mental process every time we meet someone at a business meeting, for example. The conscious process would be memory hungry and would include a list of actions and evaluations. To begin with, there would be the how far to extend our arm calculation. This would be followed by what angle to hold our hand, how much pressure to exert in the squeeze and how many shakes is sufficient.

Over time, our brains learn the handshake to such a proficient level that the sight of somebody walking towards us in the correct business context triggers the automatic shaking of the hand script.

My own research (2010) tested the level to which the handshake is an automatically controlled set of behaviours. In a study conducted in the UK, participants would approach me and in turn I would hold out my hand to shake hands. However, just as our hands were about to interlock, I'd grab the hand of the participant with my left hand, say a number out loud and then let them continue with the handshake with my right hand. During the study of 20 people, only one became aware of this apparently incongruous behaviour. The remaining 19 had no knowledge of it happening and 17 of them, when asked to think of the first number that came into their head repeated the number I'd given to them.

The second technique that our short term memory uses is chunking. This technique involves creating a strategy for making more efficient use of short term memory by grouping small bits of information into manageable chunks. A good explanation and example of chunking can be found on Wikipedia, where the process of learning telegraphic (Morse) code is explained. The operator begins learning the dot, dash code by learning each letter by its relevant dots and dashes. As the trainee gets more proficient, they are able to chunk groups of dots and dashes into words. Then as they become even more learned, they can learn (chunk) entire phrases in manageable blocks.

To give another example of chunking, consider a person learning to play the piano; they will begin by learning individual notes, A to G in each scale. Once they know these, they can begin to understand and learn chords. Pressing the piano keys C, E and G simultaneously will deliver a C major chord. As time goes on, people can learn more notes, add chords and so learn entire pieces of music. In summary, humans start by learning a relatively basic, single script then they typically go on to use it as part of more complex behavioural scripts.

For a familiar example of chunking, look no further than how we remember telephone numbers. It is somewhat difficult to remember 01827569700 However, if the digits are chunked into (in this case) three simple chunks, it instantly becomes easier to remember: 01827 569 700.

Both single scripted behaviour and chunking are widely used as part of shopping. The person who buys 20 cigarettes each morning on their way to work will more than likely have developed a single scripted behaviour as an effortless means of making their daily purchase. As a result (i.e. with no conscious awareness of the process), they will be oblivious to any references to cigarettes in displays and special offers.

Although the science is solid and a number of research projects have shown that people shopping using a single scripted behaviour are 'blind' to offers and displays, brands and retailers still try in vein to attract them. It is possible to communicate with shoppers on a single scripted behaviour, but first it is necessary to interrupt the behaviour to get attention. Ways to interrupt single scripts include the desired product not being is stock, the products or store being laid out in an unfamiliar way, or if we go to a store with which we are unfamiliar.

Retailers don't tend to like single scripted shopping, as it is difficult to increase the shopper's weight of purchase (WOP). With regard to brands, it really depends on whether the single script includes the brand owner's brand or not. If it does, then all is good, if not then their aim is to break the script. This is a process that can be very effective, but fortunately only a few retailers and brands are aware of it.

Shoppers can be influenced by actively breaking the script and then managing the shopping behaviour so that the replacement new script becomes hard wired. For example, imagine that as a shopper, you or I use a single script that involves purchasing a bar of Cadbury's Dairy Milk chocolate every time we fill our car with petrol. Mars would like to break that script so that we will consider or even buy a Mars bar with every fill up instead. In this instance, Mars need to develop a switching strategy.

For Mars to switch the Cadbury shopper in the example given, they could initiate regular re-merchandising of the confectionery fixture making the Dairy Milk harder to find or communicate some script breaking message to the shopper as they stand in a trancelike state filling their car. A third means of rewiring the shopper is to create a stronger emotional reason for the shopper to buy Mars over Cadbury. This is sometimes referred to as initiating leverage, for example linking Mars to some preferable social situation by way of a movie, advertising or product placement. The subject of emotion is perhaps the most important for retailers, brands and smart shoppers to understand and will be covered in detail later in the book.

The reason that so few brands and retailers do this is because of the time it takes to change a habit. In today's 'have it now' world, brands and retailers want instant results, not longer term shopper re-training that can often take months to embed.

Chunking is also used when shopping for a variety of different reasons. Some of us will mentally chunk recipes and then 'cook the meal' as they shop the grocery store. The image of lasagne triggers all the ingredients needed and, if in a familiar store, they are bought on a single walk up and down the aisles without any back tracking. It is probably no coincidence that menu cards are so popular as giveaways in the supermarkets, but crucially they need to be in the right location in-store, as our evidence is that once we commit to buying a particular meal solution, we usually stay loyal to it. In a similar vein, DIY stores sometimes carry 'project guides' that help shoppers to remember all they need to buy to complete a particular project in the home.

Faced with the pressures of 21st century shopping, we need to be more aware of when our brains are being overloaded and subsequently when we are making less than ideal purchasing decisions. In those situations, our brain is adopting a type of 'needs must' strategy. In other words, our brains are less concerned about coming to the best value or even the most practical purchase decision; they just need to get to some type of decision so that they can continue to cope with everything. Before handing over your cash or credit card too readily, try to evaluate why you have arrived at a particular purchase decision. It's not that the decision will be wrong, it's just a sense-check; as quite often you'll find there may be a better solution readily available.

The final section of this book offers you a range of tools to help you evaluate why you buy the things you do. In addition, it provides a further set of techniques aimed at helping you to discover how your brains are wired; the fact is that almost all purchase decisions are influenced by emotion and emotion is a topic only rarely mentioned in classical psychology text books.

Because emotions are so integral to so many of the decisions that we make, we'll cover the subject comprehensively in this book. We'll discuss just what an emotion is and to make them easier to understand, we'll also provide descriptions of how they can be measured.

At this point, it's useful to state that a lack of understanding of human emotions is often at the root cause of our less than ideal shopping and consumer marketing related decisions. Even many researchers don't fully comprehend what emotions do and what they influence, which can result in consumer and shopper research that is less than perfect. As a result, the insights presented to retailers, brands and marketers can be based on little more than the rationalised guesses of respondents like you and me to market research questions.

An understanding of human emotions is, like so many others in this book, right at the heart of why we behave as we do. Armed with this understanding, whether shopping, consuming or whatever, you will be in a much more qualified position to understand what makes you tick and why you react and behave as you do, not only in supermarkets, but also in life.

What is emotion?

It is impossible to escape the fact that as shoppers we are emotional and that shopping for the most part is not a rational and objective process. Many decisions that we make, we do so emotionally; retailers know it and brands know it. This is the wake up call for all of us who go shopping in the supermarket as typically, we'll each part with an average of £150,000 over our adult lifetime and the cold hard truth is that unless we take action, we will do so based on our emotional reactions and with little regard to rationality or reason.

It's useful to define what we mean when we talk about emotions. They are the building blocks of feelings and are with all of us, all of the time, to a greater or lesser extent. As our minds develop, we each create our own personalised inner world based on our experiences. Professor Susan Greenfield, author of *The Private Life of The Brain*, states that during periods of intense emotion, such as anger, fear or sadness, we as humans can lose our minds and revert back to the mental states we experienced as children.

In more technical terms, an emotion is the complex combined psychological and physiological response of a person to a single stimulus or set of incoming stimuli. It is the response of the brain and body to create a state of readiness to respond to a particular stimulus or set of stimuli (fight or flight for example). In humans, emotion fundamentally involves physiological arousal, expressive behaviours and conscious experience. According to Robert Plutchik, author of *Emotions and Life*, and professor emeritus at the Albert Einstein College of Medicine and adjunct professor at the University of South Florida, emotions are genetically based, unlearned behavioural adaptations that have value for the individual; they are patterned reactions rather than disorganised events.

Before there can be any form of physiological response to an incoming stimulus or set of stimuli, there has to be a form of psychological evaluation. In other words, before the hairs of the back of our neck can stand on end, our brain has to send the appropriate impulses for that physiological 'behaviour' to occur. For our brain to send out such a signal it first has to receive the stimuli that it needs to respond to; these stimuli are received from one or more of the five senses. Each of the senses is physiological by nature, so in essence, the process of an emotional reaction goes like this: 1, incoming physiological stimulus; 2, almost instantaneous psychological processing; 3, if appropriate, a signal goes back to the physiological system(s) to do something. Body first, then brain, then back to body.

How do our brains process and decode the incoming physiological stimuli? They do so by using a somewhat basic evolutionarily based calculation: Chase it to eat, chase it to mate, or will it chase me and eat me? Based on the outcome of the calculation, the brain can decide which part of the body needs the blood, oxygen and nutrients to best address the situation. In other words, our brains take even the most complex physiological stimuli, such as watching an expensively crafted scene in a 3D movie on the latest high definition, surround sound enhanced LCD television and then take it all the way back to fight, flight or fornicate.

Figure 6 - Fight, flight or fornicate responses

Emotions are built on three different psychological components, which all appear to a greater or lesser extent in all emotions. First, there is happiness or pleasure; there will be lots of happiness in glee, but hardly any in anger for example. The second aspect or component of an emotion is stimulation or arousal. Emotions of confrontation contain a high percentage of stimulation, whereas being obliging would contain a minimal amount. The third and final psychological component that exists in every emotion is control or dominance, how in control of a situation a person feels. Greed and impulsivity are both emotions that contain high levels of control while obedience and shyness would only contain much smaller amounts.

These three components of emotion: happiness, stimulation and control are the mental switches that the brain uses to prepare the body for an instinctive course of action. As an analogy, imagine that these three components of emotion are the ingredients needed to make a traditional homemade wine: grapes, sugar and yeast. Depending on how much of each ingredient is used in proportion to the other two, determines what the final wine will be like. Too much of one ingredient and the wine may turn out bitter. Get the balance wrong another way and the mixture may explode out of the barrel. However, get the balance of ingredients just right and the result is a balanced, tasty and enjoyable wine.

We are constantly receiving stimuli through our nervous systems that are in turn being instantly processed by the fight, flight or fornicate parts of our brains. On the one hand, it is important that the stimuli are correctly converted into an appropriate emotional response and on the other hand, it is possible that by manipulating the stimuli we receive, our emotional responses can be influenced and altered.

To recap, an emotion is the combined complex psychological and physiological experience that results from a person reacting to a particular single stimulus or set of stimuli they encounter. Emotions are the split second changes in mental and physical states that come directly from the evolutionary development of man.

We are all capable of experiencing a number of different emotions. There are the six universal, core emotions: happiness, fear, sadness, surprise, disgust and anger. The French philosopher René Descartes (1596–1650) first assumed that there were six primary emotions, or as he termed them, *passions*, and that all others were composed of mixtures or blends of these six. Much more recently, in 1985, Dore and Kirouac developed a 70 item questionnaire that contained an excellent summary of the cumulative theories of the six primary and universal emotions.

These are the raw instinctive emotions that govern fight or flight, kill or be killed, or procreate. These six core emotions can be charted as making up an entire 360 degree circle. They vary from hostility to affiliation on the 'X' (horizontal) axis and dominance to submission on the 'Y' (vertical) axis. We have little or no control over these universal emotions as they are managed predominately by the limbic system, one of the more primal parts of the brain.

Importantly, within the six universal emotions, there are approximately 100 further emotional variants or blends of emotions. For example, within happiness, there is pride and confidence (both towards the anger end of happiness). Then, more centrally within the happiness section is joy, glee and pleasure. Towards the fear end of happiness lie such emotions as contentment and relaxation.

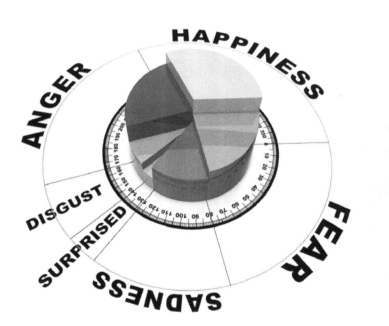

Figure 7 - Six primary emotions

Emotions manifest themselves through different physiological changes to the body, the most obvious of which are facial expressions. In addition, the body emotionally responds to a set of stimuli by autonomically triggering such changes as sweaty palms, hairs on the back of the neck standing up, and alterations in heart rate and breathing.

Emotions serve to enhance the possibilities of survival and reproduction. According to Steven Pinker, Harvard University professor and author of *How the Mind Works*: 'The ultimate function of the mind is survival and reproduction in the environment in which the mind has evolved – That is, (in the case of humans) the environment of the hunting and gathering tribes in which the human race has spent more than 99% of it's evolutionary history, before the recent invention of agriculture and civilisations only 10,000 years ago.'

Aaron Ben-Ze'ev, professor of philosophy and president of the University of Haifa provides another good explanation of emotions and states: 'Emotions direct and colour people's attention by selecting what attracts and holds attention. They regulate priorities and communicate intentions. Emotions are concerned with issues of survival and social status.' This quote illustrates just why understanding human emotions is so important for retailers, brand marketers and shoppers. Stores and brands are constantly striving to grab and hold the attention of us shoppers, be it with displays, packaging, promotions or other such attractions. Therefore, our emotions act as the gatekeeper of our awareness and attention in-store.

The aim of retailers, and in particular brands, is to form strong, meaningful and profitable associations with us as shoppers and consumers. Once we become emotionally hard wired to a brand, we represent a loyal source of future sales and revenue. The key tool brands and retailers use to connect with us shoppers is emotion, probably the most influential tool known to man!

Themes used to elicit situations for the six basic emotions*

Happiness
1. Goal oriented activities or achievement of a goal
2. Success in a new hobby or activity, or with a new friend; to see or hear new and pleasant things
3. Recognition of the familiar; to repeat a pleasant activity; to meet someone or something that is known
4. Social approval, especially (but not exclusively) from a friend, relative or esteemed person
5. Benefit in general: money, status, reward, etc.

Fear
1. Life in danger: anticipated or learned fear; danger from an event or a person
2. Threatening verbal or physical attack: punishment, insult or anger of an opponent
3. Loss of support
4. Unfamiliarity or strangeness

Sadness
1. Loss in general: death of or separation from a loved one
2. Health problems
3. To see someone crying or to perceive sadness

Surprise
1. Unexpected event
2. Unusual sensations (sights, sounds, tastes, smells or tactile)

Disgust
1. As elicited by sensations
   a. Bad or repulsive taste
   b. Bad smell
   c. Sticky or slimy to the touch
   d. Sight of someone or something repulsive, dirty or organically deteriorated
2. Inappropriate behaviour violating moral standards, habits or norms

Anger
1. Barriers, obstacles, frustrations (psychological or physical), threats from someone, social constraints and dangerous attacks
2. Insults (psychological or verbal threats)
3. To be forced to do something
4. To observe or to suffer from an unjust treatment
5. Unrelieved tension which persists and prevents need satisfaction

*Adapted from 'Identifying the Eliciting Situations of Six Fundamental Emotions' by F Y Dore and G Kirouac, 1985, *Journal of Psychology*, 119

To quantify the importance of emotions to brands in particular, John Hallward in his book *Gimme* states that the emotional brand value (the mental value) of a brand such as Coke or McDonald's is financially worth much more that the combined tangible fixed assets and stock that a company may own.

In fact, this is the very essence of what a brand is: the de-commoditisation of a commodity for the purpose of being able to charge more for it. A brand is a product, service or concept that is publicly distinguished from other similar products, services, or concepts so that it can be easily communicated and marketed. Or, to quote David Ogilvy, the famous advertising copywriter and ad agency founder, the definition of a brand is, 'The intangible sum of a product's attributes: its name, packaging, and price, its history, its reputation, and the way it's advertised.'

There are either no, or only marginal, physical differences between many competing brands of fast moving consumer goods available in supermarkets today. Advertisers differentiate them effectively by giving them what is often referred to as a 'brand personality'. In other words, they attach a unique set of emotional associations to a product that results in altering our perceptions of it as shoppers and consumers.

Retailers have recognised and responded to the enormous value potential of brands. It is widely known that they offer a range of own label, self-branded products to shoppers in direct competition to the leading supplier brands. Typically, own label (or private label as they are sometimes known) products refer to those items manufactured by a company and sold under the brand of a supermarket. For example, most supermarket chains offer alternative breakfast cereals in direct competition to the likes of Kellogg's, Weetabix and Alpen. More often than not, supermarkets make more of a profit margin from their own brand products than they do from those supplied by the leading brands.

What began as cheaper alternatives to the well known branded products have now evolved into well known brands in their own right. In the UK, there is 'Tesco Finest', Sainsbury's 'Taste the Difference', Waitrose 'Essentials' and Asda's 'Extra Special' ranges, just to name a few. These standalone own brands allow the retailers to compete for customers at different price levels. What began as a lower end alternative can now compete at the bottom, middle or top of the product range pricing matrix.

As retailers have created their own brands, they themselves are now competing for the emotional custom of us as shoppers and consumers. With so much attention on brands from both retailers and brand owners, it is surprising just how little research around emotions tends to take place within supermarket retail environments. Until relatively recently, emotions have been off retailers' radar, and still are in many cases. This is in part because historically emotions have been notoriously difficult to measure with any accuracy or reliability, and also because they didn't have a psychological 'home' in academia. However, such luminaries as Robert Plutchik, author of *Emotions and Life*, Albert Mehrabian, professor and expert in human to human non-verbal communication and Dr Paul Eckman, author of *What the Face Reveals* along with many others are helping to bring emotions centre-stage, where they rightfully belong.

I anticipate that emotions will be at the heart of more and more shopper marketing initiatives over the coming months and years. If, as expected, retailers and brands financially invest more to be able to make advanced forms of emotional connections with us as shoppers, consumers and customers, we need to recognise if and how we are being targeted.

This shouldn't be seen as an entirely negative thing, as emotions management can actually be a good thing for us. Imagine, on a wet Friday morning, the housewife, with toddlers in tow, enters the supermarket to undertake the main weekly shop. If the retailer is able to manage her emotional experience in-store, so that she leaves feeling somewhat better than when she first arrived, then it is good for her emotional state and for the value of the retailer's brand overall. Indeed, the retailer should aim to make us feel more affiliated and less hostile towards the store as it's no surprise that a combination of shopper affiliation and shopper happiness results in improved shopper satisfaction and retailer loyalty.

A significant barrier to the creation of a retail emotional nirvana is both the lack of a true understanding of emotions and the difficulties associated with quantifying and measuring them. Over the last century, there have been dozens of definitions of numerous aspects relating to human emotions; although these definitions vary, there are commonalities, predominately around a number of core facts.

First, it is widely agreed that emotions are autonomically triggered by the brain's and body's responses to a stimulus or set of stimuli being faced. Second, emotions involve psychological activity and a level of physiological activity. A third fact that experts agree on is that facial expressions are an integral part of people's emotions. Despite these agreements, it has remained difficult for a systematic study of emotions to be conducted.

One of the reasons for this difficulty is language, the different interpretations words have to individuals and to various cultures. Another difficulty is that of culture itself, in that different nationalities of people have different forms of emotions. Although it is accepted that people from all races and cultures exhibit the same six core or universal emotions, there are some differences when it comes to the much larger array of emotional blends and variants. For example, some Far East cultures consider overt expressions of emotions (both positive and negative) as a possible threat to the social order.

Overall, though, the understanding of emotions and tools to measure them are becoming more available. There are a number of emotions measurement tools that can be effectively used. For example, there is the HSC (Happiness, Stimulation and Control) scale and the PAD

(Pleasure, Arousal and Dominance) scale. Both of these tools work on the premise that an emotion has to consist of the three different components to a greater or lesser extent.

Each of the 100 or so emotions has a different combination of happiness, stimulation and control. It is possible for brand researchers to compare the emotional response to their brand to the emotional experience of using their brand and to the emotions associated with shopping for their brand. As a result, they can align using, choosing and paying in-store at the moment of truth and so drive sales and market share.

Another effective emotional measurement tool is the study of facial expressions. Dr Paul Eckman, author of *What the Face Reveals* and a number of other titles is a leading proponent of this science. Dr Eckman has developed a Facial Action Coding System (FACS) that studies people's facial expressions as indications of their emotions at that time. According to Dr Eckman, humans have some 3,000 facial expressions directly linked to emotion, despite there being less than 200 words in the English language to describe emotions. In addition, Albert Mehrabian, professor emeritus of psychology from UCLA, and best known for his publications on the relative importance of verbal and non-verbal messages was responsible for the 7%-38%-55% rule. This quantified that words themselves represent only 7% of human to human communication when related to feelings and attitudes, 38% of communication comes from the tone of voice used, and the remaining 55% (the majority) comes from non-verbal communication: body language and facial expressions. Interestingly, there are two types of facial expressions: micro and macro. The latter last from half a second to four seconds and we see them in our daily interactions with other people all of the time (a smile from the mail carrier). Micro-expressions are significantly more subtle; they occur when a person is just starting to feel an emotion. These last less than half a second and they happen when people are consciously or unconsciously trying to conceal or repress what they are feeling (when you get yet another pair of hand-knitted socks from your nan).

To conduct FACS studies, the researcher records the faces of research subjects and then plays the footage back at just 1 frame per second (between 25 and 30 times slower than normal). The reason for playing the film back so slowly is that although 'macro' facial expressions stay on the face for between two and five seconds and are easily spotted, 'micro' expressions can sometimes last for just 1/25 of a second and are much harder to detect. Because people reveal their emotions before they can construct any cognitive response to a research question, the study of micro expressions provides great insight to a person's emotional state.

This type of research is being actively carried out on shoppers (Shopping Behaviour Xplained Ltd, 2009 and 2010). During these studies, researchers asked shoppers for their attitudes towards buying and using a number of products including confectionery, hot beverages, alcohol and cigarettes. There was significant consistency in the results of each study.

Consuming the products returned the happiest, most positive, affectionate and dominant emotional connections in each case. Next came shopping for the products which ranged from pleasurable and confident through to greedy and demanding. The worst aspect of each study was when shoppers were asked their opinions of specific brands of product. In each example, shoppers emotionally demonstrated confrontation, rebelliousness and even contempt (in the case of alcoholic drinks).

Further studies of the research data revealed that it was actually the word 'brand' that was an emotionally negative trigger in the minds of shoppers. They felt as if the large brands and the brand owners in some way controlled them and as a direct result they rebelled against them. This was proven in subsequent studies when the word 'brand' was removed.

As a result of the FACS based shopper research studies, changes were made to displays and merchandising. The results were that in each case sales, or at least the share of sales of the sponsoring brands, increased substantially. A particular brand in The Netherlands showed double digit growth, as did the same brand owner's products in Hungary and in Turkey. In the hot beverages category, it has been reported that share jumped by 40% during a brief trial in the UK.

These examples demonstrate just how much of an influence human emotion has in-store. Therefore, for the brands and retailers, measuring and influencing our emotions as we shop offers significant returns on investment (ROI). For us shoppers, it demonstrates how important it is to develop strategies for minimising damaging and non-beneficial emotional engagement when choosing what to buy. Although this is not easy, there are a number of proven strategies and techniques presented in more detail later in the book.

Another indicator of the power emotion has to influence decisions, including those of us as shoppers, was reported by psychologist George Miller and more recently Janice Jenkins in her article 'Marketing Tips & Techniques' which quantified that emotion stimulates the mind as much as 3,000 times faster than rational thought. The famous Renaissance humanist, Erasmus, quantified that the ratio of emotion to reason is 24:1.

It is beyond doubt just how powerful human emotions are and that they are the key with which retailers and brands can get into our minds as shoppers and consumers. To understand more about their phenomenal power, we need to examine what emotions actually do in more detail.

What emotions do

Emotions influence every decision we make every day of our lives. Remember that an emotion is the combined psychological and physiological response to a stimulus. For example, when somebody is sad, they adopt a sad posture and a sad mentality. Motivational experts such as Anthony Robbins state that it isn't possible to *be* depressed; a person has to *do* depression.

In tests, research students have been asked to feel sad and have their physiology measured before and during sadness. There is a significant change with participants' bodies physically appearing to be closing down and turning in. When asked to adopt a proud and confident physiology and then to feel sad while doing so, those being researched simply could not.

To understand how and why emotions are as powerful as they are, it is necessary to examine what specific emotions do. One of the world's leading authorities on this was Charles Darwin. In the book *The Expression of the Emotions in Man and Animals*, first published in 1872, Darwin famously identified that human emotions are linked very much to animal behaviour and are based on evolutionary needs. Darwin recognised the universal nature of bodily, mainly facial, expressions in the book: '...the young and the old of widely different races, both with man and animals, express the same state of mind by the same bodily movements.' This connection of mental states to the neurological organization of movement was central to Darwin's concept of emotion.

I'd like to provide some examples to demonstrate how emotional expressions of the face are linked to evolutionary needs. First, and from the oldest evolutionary perspective, Darwin stated that facial expressions of humans evolved from things called branchial arches. These are gill arches that are associated in the extraction of oxygen from water. In other words, human facial expressions can actually be traced back to a time before we crawled out of the swamp.

In another example, Darwin points out that happiness is visible from much further away than any other emotion. This is because, as human beings, we have evolved to be social creatures who seek groups with which to interact and the appearance of being happy makes a person appear more approachable and less threatening. In the context for humans being social animals, blushing can also be traced back to evolution. When humans think that other people are watching them, and in particular paying attention to their faces, they mentally think of their own face and the brain (without any conscious control) sends more blood there.

Here are some other examples of the evolutionary roots of facial expressions according to Darwin: The baring of teeth when angry or in a rage stems from the gesture of a threat to bite or tear flesh off an opponent or predator. Similarly, but subtly different, the showing of a canine tooth in humans signals a preparedness to bite or enter battle. Humans signal disgust by making a particular shape with the mouth, the same shape as preventing anything from entering it while at the same time blocking the nostrils by pushing up the top lip. In evolutionary terms, people are avoiding what would have been rotten food that smelt bad.

Focussing more on the eyes, Darwin again made excellent links between emotional facial expressions and evolution. When a person partially closes their eyes so that they send out a signal of disdain, what they are actually doing from a perspective of evolution is signalling that the thing they are looking at or referring to isn't actually worthy or worth looking at.

It's clear that emotions communicate people's real feelings in a very accurate way. As Dale Carnegie famously said: 'The expression a woman wears on her face is far more important than the clothes she wears on her back.' According to Dr Eckman and colleagues, the face is the only place where the muscles are directly connected to the skin. This combined with the fact that emotional responses happen much faster than cognitive and rational thought means that facial expressions reveal the truth. On this point, Darwin also pointed out that when somebody is acting (faking a facial expression) their face moves asymmetrically and one side of the face moves more than the other. Most natural facial expressions are, according to Darwin, represented by the face symmetrically.

Not only is this valuable information if you want to know how somebody really feels, but it can also be effectively used to communicate to shoppers in-store, particularly as 'a picture speaks a thousand words'. Researchers from Shopping Behaviour Xplained Ltd carried out studies that compared responses to and sales from two almost identical in-store point of purchase display units.

One group of test units had graphics that included people 'experiencing' the products and showed their facial expressions and the other group had displays that showed the product in situ in the home but without the added emotional content. In both studies conducted within two very different categories (furnishings and satellite television) the results were much more favourable and positive towards the emotionally enhanced displays. Shoppers preferred the emotionally 'tagged' displays, scored the associated brands more positively and, importantly, bought more from them.

Emotion doesn't have to be communicated visually; retailers and brands can influence and physically alter our emotional states when we're shopping by targeting any of the senses. Different genres of music can be used to enhance the emotional associations with particular stores, departments or even products. The ears hear the music, emotional triggers fire in the long term memory and we adopt a mood state in relation to the trigger being fired. Similar reactions can be initiated using smells and aromas, tactile sensations, and even tastes. The subject of sensory communication and influence is covered in more detail later.

Emotions alter our mental and physical states, influence and drive our decision making, and they are the reasons why we react and behave as we do. Emotions are capable of changing our heart rates and level of physical activity, can induce greater physical awareness of the environment and even cause excretions of bodily fluids (tears for example). They are the driving force behind most shopping activity because emotions are designed to protect us from danger and to help us survive and further human existence on Earth. It is because of the vital importance of human emotion and the influence they have on us as shoppers that we've dedicated so much time to discussing them.

Primary and social emotions

Earlier, I introduced the six core universal emotions along with around 100 blends or variants. As a reminder, the six universal human emotions are generally recognised by academics to be happiness, fear, sadness, surprise, disgust and anger, although there is some debate that there are actually seven, eight or even ten universal human emotions.

As already stated, universal human emotions are triggered and managed by the limbic system in the brain. They exist to help their owner instinctively arrive at fight or flight, kill or be killed, and procreate opportunity decisions. Almost all of the evidence suggests that these emotions are completely out of any form of conscious control. After all, they've been hard wired in our brains since before we were humans. This means that brands and retailers could have the opportunity to communicate with us in a way that we potentially have little or no control over. Fortunately, that isn't the case and later on we'll look how we're able to filter emotions through cognition and how they then become feelings.

Universal human emotions still represent the primary means for retailers, brands, advertisers and promotional agencies to attract our attention both in and outside the shopping environment. Different forms of sensory stimuli can have a powerful emotional influence on shoppers. Luckily, many of the people with this power, and the budgets to exert it, don't fully understand how emotion works in relation to cognition and feeling.

Despite this, there are still many examples of shoppers being involuntarily 'forced' to make an emotional snap decision. Often, retailers project moving images onto the pavements outside their store windows using what are referred to as 'Gobo' units. Although these moving images are initially only seen in the peripheral vision of passers-by, what they do is to cause the person to step round or over the image or to stop just for a moment while they calculate the danger from the projected image and whether they might trip over something. At that moment, the retailer has the attention of another passer-by.

Another technique that relies on emotion to attract attention is the coupon dispenser in the supermarket which has an apparently innocuous flashing red LED light. Once again, the shopper is momentarily awoken from their trance to process what this means. Red could mean danger, blood, heat, the womb, etc.

On many occasions, something that appears innocent such as a single red flashing light is actually an attempt by the retailer and/or the brand to engage the shopper at a mental level that they can't ignore (for a split second anyway).

As already mentioned, there are two different types of human emotions: Universal, primary ones – which we've already discussed – and the blends and variants, within which are a number of more modern, social emotions. Lone Frank lists in her book *Mindfield* that the key social emotions are: pride, respect, admiration, generosity, contempt (this one may even be a universal primary emotion), shame and guilt.

Unlike the universal emotions that are primarily involved with survival, social emotions are much more related to how we perceive and are perceived by others and are more cultural in nature. Although there are around 100 human emotions, of which the universals only account for six and the social ones another six or seven, all one hundred are universal, social or a combination of the two.

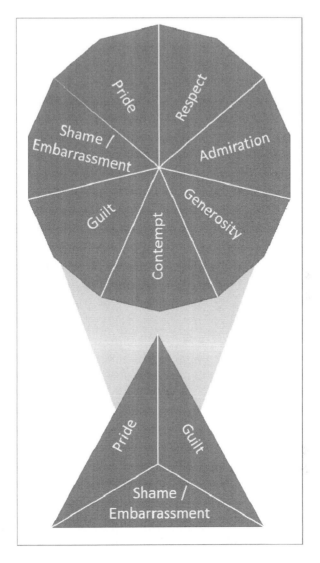

Figure 8 - Social emotions

These social emotions are a powerful ally to most retail and brand communications people and a considerable threat to us as shoppers. Being able to attract our attention in the supermarket by triggering a universal emotional reaction is one thing, but being able to force us to make a cultural judgement or decision is arguably more powerful and definitely easier to attain.

The influencing power of social emotions is significantly greater than that of the universal ones. An image of a sad puppy waiting for his master to return home pulls on the heartstrings of pet owners. Communicate this in-store next to the pet snacks and treats and the result is a guaranteed technique to increase sales and weight of purchase. Although all social emotions offer powerful communications buttons for retailers to press, there are three that are triggered most often in the supermarket environment.

Pride: If an item in-store triggers the emotion of pride, then that's well on the way to being a sale. Motor manufacturers are particularly fond of portraying their brands associated with proud motorists.

Guilt: The second of the top three is guilt, and look no further than the puppy example to understand how easy it is to communicate guilt in-store at the moment of truth.

Embarrassment: This manifests itself in numerous categories, one of the most common being deodorant and toothpaste. The threat of having an anti-social smell either from the skin or the breath is enough to send millions of us scurrying down the soap, deodorant and oral care aisles.

Social emotions aren't as old as their universal counterparts and have only really been around since the predecessors to man decided it was beneficial to operate together in groups. There are varying estimates as to how old social emotions are, some say that as long ago as 200,000,000 years ago when mammals first became warm blooded (and modern elephants do exhibit many social tendencies toward their herd). Other estimates are significantly more recent: For example, anatomically modern humans are believed to have originated in Africa about 200,000 years ago, reaching full behavioural modernity around 50,000 years ago. Suffice to say, social emotions are an output of the brains of modern men and women and exist to ensure that their owners aren't excluded from the social circle or society.

One problem for those working with human emotions is simply the semantics of language: First, different cultures have different explanations of different emotions. Second, and perhaps more importantly, is the fact that the combined weight of evidence indicates that an emotion is the instant and momentary response to the stimuli a person is facing. But, humans are more developed than most other animals in terms of mental capacity. Therefore, we are able to take our own, uncontrolled emotional response and cognitively assess the situation before coming to a more reasoned course of action. In this next section, we'll discuss a uniquely human extension of emotion, the rationalised response to an emotional impulse that results in a more reasoned feeling.

Emotions through cognition to feeling

Until now, we've described emotions in terms of what they are and what they do. It's important to understand though that emotions and feelings are not the same thing. An emotion is an instantaneous reaction to a set of stimuli. The reaction is psychological and physiological. An emotion is the brain's process of putting both the brain and the body in a state of readiness for any impending situation.

After the emotional response, and only afterwards, your mind evaluates the emotion and then the brain and body adopt the 'refined' feeling. So, whereas an emotion is instinctive, a feeling occurs when the emotion has been cognitively evaluated and a more considered response is obtained.

It's important to understand how a raw emotion passes through cognition and how it then becomes a feeling. Our initial response to a stimulus or set of stimuli hitting the nervous system is normally handled by the limbic system. This response is handled autonomically, without any conscious control or input. This uncontrollable response happens extremely quickly and lasts for only a short time, depending on the severity of the stimulus. The pre-frontal cortex then gets involved and acts as a type of negotiator. This part of the brain weighs up the situation and evaluates the options while the body waits in a form of readiness (freeze, fight, flight or procreate).

The cortex relies on different types of memory that combine to create what we collectively know as beliefs or codes by which we live our lives. These codes could be cultural, such as it is not generally acceptable to go to the supermarket in the nude. Other forms of belief code relate to survival, for example, humans learn that it is detrimental to their health if they, when seeking meat for the Sunday roast, decide to cook one of their own limbs. In general psychological terms, beliefs are the simplest form of mental representation (learned ideas and concepts) and therefore one of the integral components of conscious thought.

Beliefs are typically divided into core beliefs (those that the thinker may be actively thinking about) and character related beliefs (those with which a thinker may concur, but that have never previously been thought about), and are not just religious or political beliefs. For example, if asked 'Is it a firmly held belief that elephants wear bedroom slippers?' A person would probably answer that they do not, despite being very unlikely to have thought about this situation before.

Having briefly discussed beliefs and what they are, let's turn our attention to how beliefs are formed. Psychologists who specialise in studying beliefs suggest that they can form in a number of ways. From our early development, humans tend to learn and accept (internalise) the beliefs of the people around us during childhood. These beliefs may be adopted as core, character or cultural, or a combination of two or three. Albert Einstein once said that: 'Common sense is the collection of prejudices acquired by age of eighteen.' For example, most individuals grow up to believe in the religion they were taught in childhood.

We can also adopt beliefs by accepting and 'taking as read' the beliefs of either a charismatic leader or a celebrity; these beliefs are still internalised even if they contradict our previously held beliefs, and might produce actions that are not in a person's own self-interest. For example, why did many teenagers and adolescents suddenly begin wearing jeans so low down that their underwear is often in clear view of the world? Because their peers and 'gang culture' wore their denims this way, there was a general adoption of the perception that wearing jeans in this way makes someone look tough. The advantages of this perception (if it were actual reality), are that it communicates life preserving (don't mess with me) qualities and that being a seasoned 'hard man' is thought of as being attractive to the opposite sex, as the baggy jeans signal a fit and able male.

So, where did this fashion statement come from and why was it adopted as a belief by so many people in the first place? It is thought to have originated in the prisons of the United States: When new inmates were first locked up, they would have their belts taken away so that they couldn't use them to harm themselves or others. As a result, the typical prison issue jeans would hang loosely around the inmates' nether regions. This translates to street fashion as follows: Prisoners wear their jeans low down their butts; prisoners are perceived as being tough, hard men. Therefore, it follows that by wearing a pair of jeans low down, somebody will look tougher or more able to take care of themselves, even if the jean clad teenager is shopping in Tesco with his mum and little sister!

A commonly held hypothesis is that much of modern day consumerism is interlinked with our belief systems as consumers. There is a train of thought that links wearing a replica football shirt, such as that of David Beckham, to the wearer perceiving that they are seen by society as having similar beliefs to the star himself. So, the person wearing the Beckham football shirt perceives that others see him as attractive, successful, a good person to be with and an above average mate. Of course, there may be a significant gap between perception and reality.

The next aspect of belief we'll explore is whether it is voluntary. Sensible, rational human beings need to reconcile their actual reality with any said belief; therefore, if your perception is that a belief is not present or possible, it means that you must either change the belief or oppose it. Many industries recognise this and actively target people's belief systems. One such business sector that concentrates on this is the advertising industry, which is a firm believer that repetition forms beliefs, as do associations of beliefs with images of happiness, sex, love and other strong positive emotions.

This is the link between emotions and beliefs. A person responds emotionally at first to a set of incoming stimuli. Then using cognition, they consider the options, compare with past experiences and then, importantly, run it by their belief systems before committing to their final course of action.

Even very self-aware people, who are conscious of the process by which their own beliefs form, can strongly cling to adopted beliefs and act on them even if they are against their own self-interest. This often leads to people changing their beliefs; even those wired in from childhood can be changed by advertisers, life experiences, celebrity endorsement or brain injury. In Anna Rowley's *Leadership Theory*, she states 'People want their beliefs to change. It's proof that they are keeping their eyes open, living fully, and welcoming everything that the world and people around you can teach them.' People's beliefs should and do evolve and become more refined as they become more experienced in life itself.

There are numerous belief related consequences to shopping. Many of us still believe that 'a Mars a day helps you work rest and play', because that is what the advertisers told us over and over again, many years ago. Someone buying their lunch can justify adding a Mars bar to their Healthy Options cottage cheese crisp bread lunch because it will help them get through the day, not just mentally, but physiologically as well: Calories turn into energy and energy is needed to get through the day; enough justification then!

From a shopping perspective, along with many other viewpoints, an emotion is the uncontrollable, instinctive response that occurs as a direct result of external stimuli hitting the nervous system via any of the five senses. We then use our well-developed pre-frontal cortex to regulate our response by pausing it while more of the options are evaluated. We are able to consult with our own beliefs as well as information stored in our memories as part of the process to decide the preferred action to take. Once the final course of action has been decided, the pre-frontal cortex communicates back to the limbic system and to the nervous system on how best to react to the original incoming stimuli.

The resultant physiological and mental state combine to create a feeling that can last just a few moments or considerably longer depending on the intensity and duration of the stimuli and the result of the course of action.

This three stage process is what determines many of our purchase decisions in-store and throughout life in general. It offers numerous opportunities to both retailers and brands during which they can attract our attention via a trigger and emotional response. They can then feed our cognition with reasons why a certain course of action is better than the others available. Finally, we can be encouraged to arrive at the right feeling and so make the preferred purchasing choice.

For example, imagine you are walking in a trance-like state up and down the aisles of the supermarket; suddenly you chance upon a large card promotional display that is linking a famous chocolate bar with a recently released film: *Sex and the City*. Because the display in question is a short term promotional fixture, it attracts your attention and so generates an emotional response: Because it is something different (possible threat, meal or mate) it requires your attention and becomes something you have to evaluate. The momentary limbic system assessment of the promotional material uses your cerebral cortex and your pre-frontal cortex helps you to realise that a large card box is no threat or mating opportunity. However, it does offer a gatherer related benefit by way of 'low hanging' food.

At pretty much the same time as the cerebral cortex gets involved, and just a split second after you see the display, the emotional imagery also finds its way into the pre-frontal cortex where it triggers feelings from within the long term memory. Let battle commence: now that the promotional display can be viewed in its 21st century context, i.e. in the aisle of a supermarket where neither fighting, fleeing or procreating are encouraged, different choices emerge. You make connections between buying and consuming a chocolate bar with all the beliefs and feelings coming from the long term memory which are enhanced by the way they perceive the film experience of *Sex and the City*.

No longer is it just a bar of chocolate, high in calories and bad for the teeth. This 'commodity' now represents an escape from reality, a chance to leave day to day drudgery. The exact feelings that it elicits can vary, but for many people, women in particular, the response is the same. You start thinking of numerous emotional, belief related and feelings based experiences from a brief rebellion against your everyday life, through to spoiling yourself with a well earned treat.

Many women faced with this scenario will also mentally imagine aspects of control over men, sexual freedom and a host of other emotions, feelings and moods. All this becomes available from a small brown block of a commodity that is both insignificant in nature and minimal in terms of cost. Why? Because it's no longer just a commodity, it's become emotional.

Looking at another slightly less supermarket oriented example, why would anyone possibly buy a Hummer? It's a relatively unreliable automobile that is uneconomical to run, too large to be a practical tool for simple transportation and that is likely to lose its value faster than most other cars? This vehicular monster triggers immediate responses both from potential and existing owners. Like many four wheel drives, it offers a perceived significance to the driver. They are in a bigger box, physically higher up compared to other mere mortals and they believe that they are exhibiting wealth, status and a host of other attributes that they want others to perceive about them. It's fascinating to view a driver's facial expressions whist controlling their automotive charges and equally entertaining to observe the facial expressions of those looking down their noses and physically up at the drivers of these machines.

To summarise then: From a shopping perspective, an emotion triggers cognition that creates a feeling. It is this feeling that is the combined physiological and mental state to which we as shoppers respond. To understand why we respond to such feelings, let's first introduce, and then advance, Maslow's famous 'Hierarchy of Needs'. In exploring additional information about human decision making, I will argue that although Maslow was definitely on to something with his hierarchy of needs, the needs of human beings are actually somewhat more advanced.

Advancing Maslow's hierarchy of needs

We'll start by defining Maslow's hierarchy of needs, which has become common knowledge and a mantra of sorts among marketers and advertisers. Abraham Maslow first published his hierarchy of needs in his 1943 paper 'A theory of Human Emotion'. This hierarchy applies to human needs but as you will observe, it is also apparently well suited to the needs of shoppers. In the book *Why We Shop*, by Jim Pooler, the hierarchy is applied to five different levels of shopping.

Abraham Maslow's hierarchy of needs are as follows; at the most basic level, the initial human need is physiological: breathing, food, water, sex, sleep, homeostasis and excretion. Once this base level has been met, the next fundamental human need is safety: security of the body, employment, resources, morality, family, health and property. The third most important of Maslow's five layers of human needs concerns love and belonging, including friendship, family and sexual intimacy. Next comes esteem: self-esteem, confidence, achievement, respect of others and respect from others. The fifth and final need is self-actualisation: morality, creativity, spontaneity, problem solving, lack of prejudice and acceptance of facts.

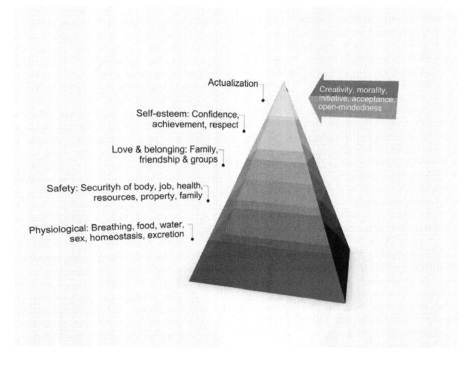

Figure 9 - Maslow's hierarchy of needs

These five needs are often illustrated in the form a pyramid with the lower four needs containing what Maslow referred to as 'deficiency' or 'd' needs, specifically: esteem, friendship and love, security, and physical needs. With the exception of the lowest (physiological) needs, if these 'deficiency needs' are not met, the body gives no physical indication but the individual feels anxious and tense.

On the top of the pyramid sits self-actualisation. Abraham Maslow explicitly defines self-actualisation to be 'the desire for self-fulfilment, namely the tendency for the person to reach his or her full potential'.

In *Why We Shop*, Jim Pooler states that it is easy to apply the hierarchy of needs to shopping. In the first instance, there is shopping for physical survival needs; by this Pooler means basic food and clothing products. Shopping for the basics is often very much a chore, a tiresome task that has to be carried out over and over again. This form of shopping often becomes managed by the short term working memory and involves much single scripted behaviour related to the selecting of repeatedly purchased items.

According to Pooler, the second level of shopping is for health and security products. In many cases, this is indistinguishable from the first level of shopping for physical survival needs and includes everyday health products like razors, bandages, toilet paper and soap. Much of the shopping for basic health and security products is often handled by the short tem memory and carried out using chunked and single scripted behaviours. Once shoppers have learnt how to buy toilet paper, there really isn't any reason to burden the brain with more than the least amount of effort needed to buy it again. However, for the less frequently purchased health and security items, more mental activity is needed. An example would be cough medicine which needs analysis of which is the best type to buy and consideration of which are the most trusted brands.

The third level of shopping in Jim Pooler's adapted hierarchy of needs concerns shopping for items that satisfy social needs including those that lead to a greater sense of belonging and increased feelings of affection. This level is all about shopping to create a sense of belonging and identity and is much more considered. Additionally, it is far more reliant on emotion, feelings and delivering a sense of belonging either in reality or just perception. Retailers and marketers realise that once feelings and emotion are involved, then they have the power to influence, persuade and even deceive. Whether the item in question is the latest type of sports training shoe or a new model of car, the marketers can and do position things as a way for the owners (us shoppers) to better 'fit in'. As we are evolutionarily wired to be social creatures and to survive in social groups, the need for a sense of belonging is very high. Although it isn't actually possible to achieve this solely from purchasing particular possessions, these items are important in helping us to create our own identity within our social group.

Jim Pooler's fourth level of shopping is concerned with us shopping for products that meet our self-esteem needs. This is the level of shopping that moulds how we want the rest of society to see us. For most of us, in these times of conspicuous consumption, owning and buying things that make us feel good about ourselves leads to an increase in our self-esteem and self-confidence. Shopping for self-esteem is very much about shopping for showing off. We'll tend to consume the product extrovertly and in ways that we hope others will notice and perceive that we'll be better thought of as a result. Shopping for self-esteem is shopping to define oneself. Therefore, the purchase process is often an experience where you are made to feel special by way of exclusive retail environments, pampering shop staff, and more often than not, a high price. When we are out and about self-esteem shopping we'll often adopt what is known as an experiential mode of shopping. That is we'll use more than just visual cues to make our purchase decisions. We will try on clothes, listen to the latest Apple product or have the store staff apply cosmetics to us. During this process, we are using the experiential experience to induce an emotionally-led state change to alter how we feel. Once we feel how we want to feel in front of others in our social group, the sale is almost guaranteed.

This leads naturally on to the fifth of Jim Pooler's level of shopping, the level at which self-actualisation takes place. In this context, self-actualisation means personal growth and accomplishment, and refers to us as shoppers attaining a sense of self-fulfilment.

This fifth level of shopping is often referred to as shopping for pure indulgence. It isn't easy to pinpoint the exact feelings of joy and pleasure that come from this type of shopping, but almost all of us will have experienced it at some time or another. The purpose of this shopping isn't just to reward oneself for one's efforts; it's about more than self-indulgence and often involves buying symbols or representations of the success and achievements we have in our lives. For example, rewarding yourself with a designer handbag or pair of jeans, both of which are enjoyable and communicate our success and achievement to others.

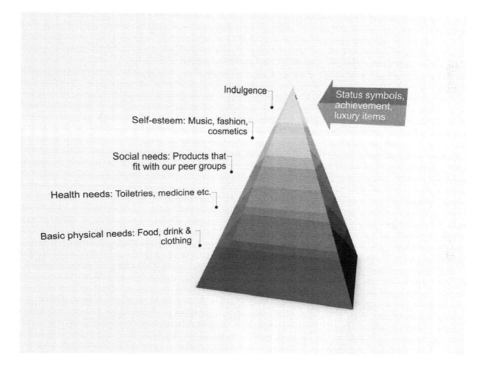

Figure 10 - The hierarchy of shopping needs

Shopping for self-actualisation is similar to shopping for self-esteem needs (level 4 shopping) in that the actual path to purchase has to actively build and enhance the perceived ownership experience. When we are self-actualisation shopping, we want the retail environment, store staff and product display to enhance the brand values of the item. These values are those emotional and feelings based connections that marketers and advertisers have expensively nurtured over the months and years.

The evolution of shopping needs began with Maslow's hierarchy of needs and was then adapted to Jim Pooler's five levels of shopping, although this still doesn't fully align basic human needs with modern day consumerist activity. Next on the journey to understanding shopping motives is a relatively new set of drivers, which on the surface appear to better explain why we shoppers buy many of the things that we do.

The central six fitness indicators

Before introducing the 'central six', or the six universal fitness indicators that drive most purchase decisions from an evolutionary psychological point of view, consider the following. Human beings are remarkably similar to each other. Each has a similar number of chromosomes (23), just over 600 muscles, more than 200 bones and, according to Geoffrey Miller, can expect to take 600 million breaths over the average lifespan. But, as American psychologist William James points out: 'There is very little difference between one man and another, but what there is, is very important.'

Over the last 100 years, numerous psychologists have identified six different aspects of human behaviour that are the key differences that distinguish human minds from each other. These six traits can be accurately measured and each person will have a different combination of them; a lot can be learnt about a person if their scores for the six fitness indicators are known.

Geoffrey Miller, in his book *Must-Have*, refers to the six fitness indicators as follows: general intelligence, openness to experience, consciousness, extraversion, agreeableness and emotional stability.

These core fitness indicators are an excellent means of linking the evolutionary needs of humankind (survival, mating and sociability) with modern day consumer narcissism: The personality trait of egotism, vanity, conceit or simple selfishness. Applied to a social group, it is sometimes used to denote elitism or an indifference to the plight of others. On the one hand, as humans we are wired to find mates, and find the best mates possible. For the men among us this means finding women who will produce a number of good offspring and for the women among us, it is more to do with finding mates that will help produce the strongest and fittest children and who will care and protect most effectively.

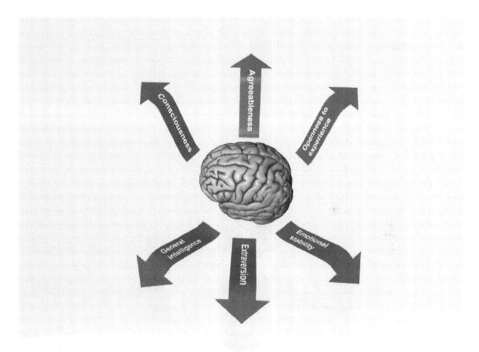

Figure 11 - The central six fitness indicators

This helps to explain why so many women put themselves through what may seem to be strange, time-consuming or painful behaviour. For example, stiletto heels give a woman the appearance of longer legs and make her appear taller. From an evolutionary perspective, a somewhat different picture is presented. In addition to the high heels making women physically taller, they also have the effect of forcing their backs to arch which in turn pushes the chest (bosom) forward and at the same time, pushes the buttocks backwards. The overall result of women wearing high heels is to accentuate the female form, and as fashion historian Caroline Cox wrote: 'Men like an exaggerated female form.' The trouble is that when all women wear high heels, the benefit is cancelled out and women have to continue to wear uncomfortable high heels to avoid appearing visually inferior.

Another example of women exaggerating their own form is through cosmetics, from making the eyes look larger to presenting fuller and redder lips. However, only part of this is to do with exaggeration of facial features; according to many sources, the evolutionary purpose of wearing many cosmetics is to make the wearer look as though they are at their most likely to become pregnant.

Men are equally likely to use modern day consumer goods for some evolution related sexually beneficial reason. Men are evolutionarily hard wired to mate with lots of different partners as this way they can be more assured of passing on their genes. That's the evolutionary part, but it translates in the modern day to a host of consumer goods purchases. Any number of advertisers have recognised and exploited the fact that 'sex sells'. Whether it's the automobile that can turn even the dullest and puniest of men into an instant sex god, or the deodorant that is guaranteed to make you irresistible, or so the advertisers tell us.

In essence, almost any purchase we make is to meet one of the six fitness indicators, and they offer a considerable advancement of the thinking behind Maslow's hierarchy of needs.

Looking at the central six in more detail, the first is general intelligence, which appears to be a relatively good guide or index to genetic quality. According to Miller, general intelligence correlates positively with overall brain size, speed of performing motor tasks, physical health, mental health, sperm quality and therefore romantic attractiveness. It's no coincidence that as shoppers we are targeted with intelligence related claims about products: There are smart foods, brain foods, energy drinks and even smart drugs. Even some children's toys and games are marketed as being good for 'constructive play' or brain training.

What apparently goes against the logic of buying intelligence boosting products is the fact that we'll often pay more for a status symbol that tells others just how intelligent we are. A good example is the multifunction wristwatch, which costs serious money to buy and yet is only really appreciated by the wearer. They are of the belief that the watch helps to communicate to others just how intelligent they are, but unfortunately, as studies have shown, generally nobody really notices what brand or type of watch another human is wearing.

This leads to an apparent conclusion that 'badges' of general intelligence appear to be nothing but expensive wastes of money. However, this isn't always the case; following the purpose through to the natural conclusion, they are worth the investment because of the added confidence and altered mental state they give the wearer. The wearer of the expensive multipurpose pilot's watch might have the added confidence to ask more girls out on dates and the law of averages suggests that the more dates a man has, the greater his chance of a sexual encounter. It follows that the more sexual encounters, the greater the potential chance of ensuring the next generation of wrist watch loving consumer narcissists. This is an example of how consumer goods can help humans improve their own social standing, in their own minds at least.

The second of the central six fitness indicators is extraversion, which indicates the degree to which a person is outgoing, friendly, talkative and socially confident. Extraverts tend to enjoy leading, prefer to be active and exhibit higher levels of self-confidence. People who are low in extraversion prefer to work alone, tend to be physically passive and are less trusting; low extraversion is associated with negativity and shyness.

As a fitness indicator, extraversion manifests itself as a means for men and women to stand out from the crowd in order to be seen. Males want to be perceived as a potential mate and will often go to considerable lengths in terms of extraversion. Elaborate dancing routines at nightclubs, appearing to be the centre of attention at parties, and customising or individualising their cars with things like extra loud exhausts, special paint jobs and deafeningly powerful in-car audio (presumably, so that the music can to be heard above the sound of the exhaust) are all ways of appearing more extraverted.

Females are also naturally more extravert in social situations than they once were. This may have evolutionary roots as women have historically been more prone to group activity, while males have been forced to consider other males as a threat or a challenge. Females tended to share the caring for children and to work as more of a team within the social group.

A much more recent phenomenon concerns younger women who can exhibit extraversion by adopting behaviour historically associated with men, so-called 'ladettes' who populate bars and clubs in many UK cities at weekends. These very extravert females party and drink wildly, often with scant regard to health, dignity or wellbeing.

When shopping, we exhibit extraversion by purchasing products that proclaim our willingness to be outgoing. For example, take a look at the way middle aged men dress in public: at work, in restaurants and bars and even while out shopping, we typically dress conservatively to 'fit in'. But on some occasions some of us will dress in pink shirts and white and blue checked trousers just to play a round of golf. This considerably outlandish act has little or nothing to do with the activity; it does, however, indicate to the other players that the normally mild-mannered office clerk or shopping behaviour consultant is the outgoing, witty, socially confident person whom it would be good to be around. Whether this is perception or reality is open to question. But it does sell a lot of very brightly coloured golf clothes.

Another clothing related example can be seen among holiday makers abroad. Whether it's British tourists in Spain, or American sightseers on a trip to London, there often appears to be an uncontrollable desire to dress preposterously. On vacation, holiday makers can play the role of somebody who is more extraverted and can dress to reflect their more positive inner emotions, feelings and moods. As a result, they adopt a dress code that many wouldn't dare wear in their local neighbourhood. We tend to dress emotionally as well as shop that way.

Extraversion is also linked to men achieving more sexual encounters and women finding better quality mates. In both cases, the principal of needing to be seen to have a chance of being selected is often behind acts of extraversion from an evolutionary perspective.

Openness is the third of Geoffrey Miller's fitness indicators and relates to the curiosity, novelty seeking and broadmindedness of people. Depending on our openness, we'll tend to perceive others, who we see as less open, as dull, tedious or boring. Conversely, we'll probably regard those who appear more open than us as threats; bizarre, eccentric and even downright mad. Although many of us have a tendency to try to appear more open than we are, the truth is that most of us have a natural comfort level of openness and we seek others of a similar nature.

From an evolutionary perspective, we have to be open enough to become parts of social groups; however, we must fit within the group and not be either a burden to it or a disruptive influence. Miller cites evidence from a number of studies that indicate that a lack of openness and some level of xenophobia may well be linked, again from an evolutionary standpoint. We have what is known as an adaptive immune system. This is what protects us from many germs we come into contact with daily. Anecdotally, those of us who come into contact with more germs (teachers and those in frontline medical professions) develop stronger defences against these germs, but there is little or no evidence to say whether we then develop more extravert personalities.

In the retail scenario, retailers and brand marketers go to considerable lengths to demonstrate that as a result of using a particular brand, we'll be more open, extravert and the centre of attention. There are very few occasions where any brand is advertised as being the route to introversion and shyness. The marketers have to make their brands and products appear at the right level of openness; not too inwardly shy, but also not too extravert and wacky. Often it is left to viewers or readers of an advertisement to align the openness of a brand with their own perceived openness, or at least how they would like others to perceive their level of openness.

The fourth of Geoffrey Miller's six fitness indicators is conscientiousness. This is the personality trait that includes such characteristics as punctuality, reliability, integrity and trustworthiness. Conscientiousness is essentially the self-control exerted by the frontal lobes in the brain onto the much more impulsive, short term and selfish instincts of the limbic system. According to Miller, conscientiousness is slow to mature, but when it does, it inhibits the short term mating activity that tends to maximise reproductive success among younger human males.

Because conscientiousness is managed by the more recently evolved frontal lobes of the brain, it is argued that this trait wasn't needed or even prevalent in the prehistoric hunter–gatherer life.

Much of our adult life is spent trying to portray to others just how conscientious we are. Unsurprisingly, modern retailers, marketers and advertisers feed this with a wealth of goods and services that can function as conscientiousness indicators, badges that say we are indeed conscientious. Some of us will display this by always having a clean car, keeping our garden well tended or even never being seen out with unpolished shoes. This leads us into the entire personal grooming market which, according to Miller, is often misunderstood as just lots of products for enhancing and maximising physical attractiveness. However, many personal grooming and beauty products actually serve as conscientious indicators. The well shaved man, the immaculately made-up woman and the impeccably dressed shop manager all serve to communicate conscientiousness to some degree.

Numerous brands and retailer marketers use conscientiousness as a lever to help us part with money. Messages such as 'show them you care' or 'the caring, sharing Co-op' speak for themselves when seen in this context. Other strategies are considerably more subtle and frequently show the mother of the typical family making excellent (conscientious) shopping and consumption decisions while the man of the house is typically 'messing up' somewhere.

In-store, retailers and brands vie with each other to promote the product that best feeds our conscientiousness trait. Kitchen and bathroom cleaners claim to kill more germs than the others, and in the cereals aisle of the supermarket (one of the most visually busy parts of the store), claims and counter claims abound. How many breakfast cereals claim to have no *added* sugar or salt, contain wholegrain, are rich in calcium or are fortified with vitamins and minerals? Do most of us shoppers really understand the actual health benefits or are we just exhibiting conscientiousness by buying products with the longest list of apparent benefits?

As conscientiousness is a trait associated with generally working hard and being reliable and driven by success, it could be argued that those of us who exhibit the greater degree of it will make better mates. The males might be better providers for the family while the females will take better care of the young.

Geoffrey Miller refers to the fifth fitness indicator as agreeableness. He states that agreeableness is at the very heart of human altruism and social progressivism. In other words, it is the rare product of natural selection and sexual selection that allows us to rise above the instincts of most of the animal kingdom.

From a shopping perspective, agreeableness manifests itself mostly in connection with gift giving. Many retailers and brands couldn't survive if it wasn't for the ritualised gifting occasions such as birthdays, anniversaries, religious festivals, Mother's Day, Father's Day and numerous others. Supermarkets devote large areas in-store to seasonal and gifting related categories and products. Almost all gifting related types of occasions have people giving gifts to others as signs of their agreeableness.

This caring nature of humans can be observed in many aspects of modern life. Driving a gas guzzling impractical Hummer exhibits only a minimum amount of agreeableness, while caring for the planet and other humans by driving a Toyota Prius hybrid car communicates significant agreeableness.

Highly agreeable people want to get along with as many people as possible, so they tend to conform. Conversely, those who have low agreeableness tend to be dominant and assertive. To test this, Vladas Griskevicius and his team at the University of Minnesota conducted a study that compared males who had been exposed to sexually arousing images with those who weren't in any way 'sexually primed'. They were testing whether men who had been sexually primed were less agreeable and showed more assertive tendencies than the non-primed males. As suspected, the mating-primed men showed less conformity and more dominance. This is no surprise as, evolutionarily, women have a stronger preference for a mate who displays dominance, assertiveness and a degree of risk taking.

A follow up study by Griskevicius, and the aforementioned Geoffrey Miller reported that the effects of sexual priming are influenced by whether a person is evaluating subjective preferences or hard facts. Sexually primed males show strong non-conformity when making subjective choices as to which brand they prefer but show strong conformity when responding to fact based general knowledge questions.

In summary, sexually primed men (those who have been primed to think of mating) want to improve their chances by standing out from the competition. But conversely, they rely on the opinions of their peers to avoid looking less intelligent about facts. Women on the other hand show stronger conformity when sexually primed, but remain neither agreeable nor assertive when responding to factual questions. Men want to show off their rebellious nature when they want to impress women, while women want to show off their agreeableness when they want to impress a man.

Taking the findings of this research into the supermarket, some commodities are marketed as helping the male purchaser to stand out from the crowd. For this to be the most effective, it would be necessary to sexually prime the incoming male shoppers. Male shoppers would pay particular attention to product adjacencies (what categories are next to each other along the typical customer journey through the supermarket). Imagine condoms next to boxes of chocolates, or men's magazines such as GQ and FHM next to the fresh flowers in the supermarket. Based on the evidence here, sales would benefit from such creative merchandising.

Women are more interested in presenting a conformist perception of themselves and would prefer to be seen as doing the right thing in the eyes of society. In-store, this behaviour could be influenced by offering females product categories grouped by their social acceptance. For example, in the beer aisle, whereas men are happy to lug 24 can packs off to the checkouts, women would much rather be seen to purchase a more socially acceptable amount, such as one or two bottles. In a real life example, chocolate bars were on BOGOF (buy one get one free) in a chain of convenience stores. Researchers from Shopping Behaviour Xplained Ltd were carrying out a shopping behaviour study and identified that on a number of occasions, shoppers were only buying a single bar of chocolate. It was mostly women who were apparently not taking up a free product, but acting in a more socially acceptable way.

The sixth and final fitness indicator is that of emotional stability. This refers to the resilience we have, how resistant we are to stress and how quickly we can mentally recover from an emotional setback. Those of us who are emotionally stable tend to be calm, relaxed, optimistic and quick to come to terms mentally with a given situation. Those low with emotional stability are more likely to exhibit anxiousness, depression and pessimism. They are quick to anger, tend to cry with little or no encouragement and suffer from anxiety.

From an emotional standpoint, emotional stability offers both mates a more solid, reliable and dependable partner. Therefore, we tend to have a strong desire to project ourselves as being emotionally stable, both from a mating perspective and a social acceptance point of view. Within the workplace, emotional stability is often an important consideration for employers, who don't really want a neurotic and tearful person managing air traffic control at JFK airport. Conversely, those in the world of artistic professions such as actors, song writers and designers need to be more in touch with their emotions.

Emotional stability can play a major role in influencing what we do and don't buy. Excluding people who can be addicted to shopping (so-called shopaholics), even the most level headed of us are prone to make decisions based on our emotional stability, or lack of it. We may actively shop for products that display our own emotional stability; such items might include the right choice of wine and food to serve at a dinner party. Conversely, we sometimes purchase products to portray an image of emotional instability. An example of this would be buying an off the wall ringtone for our mobile phone.

Apart from buying products to feed our perception of our emotional stability, we also buy things as a result of our actual stability or lack of it at any particular moment in time. For example, the hard-working woman who has just spent 40 minutes doing a big food shop in the supermarket, upon seeing a large cream cake at the in-store bakery, thinks to hell with the diet, I need that cake!

Other products chemically influence emotional stability, including alcoholic drinks and tobacco products. These types of items have a direct impact on how a person feels. People might burst out laughing or crying for no apparent reason after a few glasses of wine; a nervous person might face up to someone more easily after a nicotine fix from a quick cigarette. These chemical items portray a less than ideal emotional stability to others and although they can address short term emotional imbalance for the user, they do little good for the way we are perceived by others.

What began as Maslow's hierarchy of needs has now developed into Geoffrey Miller's six fitness indicators, or central six. However, in my view, neither is completely correct. Maslow was right at the time, based on the knowledge he had and Jim Pooler more recently applied the Maslow hierarchy to shopping. However, Geoffrey Miller now provides a much more reasoned hierarchy of needs that incorporates modern scientific breakthroughs with a solid understanding of human evolution.

Miller says that the root of consumer capitalism lies in biology. I agree with this point, which supports the fact that humans evolved in small social groups and that image and status were central to social status and attracting mates. From this perspective, the six fitness indicators offer a solid and, for the most part, accepted argument relating to why we buy the things we do.

Miller concludes by arguing that consumerist capitalism is largely an exercise in 'gilding the lily'. His point is that humans take wondrously adaptive capacities for intelligence, kindness, creativity and beauty and then forget how to use them for making friends and attracting mates. He also states that due to this shortcoming, humans rely on goods and services to advertise their personal traits to each other.

My view is that, yes, many purchases are emotionally driven based on either Maslow's hierarchy of needs or Miller's six fitness indicators; however, whether the purchases really do alter our status within our social groups, is falling short of what it is believed to be the fundamental point of shopping for fitness indicator products. The core of my argument is that when we buy things, we do so in the firm belief that the ownership of said items alters other people's perceptions of us. Whether or not people's perceptions are actually changed in the way we believe is somewhat irrelevant. The fact that by making the purchase, we believe that the perceptions of others will be altered is the very reason why the purchase of a product actually serves a fitness indicator purpose.

As an example, the man standing at the bar in his brand new Hugo Boss jeans is chatting to a young woman in the belief that she is aware of and respectful of the fact that he is wearing a pair of quality trousers; it is the wearing of the jeans that provides him with the belief. Armed with it he has the confidence to talk to the young woman. So the investment in the clothing has indeed had a positive impact on the purchaser. Not because he looks any better for wearing the trousers, but because he believes that the woman thinks he looks better.

This is at the heart of almost any fitness indicator purchase, the fact that the shopper (you and I) is of the belief that the owning and using of a product will enhance people's perception of our general intelligence, openness to experience, consciousness, extraversion, agreeableness or emotional stability.

Retail and brand marketers are wise to this and often promote the perception of how others will feel towards somebody wearing, using or consuming a particular brand. We need to realise just how vulnerable we are to our minds that manage our purchasing desires and are shaping our perception of how the world sees us. In addition to this vulnerability and below any conscious level, our brains are constantly monitoring what is going on around us, including how we are being responded to and reacted to. At an unconscious level, our brains are constantly aware of their surroundings; as they unconsciously process and filter information, they alter their state. An analogy would be the way that the flaps on the wings and tails of airliners are constantly making minor, computer managed adjustments to make sure the correct altitude and flight path are adhered to; our brains do the same thing as we exist moment to moment.

This is referred to as priming. Every time the unconscious reacts to something, it begins to prime itself for what may be coming along next. We'll cover this remarkably powerful and hidden brain activity next.

Priming

Priming is the memory effect where exposure to a stimulus influences your response to a subsequent stimulus. What this means is that it is possible to prime shoppers before we arrive at a particular place in the supermarket and influence our behaviour when we get there. For example, large displays of special offers in supermarket reception areas prime us to expect that the store will carry lots of big deals and special offers.

In an experiment with students in the USA, participants were asked to make up sentences from what appeared to be random groups of words and once they'd finished, take them to an office at the far end of a corridor. One group of students had a number of 'slow' words embedded into their selection lists, while the other group had a series of 'faster' words. For example, the slow words included things like sedate, tranquil, lethargic and snail. Examples of the faster words included upbeat, energetic, sprint and racy. The researchers found that the students could be primed to walk at a different speed down the corridor, with those primed with the fast words taking significantly less time to get to the office.

In another, more subtle piece of research, aisles of a supermarket were adorned with graphics that contained a mixture of images and words. In the first aisle, the images were bright, sunny and of young people taking part in energetic activities; the images included words associated with younger people. In the second aisle, the graphics were more autumnal and depicted older people taking part in the types of activity associated with what people do in later years, with corresponding words in the images. The researchers measured the amount of time shoppers spent in each aisle and unsurprisingly, those in the younger, more upbeat aisle shopped faster and spent considerably less time.

There are numerous opportunities for shoppers to be primed in the modern day supermarket environment; however priming can have both a positive and negative influence. At a fundamental level, priming can determine our mood as a shopper once we arrive at the store. A traffic jam on the way to store, a row in the car with our partner or even hearing a piece on the radio about something negative to do with food retailing can all influence our mind-set when we are about to shop. Booking the summer vacation before travelling to the supermarket or receiving some good news while travelling to the store can influence us in positive ways.

Because priming is believed to occur outside of conscious awareness, it is different from memory, which relies on the direct retrieval of information. A summary of research by L L Jacoby in *The Journal of Experimental Psychology* (in 1983) confirms that the effects of priming can and do impact our decision making processes.

Some experts argue that the very layout of the supermarket and the order of the categories we face prime us before we reach a subsequent category. Some of this priming appears intentional, such as placing fresh produce at the beginning of the journey through the store. From a purely objective shopper-needs perspective, it would appear that fresh fruit and vegetables would be best located at the end of the store journey. In this way, we would be able to place those delicate things on top of the heavy cans and packs of food and non-food groceries. Since the French do this, do they place a higher value on the quality of the fresh produce than on its ability to influence our perception of the supermarket?

The fact that we are faced with the vibrantly coloured, aromatic and tactile produce almost immediately we have entered the supermarket provides us with a host of positive and multi-sensory stimuli. All the good things about food shopping are there within the first few steps of entering the store. This primes us in any number of ways, from freshness to health and from colourful to plentiful.

It's less clear whether other adjacent categories are as intentional or positive. One example is the male toiletries area in a particular UK supermarket chain. In some stores, it is located to be visible to the cashiers working on the checkouts, presumably to reduce theft. However, the conservative British male is expected to enter the aisle in full view of a number of toiletry experts (women!) and shop it in a relaxed manner. Not the most effective of priming methods!

It's important to understand how and why our feelings and moods change in any given situation, including the supermarket environment. Once we recognise that we are constantly being primed, we can then begin to address our own mental state in relation to what we are shopping for moment to moment.

One of the reasons why large overhead graphic panels that convey mood based imagery are effective is because when we are occupied with shopping, they are processed by our peripheral vision. It is also likely that they are processed subconsciously and I hypothesise that these graphics are effective because they prime us and alter our feelings and moods. They could also alter perceptions of an entire category of products, for example, cute images of puppies and kittens significantly altering emotional perceptions in the pet care section, making shoppers feel both more loving and more guilty (for having left their pets to go to the supermarket).

To conclude the subject of priming, it offers a powerful tool for retailers, brands and shoppers. However, priming can be both positive and negative and some priming lasts only a short while, while on other occasions we can remain in a particular primed mood for some time. The fact that priming takes place subconsciously is indicative of the potential power of strategically employing such initiatives.

It is difficult for us to defend against being constantly primed by our situations and environments. However, certain steps could be taken. We might use an MP3 player that plays a suitable style of music as we shop or adopt a certain posture as we stride up and down the aisles. This brings us to the next point with regard to how we shop; so far the focus has been on the brain and mind of the shopper. Our brains and minds are unable to buy anything at all as they need the help of a third component, the body. In the next section, we'll explore the role the human body plays in moulding emotions and feelings.

Human physiology

In addition to the brain and mind of the shopper, the body is influential over the purchase and decision process for a particular product. It's worth exploring the conduit that links the brain and the body, and once again, it is all to do with emotion. Emotion and the more cognitively influenced feeling are combinations of psychological and physiological states. As we've mentioned, Anthony Robbins, author of *Unlimited Power* and other books states that a person doesn't get depressed, they *do* depression. Ask someone to start thinking they are depressed and observe their physiology; their head will drop, as will the shoulders, corners of the mouth etc. Breathing will alter as will the skin tone. The brain and body work together to generate the feeling of depression.

Conversely, when we think of excitement or surprise, our heads, eyelids and shoulders all go up. Our mouths open and there is a sharp intake of breath. This gasp of air, combined with the increased heart rate is our body autonomically preparing for a form of action (fight or flight, procreation).

What is fascinating and has been demonstrated many times by Anthony Robbins is that while physiologically in a surprised pose (as related above), it is pretty much impossible to then feel depressed. Conversely, try making somebody act surprised without moving from a physiological pose of depression. Essentially, for any of us to experience an emotion and then a feeling, we have to engage both the brain and the body.

To take this point one stage further, in his book *Descartes' Error*, Antonio Damasio, says that Descartes' error was to say 'I think, therefore I am'. Descartes' entire paragraph in context: '...and remarking that this truth "I think therefore I am" was so certain and so assured that all the most extravagant suppositions brought forward by the sceptics were incapable of shaking it, I came to the conclusion that I would receive it without scruple as the first principle of the philosophy I was seeking.'

According to Damasio, 'Descartes' error was the abysmal separation between body and mind, between the sizable, dimensioned, mechanically operated, infinitely divisible body stuff, on the one hand, and the unsizable, undimensioned, un push-pullable, nondivisible mind stuff.'

Damasio was saying that the mind and body cannot be separated because they work together as a team. This is also explained in a different way by Anthony Robbins, that this combined brain and body functionality produces the mind, a suggestion supported by Steven Pinker in his book *How the Mind Works*. Darwin also summed this up very well: 'The same state of mind is expressed throughout the world with remarkable uniformity; and this fact is in itself interesting as evidence of the close similarity in bodily structure and mental disposition of all races of Mankind.' In other words, Darwin was saying that state of mind comes from combined activity of the brain with bodily activity.

Once we accept the premise that emotions, feelings, moods and states of mind come from the combined efforts of brain and body, it is relatively straightforward to take that concept into the retail arena. Retailers and brands (to a lesser extent) can influence our brains and bodies to alter our feelings and states of mind. There is plenty of anecdotal evidence that shows that most of the influence is taking place at an ad hoc level.

Some psychologists, such as C S Areni and D Kim (1994) have demonstrated associations between music played in retail outlets and subsequent wine purchases. Playing classical or pop music does not increase the amount of wine purchased so much as influence the average price of the bottles selected, with classical music leading to sales of more expensive wines. In their experiment, half of the customers shopped as classical music was piped into the store. These shoppers heard music from Mozart, Chopin and the like. The other half of the sample heard pop music from acts like Robert Plant and Rush (the research was carried out in the early nineties). The results were impressive: when classical music was playing, people purchased wine that was, on average, more than three times the price paid when the pop music was playing. The researchers concluded that shoppers subconsciously linked the music with a perception of sophistication, which led them to spend more on wine. The psychologist North also discovered that playing French or German music influences selections, with more purchases of wines from the same origin as the music.

Combining sound with smell has also been researched on numerous occasions including work by Anna S Mattila and Jochen Wirtz, as described in their paper, 'Congruency of Scent and Music as a Driver of In-Store Evaluations and Behaviour'. In their research, they examined the idea that as consumers, we perceive environmental cues in a holistic manner. They determined that shoppers need to perceive the arousing qualities of music (fast or slow tempo) as coherent with the scent (stimulating or relaxing). They identified that matching ambient stimuli leads to higher evaluations of the store environment, i.e. more positive behavioural responses and higher satisfaction levels than when the tempo and the scent don't match.

These examples are ad hoc in nature and don't appear to be any part of a strategic 'master plan'. What isn't known is whether any brands or retailers have gone as far as creating an entire brand strategy based on influencing and managing combined psychological and physiological responses to change shopper's states of mind in-store at the moment of truth. The combined evidence of this book strongly suggests that it is possible to significantly influence shoppers and bypass many of their cognitive attempts to resist.

If our brain is happy, and we are physiologically in a happy pose, then based on the evidence, our mind is happy. If we link this concept with the six fitness indicators, the potential is both astonishing and frightening, depending on your viewpoint.

As an example of how this could apply to one of the fitness indicators, it is possible for a brand to be specifically targeted at helping to increase our general intelligence. As part of the brand positioning and image, we are made to feel more intelligent in-store. Simple graphics, showing mathematical problems that we could easily answer, if repeated along the journey through the store (maybe under the guise of a child's back to school offer) will give us the perception of cleverness. This could be enhanced by using academic imagery of mortar board hats and students receiving diplomas.

Next would be an adjustment to our physiology, so that we perceive we look clever as well as think we are clever. This may be achieved through lowering the fixtures on which the intelligence enhancing brand is to be merchandised; we then approach, perceive that we are taller than we are and so feel superior and thus more intelligent. This basic example shows that it is possible to alter our psychological process and our physiology simultaneously, and at the moment of truth, present us with a brand of product that perfectly fits our state of mind and how we feel.

Next, we'll explore autonomic responses; the body's reactions to stimuli as it waits for fight, flight or fornicate direction from the brain.

Autonomic responses

When it comes to understanding our bodies as shoppers, there are a particular set of physical behaviours that we should explore: autonomic responses. These are the bodily changes that are handled by the autonomic nervous system (ANS). This is a control system that mostly functions below your level of consciousness and is mainly responsible for things like heart rate, respiration rate, salivation, perspiration, dilation of the pupils, sexual arousal and a host of other actions that you might not think are relevant to shoppers and shopping, but they are.

Autonomic responses are generated mainly by the limbic system to prepare the body to respond to its surroundings and are the first reaction a person has to almost any stimulus or set of stimuli. The actions of the ANS are often divided into 'sensory' and 'motor' subsystems, or incoming and outbound activity respectively.

If the aim of a retailer or brand is to get our attention, then a very powerful way to do so is to cause a reaction from the autonomic nervous system. This can be achieved using a number of sensory techniques, either individually or as part of a combined sensory onslaught. Fortunately for us shoppers, brands and retailers often fail to manage any autonomic response they generate. Remember that such a response is just the initial emotion automatically taking place. For it to be truly effective, the marketer needs to manage the process through cognition and into a feeling that, if done effectively, we would find very difficult to resist.

An example of autonomic behaviour might include us physically salivating when we see a picture of a freshly halved lemon. Combined with a description of the fresh sharp lemon juice dripping onto our tongues, even as you read this page, many of you will start to sense you are salivating. It is important then to attach or anchor the lemon associated salivation with something that is of benefit to the store or brand. It could be fresh shower gel, lemon cordial, gin or any number of other products. The key is that the autonomic behaviour needs to lead on to part of a bigger process; simply causing shoppers to salivate and dribble is unlikely to increase sales of lemons by itself.

Another retail-related autonomic reaction involves lighting. The pupils in our eyes adjust depending on the intensity of light in the immediate vicinity and it takes our eyes some seconds to adjust. When coming in from a sunny street into a store, for the first few seconds inside, it's likely that you'll initially be partially blinded as your eyes adjust (unless the store is very brightly lit that is). Even as we travel from department to department, the lighting may differ so much that our pupils have to make adjustments autonomically. Typically, bright white sodium lamps are used to show off the best qualities of clothing and the whiteness of underwear. If the shopper leaves that department and moves into a less well lit area, then the eyes will have to come to terms with the change.

While discussing lighting, where some retailers have missed a trick is in not fully understanding the path to purchase for clothes. If you imagine you're a shopper and are attracted to a garment that's been perfectly illuminated on the rail, you might want to try it on. Once you've tried on said garment, if you emerge from the dimly lit changing room (or worse still, look only at the mirror in the changing room) and for some reason, the garment doesn't look as good as it did either on the rail or on some stick thin mannequin, then you may change your mind and decide not to purchase.

Often, this is simply because the lighting around the changing rooms isn't the same as that which illuminates the rails of garments, and it's important for the retailer to let us try on clothes in as good a lighting condition as they were on the rail.

Because we have no control over our own autonomic reactions, it is up to the brands and retailers to help where they can. For instance, we like to view carpets and rugs in similar lighting conditions to those back in the home and the same is true of evaluating the colours of paints and home furnishings.

Sounds can also influence the autonomic reactions of shoppers. Dr Luciano Bernardi of the University di Pavio in Italy, conducted research to assess changes in the cardiovascular and respiratory systems induced by music, specifically tempo, rhythm, melodic structure, pause, individual preference and previous musical training. The results showed that breathing intensity, blood pressure and heart rate increased and mid-cerebral artery flow velocity decreased when the music was of a faster tempo and simpler rhythmic structure than the baseline. When the music was paused, research participants experienced reduced heart rate, blood pressure and breathing intensity. Musicians had greater respiratory sensitivity to the music tempo than did non-musicians.

Dr Bernardi concluded that music induces an arousal effect, predominantly related to the tempo. Slow or meditative music can induce a relaxing effect; relaxation is particularly evident during a pause. Music, especially in trained subjects, may first concentrate attention during faster rhythms, then induce relaxation during pauses or slower rhythms.

In summary, there is a key part of our shopping behaviour that we have no control over, our autonomic reactions from our limbic systems. From a brand and retailer perspective, this offers the opportunity to interrupt any shopping trance, but is only effective if the reaction is followed through to some end result. From your perspective, you need to be mindful that although always alert, parts of your brain (and body) are operating entirely on autopilot and are open to influence. Our perception of an environment or even a single object is partly based on a group of physiological sensations; some we are aware of, others that we are not. Incidentally, Feng Shui has evolved mainly because people are indeed influenced by their surroundings.

A useful analogy would be in computer terminology: If a PC is protected by anti-virus software and a firewall, then the autonomic nervous system is the bit of the system that operates outside their control like some form of hardware based BIOS (basic input/output system). This is the part that first comes to life when switching the computer on, but goes into the background once the main processors, memory and software take over.

Outside our involuntary autonomic behaviours, we'd like to think we are pretty much in control of our physical activity in-store. But the shop environment itself can influence time spent, speed of travel, awareness, attention span and a host of other factors and we'll address those later on in the book.

The five senses – How the eyes work

Continuing our exploration of the shopper as a living organism, it's useful to examine how our brains receive signals before they decide what course of action to take. Stimuli enter our brain, either at a conscious or unconscious level, by way of the central nervous system. These stimuli enter via one or more of the five senses: sight, sound, taste, touch and smell which are correspondingly referred to as visual, auditory, gustatory, kinaesthetic and olfactory. We'll study each sense from a general human and a shopper-specific perspective.

The most important sense for most of us as shoppers is sight, or vision, with more than 70% of stimuli we receive in-store being visual.

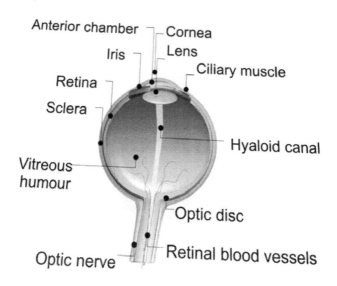

Figure 12 – The human eye

The human eye is an incredible organ and on our shopping journey, it's necessary to understand a little more about vision. Vision is a complicated process that requires input from the body (eyes) and processing by the brain. As we discuss later, 'looking' and 'seeing' are actually slightly different processes that we'll explore further, and here's a simplified explanation of how this works: The first step of vision involves light hitting neurons called photoreceptors that are housed in the retina at the back of each eye. The retina in a typical human eye contains two types of photoreceptors, 'rods' and 'cones'. These photoreceptors send impulses to a network of neurons, generating electrical impulses that the brain analyses and decodes into what people are looking at or seeing. There are some 120 million rods in the average human eye and 6 to 7 million cones, which are responsible for our ability to see colour.

Other aspects of sight include what's known as 'foveal' and 'parafoveal' vision. Foveal vision refers to what we look at with the centre of our eye and the fovea (a small area at the back of the eye, which comprises less than 1% of retinal size but takes up over 50% of the visual cortex in the brain) is responsible for sharp, central vision. We use this type of sight for reading, watching TV and pretty much any activity where focussing on detail is of primary importance. Driving is also a foveal activity, but anyone who has been driving for a while knows that the brain is also passively monitoring what happens in the peripheral vision, side and rear view mirrors etc. Typically, foveal vision is only a few degrees wide, normally a 20 degree field of vision, straight ahead.

The other type of vision is known as parafoveal vision and is responsible for analysing general vistas. It is believed, and now evidenced by people such as cognitive psychologist Manuel G Calvo of the University of La Laguna, Tenerife, Spain, that emotional images have more impact if targeted towards parafoveal vision; this accounts for why those overhead mood panels work in-store and why information laden plasma TV screens seen overhead in stores are less effective.

The subject of visual attention has been studied for more than 100 years. The studies began in the late 19th century when physician Hermann von Helmholtz identified that visual attention was a vital component of visual perception. He also realised that people were visually drawn to new and unfamiliar things that were in their foveal or parafoveal view. This is supported by numerous shopping research studies that continually confirm in-store displays, promotions and messages are almost always most noticed when they are newly installed.

In the last 100 years, we've learnt a great deal about what visual attention is and how it functions. Most recently, psychologist Stephen Kosslyn offered a refined model of visual attention. As presented in *Eye Tracking Methodology*, by Andrew Duchowski, Kosslyn describes attention as a selective aspect of perceptual processing and proposes an attentional 'window' responsible for selecting patterns, differences and contrasts from within a visual buffer. In other words, humans have a form of selective filter.

Andrew Duchowski writes about visual attention and also eye movements: 'Considering visual attention in terms of what and where, we can expect eye movements to work in a way which supports a dual attention hypothesis. That is to say, vision might behave in a cyclical process composed of switching attention between parafoveal (peripheral) to foveal and back again. Given a stimulus, such as an image, the entire scene is first seen mostly through the peripheral vision and as such is viewed in low resolution. At this stage, features of interest may pop out and so attract the attention of the foveal vision for further more detailed inspection.'

Even when attention is on a visual stimulus in foveal vision, it is believed that part of the brain also monitors parafoveal activity. This stems from evolution with humans always having to be mindful of possible predators, meals or mates.

We can assume then that most visual stimuli first attract attention from the parafoveal or peripheral vision. If there is nothing sufficiently stimulating in this part of the gaze, then it is not given any attention by our foveal vision. This means that it is processed entirely 'in the background' which again explains the power of conveying moods, sentiments or feelings via those overhead displays.

The human visual system responds more strongly to some visual stimuli than others. Edges and contrast are more likely to attract foveal attention than more blurred and similar areas. Many special offer, sale and promotional messages tend to be red and white; these two colours contrast very strongly with each other and are more likely to be noticed parafoveally and then given foveal attention and processing as well. Michael Posner and his colleagues recognised that we can voluntarily disassociate attention from the foveal direction of gaze. This means that we can look at an item or display in-store and can, without averting our foveal gaze, mentally (not visually) focus on something in our parafoveal or peripheral vision.

When our eyes scan what's in our view, they don't move around smoothly in their sockets but tend to make jerky, darting movements from one point to another. Researchers around the globe use highly advanced eye tracking equipment that can very accurately measure what visually attracts people's attention in a given scenario. At Shopping Behaviour Xplained Ltd, we use portable eye tracking equipment to analyse and understand exactly what attracts a shopper's visual attention in retail environments. The system comprises of tiny little 'spy' cameras, one focussed on the back of the cornea of the research participant's right eye, and the other on what is in front of them. The two cameras are then calibrated and it is then possible for the researchers to identify, right down to individual words on the back of food product packaging, what is being looked at and for how long.

The length of time that we look at something is important in the context of human visual attention. When our eyes dart from one point to another, each time they come to rest, the brain has the opportunity to process what is being looked at. If the time that the pupil is at rest is between 10 milliseconds and 100 milliseconds, then that is described as being a 'saccade', rapid eye movements used to reposition the fovea on a new location in the overall visual environment. According to Wayne Shebilske and S K Fisher (1985), saccades are so short in duration that during that time they render the person blind.

If the eye stays apparently motionless for more than 100 milliseconds, this is described as qualifying as a fixation, an eye movement that stabilises the retina over a stationery object of interest. Even though the eye is still moving, in a fixation it's as close to motionless as it can be. Fixations are sufficiently long for the brain to process what is being looked at and then decide on a course of action. Obviously, this all happens very quickly and a fixation is just a visual stimulus being communicated to the brain, first to the limbic system for an emotional reaction, then processed by way of cognition and resulting in a person having a feeling about what they are looking at.

The final aspect of sight that's of interest to us as shoppers is brightness and colour. It was originally believed that the parafoveal vision was not only of a lower resolution than foveal vision, but also that it only operated in black and white. More recently, Dr M Gilbert of Imperial College, London has compared a number of research studies and concluded that for high retinal illumination (brightly lit) parafoveal colour vision does not differ in essential characteristics from foveal colour vision. At low illuminations (darker or dimly lit) colour perception becomes reduced to a type of dichromatic vision (only limited colour).

The five senses – Looking or seeing

From a shopper and shopping perspective, there are considerable differences between 'looking' and 'seeing'. Although less biologically scientific than saccades and fixations, this difference still provides significant opportunities to retailers, brands and indeed to us as shoppers. As humans, we cannot process the amount of independent visual 'messages' that come from the millions of rods and cones in our retinas. Instead, we are forced to extract the meaningful patterns such as edges and contrast and it's estimated that the brain is only able to process around 5% of the information it receives from the eyes. That means that most of what is in front of us is quite simply ignored.

In this context, if something catches our eye as we shop, it qualifies as being 'looked at', but only if we then proceed to process it mentally in any way does it mean we have 'seen' it.

Here's an experiment you can try that will show your eyes and brain working in harmony, so that the visual stimuli being received by the brain can be coped with: If you look at a picture of another person's face, and switch your area of focus from one of their eyes to the other, you will be aware of your eyes moving between the two different focal points. Now, stand in front of a mirror and look at your own face. This time when you switch between looking at your own left eye to your own right eye, you'll notice that your eyes stay motionless. In other words, your brain is determining what information to focus on from everything it's receiving.

There is an excellent description of how humans look and see in James W Kalat's all-encompassing book, *Biological Psychology*. In it, he details how and why humans have to be selective about what they look at and see, and he also points out that along with shapes and contrast, humans pay more attention to things that move, compared with something that's stationary. Once again, this comes from the evolutionary need to avoid predators, find the next meal and track down future mates, all of which are likely to be moving when they first come into view.

Retailers have long known that we are more likely to notice something if it's moving. In the book *Why We Buy*, Paco Underhill points out that people tend to slow down when walking by mirrors as we are first attracted by movement, and then presumably transfixed by vanity. The moving image of ourselves captured on camera and transmitted onto a TV screen in the shop window will also slow us down.

There are various estimates on how many marketing messages we are exposed to in any given 24 hour period, ranging from 1,800 to 3,000. Researchers have quantified that the next day, each of us is only able to recall four of the messages that we looked at (as opposed to saw) the previous day. Whatever the exact numbers, the fact remains that we don't see most of what is in front of us.

Retailers and brand marketers are well aware of this selective, visual attention issue. They often put what they want us to see right in front of us; well lit, strongly contrasting and sufficiently big so as to be hard to miss. Conversely, other products and information may be merchandised away from our key sightlines, perhaps having only a few facings and being much less likely to reach our visual radars.

Many in-store promotions succeed or fail mainly because of how many of us looked at them and how many really saw them. In fact, a number of large brands actively quantify what they term 'opportunity to see'. They will compare sales from any shelf, fixture or display, with the number of shoppers who had the opportunity to buy from it (saw it) and those that did see it and went on to shop it.

We're also significantly more aware of what's below our eye lines – things that we may trip over – and tend to pay less attention to anything that may come from above.

Human conditioning also influences what we are more or less likely to look at first and then mentally process and really see. The world over, red lights are used to stop traffic and warn of danger and the same lights will momentarily stop a shopper if used in a supermarket aisle on a simple coupon dispenser or as part of a promotional display. We are conditioned to stop at solid lines across the road in front of us as we drive a car, so when solid lines are put across store aisles, not surprisingly we'll stop at them. In a research study I conducted some years ago, subtle directional lines of grey adhesive tape were applied on top of the grey carpet in a UK electrical store. These lines led the unsuspecting shoppers off the main power aisle and into a specific aisle full of audio products. Before the trial, an average of 4% of shoppers would go from the power aisle into this specific audio aisle, however, during the research, some 18% of shoppers left the main aisle and went into the audio aisle. What was of more interest was that most of the 18% would walk a few paces along the audio aisle, look up and realise they didn't want to be there, and then turn around and leave. In this experiment, I was able to make shoppers see, mentally process and respond to something without them even consciously looking at the grey lines.

In summary then, for you to be able to buy something, for the most part you have to be able to look at it. Then you need to see it mentally so that you can make some form of purchase decision. We need to recognise that our brains only see a fraction of the things that our eyes look at, and from a shopping perspective that means that we may well be missing some of the key reasons not to buy something or to buy an alternative item. It is no coincidence that what we look at and what we see aren't always the most important things for survival and procreation and brands, retailers, advertisers and marketers all employ strategies intended to manipulate what it is that catches our eye and what we are most likely to process mentally. In addition to making profitable things as visible as possible, retailers and brands occasionally try to make some items less visually noticeable in-store. An example is of the lower margin products and those footfall driving loss leaders that are heavily advertised but don't return much profit for the retailer or brand.

The five senses – Smell, hearing, touch and taste

Although 70% of stimuli entering the nervous system in-store are via our sense of sight, the other four senses of smell, hearing, touch and taste are also present and active to some extent when we're shopping. Most animal species have one sense that's more developed than others in terms of evolution. According to a Native American saying: 'A pine needle fell, the eagle saw it, the deer heard it and the bear smelled it.' Humans, unlike most other animals, have only average sensory acuity for four of the five senses with the fifth, smell, weaker in humans than most animals. Despite this, we strongly rely on all five of our senses when shopping.

To explore hearing first of all, a sound is basically a periodic compression of air, water or other media. Sounds are made up of sound waves that vary in volume and frequency that are detected by the ear, initially by the tympanic membrane and then by the other structures of the ear. The sounds are then converted into electrical impulses that travel through and are processed by the limbic system, causing an involuntary emotional reaction. Next, the impulses travel to and are processed in a more considered manner by the primary and secondary auditory cortices in the brain.

James W Kalat summarises the functions of hearing very well when he states that although people spend much of their time listening to language, they sometimes forget that the primary function of hearing has to do with simpler but extremely important issues: What is being heard? Where is it? Is it coming closer? Is it a potential mate? Is it a potential enemy? Is it potentially food, or just something irrelevant? The human auditory system is well suited to resolving these questions.

When shopping, we actively use sound to a greater or lesser extent, depending on the types of product for which we are shopping. There are the obvious examples of audio equipment including MP3 players, head phones and stereo systems, and then there are the less clear auditory considerations. The precise noise a car door makes when closing is actively managed by motor manufacturers so that it delivers the potential customer a quality 'clunk' at just the right pitch and tone. Sound is also used by shoppers to evaluate many categories and they do so without any real conscious awareness. For instance, some shoppers will shake boxes of breakfast cereals to check they are full and/or fresh, while others will shake boxes of dog biscuits and even tea bags.

Retailers often underestimate how important sounds are to us and instead the audio is used to make the store more efficient from an operations point of view. The continuous bleeping of the checkouts, Tannoy messages requesting certain members of staff go somewhere or do something and the ubiquitous code 1 or code 2 to checkouts (secret messages that mean there's a queue and so more staff are needed quickly).

Retailers, brands and shoppers need to recognise just how influential sound can be in-store. Looking at the example of music in-store, a number of studies have shown that it does influence our shopping behaviour and decision making. Field research by Yalch and Spangenberg in 1988 suggested that music affects shopping times. In their study, shoppers in a clothing store were exposed either to youth oriented foreground music or adult oriented background music. Interviews with shoppers as they were leaving the store revealed that younger shoppers felt they had shopped longer when exposed to adult oriented background music, whereas older shoppers felt they had shopped longer when exposed to the youth oriented foreground music.

Reported in *The Journal of Marketing* in 1982, Ronald E Milliman's research results suggest that music affects actual shopping times. In his study, restaurant patrons were exposed to either fast or slow tempo music; individuals tended to stay longer when listening to the slow music compared to the fast music. The additional time in the restaurant didn't result in any greater expenditure on food but did increase the amount spent on drinks. In another study, Milliman quantified that playing slower music in the supermarket increased time shoppers spent in-store by an average of 15% and increased their spending by an average of 33%.

In 1986, Milliman conducted further restaurant research in which nearly 1,400 groups of dining customers were studied over a period of eight weekends. The *Journal of Consumer Research* reported that when slow music was being played in the restaurant, shoppers took 56 minutes to eat and when fast music was played, they downed the food in just 45 minutes. In addition, the slow music led to them spending $30.47 per group on drinks compared with just $21.62 when fast music was played. On average, when slow music was played in restaurants, each dining group was worth $55.82 of gross profit, compared with $48.62 when fast music was playing.

Touch is the third of the senses that we use consciously and unconsciously when shopping. Otherwise known as somatosensation, touch relates to the physical sensation of the body and its movements through a number of sensory discriminators including aspects that determine shape, physical pressure, weight, cold, warmth and texture. Human skin has many different types of somatosensory receptors and it is likely that each contributes to a number of different kinds of touch sensation.

At a subconscious level, we're liable to make quite irrational quality judgements by linking touch with a brand, store or product. For example, the feel of the flooring (cold and hard or warm and soft) will influence how we're likely to perceive the quality of the store and the brand or product we're looking it.

What something feels like may be an important consideration when we are deciding whether or not to purchase it and we often use touch to determine quality for products like mobile phones and camcorders; I discovered several years ago that lighter objects result in a lower quality perception.

We'll often judge the perceived quality of larger electrical goods by pressing the buttons and opening/closing any doors. Some years ago, there was an active link between how slowly and smoothly a CD loaded or ejected from a player and perceived quality. Manufacturers offered hi-fi units with beautifully engineered CD insertion doors that sometimes took two to three seconds to open, and for some reason, shoppers then thought this was therefore a better quality sound system. More recently, I hypothesised that many electrical manufacturers build in delays to add to quality perceptions: Switch on a digital radio and we have to wait some seconds for it to spring to life; the same is true of many flat screen TVs and mobile phones.

The last two human senses are taste and smell, which we'll address together. Taste refers to the stimulation of the taste buds, the receptors that cover the tongue. James W Kalat, in *Biological Psychology*, states that when referring to taste (of food), people often mean flavour, which is a combination of taste and smell. This is in line with a finding from Fu, Sugai, Yoshimura and Onada in 2004, who identified that taste and smell impulses converge on the same part of the brain, the endopiriform cortex. This means that we probably combine taste and smell when making food choices.

Although the taste receptors reside on the tongue, when it comes to smell, the olfactory cells are responsible. They line the olfactory epithelium, which is located at the back of the nasal passages. Interestingly, in olfaction, there is a significant difference between men and women. On average, women detect odours more easily than their male counterparts, and the female's brain responses are stronger too. According to Herz and Inzlicht, women are much more likely than men to care about the smell of a potential romantic partner; no surprise there then!

The human olfactory system, concerned with all things aroma, scent and smell related, is able to recognise smells from the moment we are born. It concentrates on picking up olfactory danger signals such as rotten food or stale milk. This olfactory system is wired directly to the part of the brain that contains the pleasure and survival centres. Smell itself is an 'old' sense in evolutionary terms with relatively few connections to the left cerebral cortex, which is the area of the brain that contains language centres. On the other hand, smell has many more connections with the older parts of the brain that regulate emotion, including parts of the reptilian brain and the limbic system.

As a result, it is argued that we do not rationalise or verbalise what we smell, but have an immediate reaction to a particular smell and a subsequent tendency to act on that reaction. Or as it is succinctly put by Malmar and Vodvarka in their book, *Sensory Design*: 'Smelling something generally leads to emotionally coloured and even instinctive actions.'

Because olfactory stimuli don't pass though any mental filtering system in the brain, we tend to evaluate smells purely at face value. This means that the olfactory system can make a link between behaviour and the subsequent reward (meal or mate). Also, because the olfactory system is wired directly to part of the limbic system, that part of the brain that determines pleasure and disgust, it is a powerful trigger for retailers and brands to pull on, metaphorically. They do so by feeding subtle olfactory stimuli up our noses and into our brains, such as fresh bread in the supermarket, a newly mown lawn in the sports store and countless others.

With regard to smell, context becomes all important. Often, we have to rely on other senses to be able to confirm what a smell actually is: Our sense of smell alone might be unable to determine a ripe camembert cheese from a pair of smelly trainers, but in the context of an upmarket delicatessen or a bowling alley changing room, the meaning of the smell is significantly more obvious.

In summarising the five human senses, although we shop by primarily using visual cues in-store, we also rely on all the other senses to some degree and understanding how we perceive with all of our senses can help us develop more effective ways to deal with these stimuli. In fact, part of how we react to what our senses are telling us is directly related to our gender.

Men and women

As we come to the end of this part of the book, discussing the brain, mind and body and how they affect us when we shop, we'll look at the key differences between men and women. These differences come from both an evolutionary and a cultural perspective.

To begin with, there are our obvious physiological differences. Men will generally have a larger build and be taller than women, which in retail means that men will often look at different shelf heights than women.

From an evolutionary perspective, in the days of hunting and gathering, men had to be able to throw a spear at a moving animal to bring it down and males are more adept at seeing only what is directly in front of them, right in the centre of their foveal vision. This evolutionary difference may explain why men sometimes can't see the butter in the fridge unless it's clearly labelled and right in front of them. Women, on the other hand, were busy gathering nuts and berries while keeping an eye on the family and social group. This lead to a wider peripheral vision than men, and why some say that women have 'eyes in the back of their heads'.

There are also distinct physiological differences between the visual systems of men and women, and scientists have found that most women's eyes have a more complex structure, although it's not yet clear how this difference may influence colour perception. The higher probability of colour-blindness in men suggests that there are genetic differences in colour perception. In 2006 in the United States, about 7% of men could not distinguish red from green, compared to 0.4% of women.

Anne Moir, PhD and David Jessel write in *Brain Sex*: 'Women see better in the dark. They are more sensitive to the red end of the spectrum, seeing more red hues there than men, and have a better visual memory. Men see better than women in bright light. Intriguing results also show that men tend to be literally blinkered; they see in a narrow field – mild tunnel vision – with greater concentration on depth [evolved from hunting as mentioned earlier] and have a better sense of perspective than women. Women, however, quite literally take in the bigger picture. They have wider peripheral vision, because they have more of the receptor rods and cones in the retina, at the back of the eyeball, to receive a wider arc of visual input.'

Taking the subject of gender differences in vision into the retail arena, men see what's in front of their noses, while women can be aware of things all around them. Research by Shopping Behaviour Xplained Ltd revealed that women shopping a one-metre wide, free standing cosmetics fixture were able to cognitively evaluate the display next to it without looking at it directly.

There are also differences in what attracts the attention of men and women in-store. When eye tracking was used to study people shopping for consumer magazines, the results showed that women tended to look at the images of people on the covers of the publications while men took more notice of the words detailing articles inside.

This is supported by research (unattributed, but reported by Anne Moir and David Jessel) into what boys and girls look at. A group of children were given a special type of sight test. They looked through a contraption rather like a pair of binoculars, which showed the left and right eye two different images at the same time. One was of an object, the other of a person. The children had been shown exactly the same images, but when asked what they had seen, boys reported seeing significantly more objects than people, and girls more people than objects.

There are a number of interesting and relevant shopping related differences between male and female brains. Typically, men tend to process better in the left hemisphere of the brain while women tend to process equally well between the two hemispheres. This difference explains why men are generally stronger with left-brained, logical activities and approach problem-solving from a task-oriented perspective while women typically solve problems more creatively and are more aware of feelings while communicating.

In the store, men tend to approach shopping as some form of military operation that has to be completed as quickly as possible with the minimal amount of effort and spend; conversely, women prefer to evaluate all of the available options (pairs of shoes) before making a final purchasing decision (sometimes the first pair looked at!). Although that example is slightly tongue in cheek, the principle is that men shop as a task, women shop to solve a problem creatively.

Psychologist Shelley E Taylor states that men tend to have a 'fight or flight' response to stress situations while women approach these situations with a 'tend and befriend' strategy. She says that that during times of stress, women take care of themselves and their children (tending) and form strong group bonds (befriending). Anecdotally, this may in part explain why there are more female shop assistants than males and perhaps why many believe that women make better store staff.

Further evidence that women are better suited to working in a retail environment comes from the fact that females typically have a larger deep limbic system than men. This allows them to be more in touch with their feelings and better able to express them, which promotes bonding with others. Essentially, female shop assistants are better equipped evolutionarily to understand what it is that the shopper wants; they communicate more effectively and are adept at making emotional connections with shoppers.

From a shopping perspective, it really is the case that men are from Mars and women are from Venus and have different needs in-store. Unfortunately, too many retailers try to be all things to all men… and women, without fully understanding how to optimise their retail selling space for either.

How the brain, mind and body shop, a summary

In this first part of the book, you've been taken on a journey around and through our brains, minds and bodies, first as humans and specifically as shoppers. We began by exploring that most astonishing of organs, the 1.5 kilograms of grey matter that we call the brain.

We learnt that our ancestral brain system has been evolving for hundreds of millions of years, with cognitive reasoning being a very recent invention. What this means is that although our human brains are wonderfully advanced, they are just not particularly well adapted to shopping and modern living/retail environments.

We explored how it is that we have evolved differently from other animals and have a unique ability to use cognitive means of situation evaluation. We're able to choose actively between alternative responses to situations, much more so than other members of the animal kingdom.

Despite this, from an evolutionary perspective, and specifically as shoppers, we haven't evolved at all. Quite simply, shops haven't been around anywhere near long enough for evolution to occur and we still shop from an evolutionary standpoint of a time before shops existed. In other words, the human race has yet to become fully accustomed to the supermarket.

We don't just have a single, unified brain; in fact, humans have three brains: the old or reptilian brain, the limbic system, and the cortices or higher brain. The role of the reptilian brain and the limbic system are to keep their owner alive and to ensure that the next generation will come to pass. Our higher brain assesses the input from the lower brains and takes a more thoughtful look at the situation. This additional and more recently evolved part of the brain is what separates instinctive animal behaviour from more 'intelligent' and 'sensible' human activity.

The different types of human memory were explored in detail: The short term memory which handles the mundane minute to minute decisions, but which has limited capacity and can only process seven plus or minus two pieces of information at any time. In addition, we also possess a much more powerful long term memory, which is basically a system for permanently storing, managing and retrieving information for later use. Information stored in the long term memory could be available for a lifetime.

We examined how the limited short term working memory optimises it's capabilities by learning many single scripted behaviours, a group of behaviours or actions that can be carried out below any conscious level and that can be triggered by a single stimulus. We also explored chunking which involves creating a strategy for making more efficient use of short-term memory by grouping small bits of information into manageable chunks.

Next, we looked at the ways retailers, and particularly brands, aim to form strong, meaningful and profitable associations with us as shoppers and consumers. Once we are hard wired to a brand, then we represent a loyal source of future sales. The key tool brands and retailers use to connect with us is emotion, probably the most influential tool known to man.

The fact is that we are emotional by nature and shopping is not for the most part any form of rational or objective process; decisions are made emotionally. However, emotion is only the first step towards mentally making a purchase and after the emotional response, our cognition evaluates the situation; only then do our brains and bodies adopt the 'refined' feeling.

Darwin identified that human emotions are very strongly linked to animal behaviour and evolutionary needs. Emotions are capable of changing our physiology, can induce greater physical awareness of the environment and even cause excretions of bodily fluids (tears for example). They are the driving force behind most activity because emotions are designed to protect us from danger, help us survive and further human existence on Earth.

Two different forms of emotions were examined: Universal, primary emotions and the more recent social emotions. Being able to attract the attention of a shopper by triggering a universal emotional reaction is one thing, but being able to force us to make cultural judgements or decisions based on triggering a subsequent social emotional reaction is arguably more powerful and definitely easier to attain.

We can summarise this as: Stimuli to emotions to feelings via cognitive consideration and evaluation from a shopping perspective; the emotion triggers cognition that in turn creates a feeling. This feeling determines the decision we make in the aisle of the supermarket.

The evolution of shopping needs began with Maslow's hierarchy of needs, which was then adapted to Jim Pooler's five levels of shopping. Next we refined this further by introducing the six fitness indicators: general intelligence, openness to experience, consciousness, extraversion, agreeableness and emotional stability.

These core fitness indicators are an excellent means of linking the evolutionary needs of the human species (survival, mating and sociability) with modern day consumer narcissism. Shoppers who buy certain items do so in the firm belief that ownership of said items alters other people's perceptions of them. Whether or not people's perceptions are actually changed in the way the purchaser believes is somewhat irrelevant. The fact that the shopper making the purchase believes that perceptions will be altered is the very reason why the purchase of a product actually serves a fitness indicator purpose.

We then examined the ways in which our bodies influence the path to purchase and decision process for a particular product. How we shop depends very much on both psychology *and* physiology. If your brain is happy, and you physiologically adopt a happy pose, then based on the evidence your mind is happy.

We introduced an entirely involuntary physiological process, the autonomic response, which is generated mainly from the limbic system as a preparation of the body in response to an incoming set of stimuli. It is the first reaction a person makes to almost any particular given stimulus or set of stimuli.

Incoming stimuli enter our bodies and then brains by way of one or more of the five senses: sight, sound, taste, touch or smell. We explored vision, seeing and looking in some depth as more than 70% of stimuli that we receive when shopping, we do so visually. We then examined the other senses in the context of shoppers and shopping.

Finally, we looked briefly at the differences between men and women when shopping.

To understand how we are influenced and targeted, it's crucial to realise how we've evolved, why we still act on instincts and to be mindful of the ways we react. We are truly wonderful beings, but when it comes to being shoppers, we are still yet to develop fully.

It is no surprise that retailers and brands continue to invest heavily to better understand how shoppers (those who pay their wages when all is said and done) function. They are particularly keen to understand what drives us, what motivates us, particularly when we are among thousands of products to buy and take away from the store.

In the next section, we'll explore some of the ways the retail environment is used to influence our purchasing decisions. We can take solace in the fact that it is not only shoppers' brains that have not yet adapted to being efficient in-store, but also the brains of retailers and brands that haven't yet fully evolved to sell all that well either. Remember the quotation from earlier: 'If the human brain were so simple that we could understand it, we would be so simple that we couldn't.' That applies to shoppers and shopkeepers, brand owners and marketing people.

Section 2
How shoppers are targeted

Introduction

Now that we have a good understanding of how and why our brains, minds and bodies function as they do when we're shopping, we'll examine in detail how the retailers and brands go about influencing our purchasing decisions.

Although supermarkets are sometimes portrayed in a bad light, this section will present a different scenario: The stores provide what we as shoppers want in the 21st century (albeit not perfectly), but unfortunately, we are thousands of years away from evolving into efficient supermarket shoppers.

We'll analyse the physical environment of the supermarket, in particular how we're targeted in-store and how we typically respond, both positively and negatively. We'll review further evidence that the modern supermarket is an environment that we aren't sufficiently equipped to cope with and how this can lead us to some flawed decision making.

To provide a useful context, we'll summarise the history of the supermarket and discover such things as how the original stores addressed the problem of shoppers leaving with items that they hadn't paid for. We'll also cover the different types of supermarkets and how they're categorised.

Brands are a central part of shopping so we'll examine just what a brand is and how it's packaged and advertised to align emotionally with our perceptions and aspirations. We'll discover that even before arriving at the store, we've already been 'conditioned' to regard certain brands and products in certain ways.

In the pages ahead, we'll embark on a shopping trip with a difference. We'll look at what's happening in-store, both in terms of how we as shoppers behave and are influenced, and what aspects of the store, products, packaging, etc. have an influence over us. How are shop windows used? How does the store and merchandise engage and involve us at different levels? We'll quantify the importance of our own first impressions and how this impacts on our shopping and buying behaviours. We'll also explore the subject of other shoppers and their influence and discover why we act, feel and behave more exaggeratedly in a group compared with when we're alone.

A central subject for any serious retail organisation is category management, and although this aspect of retail has been around for a number of years, it's often incorrectly used or understood. We'll explore why this might be and provide an actual definition of what category management is all about.

Next in the spotlight is the complex subject of product packaging; now, more than ever before, brands are given fewer and fewer opportunities to communicate directly with us from the shop floor. A key aspect of shopper marketing is shopper communications; discovering how and where in the modern day supermarkets brands still have opportunities to make direct communication connections with shoppers.

No book on supermarket shopping would be complete without reference to the subject of pricing. One thing that almost all supermarkets have in common is that they are known for providing quality goods at what are perceived to be competitive prices. Find out how and why so many prices vary across different supermarket chains and more importantly why the subject of price and price sensitivity is more important to retailers and brands than it is to most shoppers.

Price alone means little unless it's discussed in the context of value and we'll explore the fact that value often means different things to retailers compared with what it means to shoppers. Find out why retailers and brands should consider how they can further add value by more appropriately meeting our central six fitness indicator related needs.

Advancing the price and value discussion, we'll examine why, if some store chains are cheaper than others, all the shoppers don't go there? What is it that attracts some of us to Waitrose, Marks & Spencer and the like? Find out why we prefer supermarkets that are shopped by people similar to how we perceive ourselves to be and discover why many adults develop their loyalty to a particular chain of supermarkets while they are still children.

We'll explore the details of how, when you first arrive at the supermarket, you are most likely to react when faced with an arena crammed full of imagery, logos, words, strap lines, video and audio plus a host of other attempts to attract your valued attention.

We'll look at the three forms of in-store information; find out what they are and which are beneficial for shoppers and which are more valuable to the retailers and brands. We'll also attempt to quantify how many messages each of is likely to be exposed to each time we visit the supermarket.

Finally, we'll examine the subject of adjacencies and why it is that the products that are often next to each other in the supermarkets aren't always the ones we as shoppers want to see side by side.

We'll begin though, by defining what a supermarket actually is.

What is a supermarket?

The *Oxford English Dictionary* defines a supermarket as: 'A large self-service shop selling food and household goods'. This means that they typically offer a wide selection of food and drink products and a variety of non-food items including cleaning products, healthcare items, medicines, clothes and home wares. In recent times, supermarkets have also started selling electrical goods and other big ticket products and many are branching out into financial services including credit cards, banking and insurance policies.

Typically, there are three types of supermarket, categorised by size. The smaller stores are often referred to as neighbourhood or convenience stores and according to the National Association of Convenience Stores, this type of store is a retail business with a primary emphasis on providing the public a convenient location to quickly purchase a wide array of consumable products (predominantly grocery and fuel) and services. Typically, a convenience store has up to 5,000 square feet of retail selling space and sells predominately food and drink, plus a minimal selection of non-food lines.

The next largest type of supermarket is the midsized supermarket or traditional store that sells anywhere between 30,000 and 50,000 different items. Typically they have anywhere between 10,000 and 50,000 square feet of retail selling space. These stores tend to sell a wider range of food and non-food items than the smaller neighbourhood outlets. Historically, they tended to be the largest supermarkets of 30 years ago – often in town centres. They aren't able to grow in floor space due to other stores to either side and because many of them don't have car parks, they aren't as well equipped to cater for the modern day big shop.

The largest supermarkets are known as hypermarkets; these larger, full-service stores are a supermarket combined with a department store, selling a very wide range of products, big ticket items, services and more. They often include restaurants, crèches, photo development counters, pharmacies and petrol stations.

Supermarkets have a reputation for selling products at reduced margins, due to their ability to bulk buy from suppliers and negotiate better deals. Almost all supermarkets are self-service; we as shoppers are allowed to walk around the warehouse sized room full of aisles and aisles of products and help ourselves to anything we want.

At the end of the shop, when we have collected everything we want (and often other things that we didn't really need) we then head for the checkout. This will generally be one of a long line of tills, each manned by a member of staff. We'll dutifully place our goods onto a conveyor belt and after the member of staff has scanned each one, we'll pay, put them in boxes or bags and take them home.

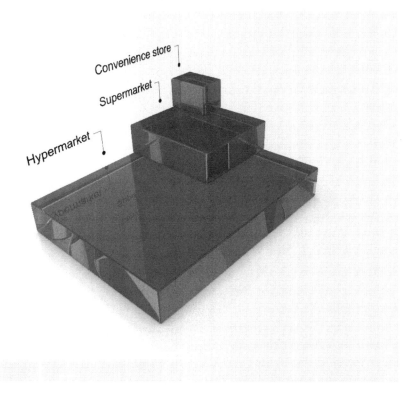

Figure 13 - Comparison of shop sizes

Some stores have other ways of checking out goods; we can use a personal handheld scanning device to compile our own list of products and then just authorise a credit or debit card payment afterwards. We can also scan our goods through self-service checkouts. With this process, there is no need for any store staff intervention. However, there is a need for trust, which can present issues and challenges; just ask the supermarket managers in France what they think of the typical British supermarket shopper (put it this way, they sometimes don't entirely trust our honesty).

In the early days of food retailing, customers first listed the items they wanted and then waited for them to be fetched by an assistant from shelves behind the shopkeeper's counter. In those days, most foods and merchandise did not come in individually wrapped, consumer-sized packages, so an assistant had to measure out and wrap the precise amount desired by the shopper. These practices were labour intensive and quite expensive. The shopping process itself was slow, as the number of customers who could be attended to at any time was limited by the number of shop staff working in the store.

The idea of the self-service grocery store was developed by an American entrepreneur, Clarence Saunders and his Piggly Wiggly stores. He opened his first store in Memphis, Tennessee, in 1916 and other grocers soon adopted the self-service format. Clarence Saunders worked for most of his life trying to develop a truly automated store, first developing Piggly Wiggly, then the Keedoozle, and Foodelectric store concepts. At its peak, the company was operating 2,660 stores and posting sales of $180 million a year.

The early self-service stores didn't sell perishable items such as fruit, vegetables or meat and so weren't truly what we now know as supermarkets. There's been much debate on the origin of supermarkets as we know them. Contenders included King Cullen, Ralph's in California and Weingarten's Big Food Markets. To answer this question, the Food Marketing Institute in conjunction with the Smithsonian Institution and with funding from H.J. Heinz, studied the issue and came to the following conclusions. First, they defined the attributes of a supermarket as being 'self-service, separate product departments, discount pricing, marketing and volume selling'.

Subsequently, they determined that the first true supermarket was in the United States and was opened by Michael J Cullen, on August 4, 1930, inside a 6,000 square foot former garage in Jamaica, Queens in New York City. The store was named King Kullen, cleverly linking King Kong with Michael Cullen. Although Clarence Saunders had brought the world self-service, uniform stores and nationwide marketing, Michael J Cullen built on this idea by adding separate food departments, selling large volumes of food at discount prices and by adding a car park.

In the early days, there was an unforeseen problem with these large self-service emporia; some shoppers would leave the store without paying for some of their items, and would attempt to conceal products about their person. Before the age of the store detective, the pioneers of retail devised a cunning means of minimising theft (now referred to as shrinkage): They designed checkout kiosks and then placed them in a row, fairly close together. This meant that the shoppers almost had to squeeze between two checkout operatives before leaving the store; in theory this allowed the staff to scan them visually for any unnatural lumps and bumps.

Another issue arising from the invention of supermarkets was that shoppers were able to make their own choices between different makes (brands) of similar products. As a direct result, packaging and brand recognition became very important, so much so that an entire industry now operates under the banner of being brand related: From research to design, to advertising to packaging.

It could be argued that because the industry has become so large and disparate, the true meaning of what a brand is has been somewhat forgotten.

What is a brand?

Earlier, we described a brand as the de-commoditisation of a commodity for the purposes of charging more for it. In truth, there is much more to brands than this. Originally, a brand was a way for a farmer to be able to mark his own cattle by means of a red hot branding iron so that a farmer could identify his cattle when they had been mingling with other herds on the prairies. It could also help identify any rustling activity, because it's not easy to remove a permanent scar from the hide of a steer.

Nowadays, a brand is a name given to a particular product, or as an umbrella name for a range of goods or services, such as Coca-Cola, Marlboro, Gillette, Disney, Google, Colgate or Apple. There are typically two different aspects that make up a brand.

If you think of a brand, it will typically start with the tangible brand assets, such as the name, logo, set of colours and shape. These all help us recognise a particular brand, but in the world of branding, this is just the tip of the iceberg. The much more valuable assets lie below the surface and relate to our mental associations with a brand. These are the hard earned emotional links to any of the tangible assets. It is these associations that differentiate a product or service, which is often no more than a commodity, from competing brands and products. The subsequent value of a brand can often be much more than the basic value of materials and tangible assets. Brand owners and marketers go to great lengths to create what are known as brand plans and these are often produced before a product even becomes branded. In other words, an organisation will recognise a gap in the market and go about researching it and then offering the ideal brand to fill it. Once the market position has been identified, the brand plan will be developed and will typically include elements like a brand promise, one line that encapsulates what that product represents. They will also think carefully about brand positioning, is it exclusive, mainstream or value? And who are the target customers? These are just three of a comprehensive set of considerations that make up the majority of brand plans.

After a thorough and meticulous process, a brand appears on shelf in a store. And for many, this is where it will live or die. Somewhere between 70% and 90% of new product launches end up in failure (figures vary depending of source). Despite this, thousands of launches take place every year and billions of dollars are invested into research, development, marketing and manufacture, so it's clear that the rewards must be there for the select few that do succeed. As a crude calculation, here's a basic explanation relating to why so many organisations continue to launch new products, remembering that brands themselves are a set of emotional associations. Imagine, for the sake of argument, around 80% of new product launches fail. On the other hand, the financial value of successful brands such as Coca-Cola and McDonald's is somewhere around five times the value of tangible assets and stock. On the surface it would appear that these big brand companies get odds of five to one that their new launch will be a success and if it is, they can expect the value of it to increase by five times. This represents sound business logic, albeit presented in a remarkably simplistic form here.

Bringing the subject of branding back into the topic of shopping, the brand, like emotion, is always a part of the decision process. Why? Because brand is emotion and emotion is brand.

As consumers we have definite likes and dislikes in terms of luxury goods brands, which is partly understandable. Some of us are also staunchly brand loyal in areas such as the bottled water and bread aisles of the supermarket and fuel for the car. Given the time and the inclination, a useful analysis is for us to identify what it is about a brand we buy and then calculate the true value versus worth of the item.

For example, is Evian water (which interestingly spells naïve, backwards) at 39p per litre (mysupermarket.com) really more than twice as good as Tesco Perthshire Mountain Spring water (17p per litre)? To some it most certainly is, depending on the emotional connections they have with Evian.

Personally, I'm fond of the Cape Town area of South Africa, having both worked and holidayed there a number of times. Therefore, I have strong emotional associations with a brand of lager called Castle, and a particular brand of red wine (Boschendal Manor), both of South African origin. When either of these items is available in the UK, I know I will choose them over any other brand in that store. They might be more expensive than other brands, and I probably couldn't pick out either in blind taste tests. However, the emotional connection with downing a bottle of Castle on the Waterfront in Cape Town, or having a glass of the Boschendal Manor red wine while picnicking in the grounds of Boschendal Manor itself are just too strong.

We are constantly making emotional connections with particular brands, some good and some bad. Retailers and brands need to understand fully how their products and those of their competitors are emotionally wired into our minds. For us as shoppers, it's more a case of self-evaluation and understanding why we prefer some brands over others, as with my own South African beer and wine preferences.

There are very few examples of a brand having a monopoly so we have a choice in almost everything we buy. To underline further the importance of retailers and brands emotionally aligning with us as consumers, consider the odds of a particular product finding its way into the typical shopper's trolley: The average large supermarket has in the region of 50,000 different types of product available for us to buy and conversely, the average supermarket trolley goes through the checkout process containing less than 100 items. Therefore, any single product has, on a level playing field, a 1 in 500 chance of being selected. Or to put it another way, if we assume that we spend on average 40 minutes in the supermarket doing the weekly big shop, then each of those 50,000 lines has just 0.48 of a second to connect with us. That's how important branding is in the supermarket!

From our perspective, things are different; we have choice and lots of it. We can be selective in what we choose to buy and the brands we decide to align with emotionally or aspire to. We can and do have the power to select or reject almost any brand we want. Every single brand should recognise what is happening in modern retail and the diverse choice that shoppers have.

First impressions inside the supermarket

When we arrive at the store, we're normally faced with several external messages. These could be on poster hoardings, light boxes or in the store windows; even before getting to the products, our brains are being asked to make decisions.

How we perceive these external messages depends in part on whether the store is one that we regularly pass by or frequent. If not, we tend to be more aware and take on board more of the messages aimed at us. This type of shopping is often known as infrequent or conscious shopping.

The other form of shopping is frequent shopping; this occurs when we're in familiar surroundings that contain messages we've seen and mentally processed before. This message processing is another human behavioural aspect that's very relevant to shoppers and shopping.

Because we're overwhelmed by visual imagery, every day, and as our brains are only able to process 5% of the information sent to them by our eyes, we're forced to filter out most of what's in front of us. The things that are most likely to get noticed and processed are objects that may be threats, meals or mates.

We're wired to spot things that are unfamiliar and different, and from a shopping perspective this means we're more likely to notice contrasting objects or things that have recently changed. A new poster will receive more than average attention, but for how long is the main question? If the message is in a window that we walk past every day, then its impact will be nullified after just a couple of days. Conversely, the same message in a Duty Free store at an airport will receive the attention of 'infrequent for the most part' travellers for up to a year or even more.

In a study by us at Shopping Behaviour Xplained Ltd, we measured the value of posters in the windows of banks on British High Streets.

Our researchers counted every passer-by that looked or stopped and looked at specific messages in the windows. Unsurprisingly, after just a few days, hardly anyone bothered to look at the still relatively new message. In other words, they'd seen it, checked it and filtered it out as it wasn't a threat, meal or mate.

The more important finding from the research came after the poster had been in situ for three weeks. Our researchers simply replaced the posters with others that were identical apart from the fact that the colours were switched; in other words, what had originally been red on a white background became yellow on a red background. Suddenly, interest in the messages was back to the same as it was immediately the original messages had been installed. Once again, this interest quickly tailed off and only lasted a few days.

Shopper facing communications each have a 'media value', calculated on a number of factors.

First, there is 'opportunity to see'; this refers to how many people pass by a message. The second factor is 'look', the number of passers-by who actively look at a piece of communication. The third media value component is 'time in view', how long do passers-by have the message in view, so as to absorb its content.

Several things can influence one or more of these factors. For example, many store windows are parallel to pavements, roads or shopping mall walkways, so people pass by looking straight ahead, the windows never enter foveal vision and the information would have a relatively low media value. In most cases where the messages are in store windows, passers-by would have to turn their heads ninety degrees to look at the message. In these cases, the communicator often tries to 'grab' the attention. They may use big, bright materials or employ flashing lights or other forms of movement. Another underused communication technique would be to present the information perpendicular to the route shoppers and passers-by are travelling along; a simple and cost effective means of raising a media value. A good example are those annoying 'A-frame' signs outside stores that tend to block pavements but that enable stores and brands to present information directly in the sightlines of those approaching along the roads and pavements.

It is the responsibility of the retailer and the brand to get their messages to stand out from all the other visible cues vying for our attention, both outside and inside the store. We, on the other hand, need to develop a strategy for most effectively scanning what's around us. Remember that once we are engaged in frequent shopping, messages, added value and other beneficial details can easily get missed.

Another aspect we need to consider around messaging and information, both on the approach and in the early part of the store itself, is the speed at which we arrive. For example, as you drive into the motorway service area for a quick snack, your brain is still mentally travelling at 70 miles an hour. You'll be mentally alert and much more aware of your surroundings. Additionally, you'll tend to move faster and it will take you several paces to process and respond to a particular message in the forecourt shop. It normally takes the brain a few minutes to relax and slow down after driving at speed. Conversely, if you amble into the local newsagent having been walking along the street, you are mentally travelling at just 2 or 3 miles per hour; you'll be less alert and harder to influence because of this. However, when you do react, you are likely to be physically close to the source of the message.

Retailers want us to buy as many of their wares as possible. A technique that's been widely used for many years is to slow us down and get us interacting with products as near to the shop door as possible. This area of the store is sometimes referred to as a deceleration zone and when we're in it, we begin to become acclimatised to our surroundings. In addition to slowing down, our eyes are able to adjust to the light inside.

Some retailers make their deceleration zones even more effective by stopping shoppers from walking through them in a straight line. Promotional displays of new release DVDs or big pallets of seasonal special offers are often placed smack bang in the middle of where we want to walk. Another technique is to have electrically operated self-opening doors; revolving, sliding or hinged. These often revolve or open slowly, taking up valuable seconds during which we can begin to acclimatise and 'tune in' to the supermarket shopping process ahead.

The psychology of crowds

In the supermarket, you'll find lots of people in the same place at the same time. This leads to a related school of behaviour known as 'the psychology of crowds'. According to Stephen Reicher, from the School of Psychology at the University of St Andrews in Scotland: 'Crowds are the elephant man of the social sciences. They are viewed as something strange, something pathological and something monstrous. At the same time they are viewed with awe and with fascination.' In his paper 'The Psychology of Crowd Dynamics', Reicher explains that the crowd provides an arena to study social (psychological) processes and analysis of crowds goes a long way towards understanding the general bases of human social behaviour.

Researcher Floyd Allport, professor of social psychology and political psychology at Syracuse University saw individuals as behaving on the basis of enduring response tendencies deriving from their cultural conditioning. In other words, people tend to behave in ways that ensure their survival but they do so while remaining culturally acceptable. This conditioning was built on a number of fundamental reflexes including withdrawing from danger, the need for nutrition and the need for love. When there are more stimuli, for example, through being with others in a supermarket, these pre-existing tendencies are magnified. In general, collective behaviour occurs when there is a coming together of individuals who are of similar cultural character and the supermarket aisles can influence behaviour by putting many socially and culturally similar people into the same space and then presenting each with consistent stimuli.

We know that we tend to behave differently in groups than we do when we're alone. For example, we laugh more at comedy in a comedy club, we cry more at tear jerkers when in a cinema and we'll dance more energetically at a nightclub than we would in the privacy of our own home. We've also discussed how emotions, along with cognitions and feelings, drive and influence our behaviour and the behaviour of those around us.

Why do we tend to feel and behave in a more extreme manner in a group, compared to when we're alone? We know that emotion is contagious: 'Smile and the world smiles with you'. If we see someone smile, we're more likely to smile ourselves.

To answer the question of why we tend to act, feel and behave more exaggeratedly when in a group, we look to evolution once again for the answer. Most emotions and feelings predate language, so we're wired more strongly to emote and feel than we are to explain emotion and feeling verbally. In the hunter–gatherer days, our ancestors would travel round in groups for their own safety; many eyes and ears are more effective than just a pair of each. Groups were more likely to spot threats and potential food earlier. However, as this happened before language had been invented, how could they inform others in their group? This is where emotions, and in particular facial expressions, come into their own.

Our brains have a mechanism designed solely for reading facial expressions, the fusiform gyrus. It feeds these signals to our amygdalas, parts of the limbic system which make up the early warning system of the brain. This mechanism makes a very important determination, it either switches on or off people's defence mechanisms and does so autonomically in about a tenth of a second (the same timing, interestingly, that humans nowadays use to recognise favoured brands). A look of fear, terror or alarm can alert others around a person in a fraction of a second, whereas language, which uses more recently evolved portions of the brain, can't respond nearly as quickly.

This alarm system alerts those around us using emotional signals, including facial expressions and we are tuned to pick up any strong emotion and pass it along. Groups that feel the same way about things tend to be a better survival unit than those that don't. If we want to survive, as part of a group we need to have other group members ready for action and the fastest way to do this is to spread the same emotion through the crowd quickly.

It follows that within the supermarket, it is possible to generate a mild form of mass hysteria. As evidence, look at what happens when the department stores first go into sale mode in January: Hoards of people charge around and aggressively snap up 'apparent' bargains. I say apparent, because I know of at least one (non-supermarket) retailer that buys in cheap products just to 'enhance' the offers available in the sale. Many of these items aren't bargains at all and actually return a healthy margin, despite appearing to be heavily discounted.

Supermarkets typically have a 'power aisle' that runs along the central spine of the store, from one end to the other. It's normally the busiest aisle in-store and it's no surprise then that so many special offers are located on the numerous gondola ends that face into the power aisle. In fact, brand owners will pay good money just to secure their products on these ends. Looking at the psychology of crowds it's reasonable to assume that a lot of special offers near to each other will be more effective than the odd promotional fixture dotted around the store. The power aisle is effective partly because the many special offer gondola ends create a corral that crowds numerous shoppers together who will then respond to the special offers both emotionally and quickly.

When conducting research in and around Johannesburg, researchers from Shopping Behaviour Xplained Ltd witnessed a unique phenomenon. Shoppers, typically poor by appearance, would spend time browsing all of the supermarket aisles. They would select products and place them into their trolleys. At the end of their journey round the store they didn't head for the checkouts or attempt theft, instead, they would calmly abandon the trolley full of groceries and leave the store empty handed. Although a number of hypotheses have been put forward as to why this strange behaviour occurs, the accepted belief is that poorer shoppers (those who can't actually afford to buy a trolley full of consumer goods) take part in a form of pretend shopping. Although the psychological or evolutionary purpose is unknown, it could be associated with evolutionary based social group behaviour and dynamics.

From a negative perspective, numerous queues at a line of supermarket checkouts are likely to generate exaggerated feelings of anger and frustration. The psychology of a crowd of supermarket shoppers should be an important consideration for retailers, designers, brand owners and marketers. A group of shoppers is likely to be more emotional than a lone individual; this is potentially very powerful both positively and negatively.

When we're shopping, we need to be mindful of the influence other shoppers are having on us. Is the special offer really that good? Or could it be that the added interest in the deal comes in part from the emotional responses of others in the same corral/crowd? Remember that we're always able to influence ourselves and each other when shopping.

Many aspects of the supermarket are designed specifically for the purpose of selling us groceries. One widely used process is category management, or how products are scientifically grouped and laid out in the aisles; this is the subject we'll explore next.

Category management

The term category management has been around in retail for a number of years, but it is often used incorrectly or isn't properly understood, so we'll start with a definition. Category management is a retailing process in which all the similar products from a retailer's entire product range are grouped together in things called categories. Examples of supermarket categories would be: hot beverages (tea, coffee and the like), beers, wines and spirits, pet food, and laundry (washing powders, fabric softeners, etc.).

Each of these categories is then jointly managed by the retailers and brand suppliers as separate businesses. Typically, within a large supermarket organisation, each category will have its own sales and profit margin targets. Importantly, category management is meant to be a collaboration between retailers and their suppliers, although this isn't always the case. Each is supposed to propose changes such as revised product layouts or the introduction of new products only if they improve the performance of the entire category in some way.

According to the Institute of Grocery Distribution, category management is defined as: 'The strategic management of product groups through trade partnerships which aims to maximise sales and profit by satisfying consumer and shopper needs.' They go on to say that category management provides shoppers with the items they want, where they want them and at the time they want them. Therefore, products are grouped together into categories that reflect customer needs based on how products are used, consumed and purchased.

Successful category management has traditionally drawn on the latest industry and consumer trends; it leverages available research and sales data (till roll analysis) and typically combines expertise from the retailers and the best performing and most established brands in the category, such as Coca-Cola and PepsiCo in the carbonated drinks category.

One aspect of category management that only receives lip service most of the time is that it supports our needs as shoppers. In other words, what do we want from the category in return for us investing our attention, time and money in purchasing products from it?

There are a number of reasons why our needs as shoppers aren't always met and this is partly our own fault. First, we don't always know what we want or can't verbalise our true needs. As a significant proportion of shopping activity is handled by the short term memory, as soon as we leave the aisle, we've forgotten the mechanics of how we shopped it. This also means that we've forgotten any minor inconveniences we experienced, unless we experienced an emotion at the time. Second, we tend to become conditioned to shopping our local supermarket; we learn how to shop it, therefore when asked what changes we'd like, we typically just respond by rationalising and just requesting reductions in price.

However, to create genuinely shopper oriented category management, it's necessary to go beyond the rationalised 'guesses' of shoppers which are typically gleaned from some survey or focus group. Progressive category managers need to understand what shoppers really want from the category, what problems they encounter when shopping it and how to optimise not only sales, but also shopper satisfaction.

To achieve deeper and more meaningful insights into what shoppers really want, a good starting point is to observe them and not just by standing and watching as much of what happens could be missed. Effective observation involves analysis of shopper behaviour using CCTV cameras and recording equipment. Analysts are then able to study the data frame by frame and pick up the smallest details of problems shoppers are facing.

In one such example, when our researchers studied shoppers interacting with the laundry aisles of a number of supermarkets in and around Johannesburg, they identified a problem that then turned into a shopper focussed solution and opportunity. In stores in the poorer areas and townships, shoppers were seen to shop for washing powder and soap apparently without any difficulty, finding their products and selecting them in a grab & go manner. However, when it came to the fabric conditioners, shoppers exhibited considerable frustration and aspects of inexperienced shopping.

After studying the data and comparing how shoppers behaved in the aisle, we identified the problem and validated it by speaking to shoppers in subsequent research in-store: These poorer shoppers didn't have hot water, so they would mostly buy cold water washing soaps. At the time, there wasn't a fabric conditioner specifically targeted for use in cold water. Since then, such a conditioner has been developed and retailers, brands and shoppers have all benefited from its creation.

This development came directly from CCTV-based observation of the problems shoppers were experiencing in the aisle. As shoppers, we shouldn't be alarmed at this because what the category managers want to achieve is a category more in line with our actual (as opposed to stated) shopper needs.

In another example, we were filming shoppers as they interacted with a particular brand of cosmetics displays in UK beauty stores. The brand owner was testing a new type of display, capable of housing significantly more products for shoppers to test in a single one metre wide fixture. The display used a number of self-closing drawers that shoppers could open and then by lifting flaps inside each drawer, expose and test more shades, colours and variants of products.

In original research, consisting only of interviews, there were no apparent problems with the prototype, so the units went into production. Later CCTV observation recognised an important, but previously unforeseen issue: Most shoppers arrived at the fixture carrying handbags and other bags of shopping, so they only had one hand free to use the cosmetics stand. To access the increased range of products, shoppers needed to be able to open a self-closing drawer and hold it open (one hand) then lift a flap inside (two hands) and finally test the products within (three or even four hands). Unfortunately, this issue was only uncovered after hundreds of the displays had been manufactured and distributed throughout the UK!

Another aspect of category management that often results in our needs as shoppers being ignored or underrepresented is the nature of trading relationships between retailers and brands. Typically, the retail partner is represented by a buyer who buys the goods that a store sells to its customers. Buyers working for large supermarkets each specialise in a single category. Buying teams often consist of a buying director or trading director, a buyer and an assistant buyer.

On the other side of the negotiating table is the key or national account manager from the brand supplier and it is the negotiations between these opposing 'factions' that determines the products a store will offer to its customers and how much they will cost. The current trading relationships tend to be very commercially focussed, with buying targeted to meet sales, profit and margin goals. There isn't enough focus on the softer, more emotionally based shopper satisfaction or even shoppability targets. Effective category management needs to include what the shopper wants from the category. After all, it is our money that eventually pays the wages of those employed by the retailer and the brand supplier.

When retailers and brands realise there is more to life than 'price, price, price', I fully expect that stores will start to replace some of their drab functionality with design aspects that engage with shoppers at an emotional level. I believe that's the future of category management; it will be replaced with a term called shopper marketing, which by definition is the understanding of how target consumers behave as shoppers, and using this understanding for everyone's benefit; consumers, retailers and brands alike.

Packaging unwrapped

As we've shown, a key aspect of shopper marketing is communications, but in the modern day supermarket, brands have fewer opportunities to communicate with us, the shoppers. There are fewer brand specific displays in supermarkets and some have introduced 'clear floor' policies: This rule states that branded displays aren't to be used on the shop floor unless there's a specific, shopper related reason for them to be there. Of course, on some occasions a brand has deep enough pockets to buy their way out of obeying a clear floor policy!

There are two specific in-store areas where brands still have control with regards to how they can directly communicate with shoppers: shelf ready packaging (SRP) and product packaging itself. The first, shelf ready packaging, also known as retail ready packaging, are those cardboard trays that hold a number of packs of the same product. They were introduced a few years ago when retail supply chains identified an opportunity to improve their operational efficiencies significantly by focussing on the last 50 feet of a product's journey from the supermarket warehouse to the shopping trolley. Shelf ready packaging makes it easier for store staff to pick up a group of items and it's also simpler to display the items on the shelf.

When SRP was first introduced, there were numerous examples of dramatic changes in product performance. In one interesting example, the entire hair care category was studied using a number of specialist shopper research methodologies, including camera based observation. Each store was first studied with none of the products in SRP, and then again with the majority of the category merchandised in SRP (cardboard outers). The results were surprising: The share of sales for a particular brand that had been put into SRP rose by more than 30% in each store, while sales of another brand, also housed in SRP dropped by as much as 70%. Although the only change was the introduction of these 'innocuous' cardboard outers, these alarming sales changes meant that we needed further research.

We discovered that simply covering the bottom inch of a well known product in-store sufficiently alters its appearance making it harder for shoppers to locate as part of any single scripted behaviour. In other words, they were forced to engage with the category again and took more interest in other products that were available.

In another somewhat surprising finding, one of the brands of shampoo was placed in the same one inch high card trays and positioned on a shelf in-store. Sales of the brand significantly increased after the introduction of SRP, but why? In what might be a design error, the SRP that this particular brand used prevented shoppers from being able to read if the product was for greasy hair, dry hair, etc. The fact that shoppers had to pick up products to see if they were the right type resulted in the sales going up, as a product in the hand is half way towards being in the trolley. Although this wasn't a shopper oriented initiative, it still resulted in an increase in sales share for that brand.

This early study on the impact of shelf ready packaging also highlighted interesting correlations between certain categories and specific colours; simply switching the colour of the shelf ready packaging resulted in significant variations in sales share.

An unforeseen side effect of the introduction of SRP is that the sight of so much brown, corrugated card on shelves results in an increased perception of commoditisation in the minds of shoppers. Fewer branded displays in-store, combined with a significant increase in the amount of shopper facing brown cardboard results in the store looking less like a wondrous emporium of thousands of different products and more like a warehouse. Is it any coincidence that a 21st century, leading edge supermarket now looks more like the now defunct Kwik Save; a pile it high, sell it cheap chain of supermarkets that displayed products still in the large cardboard boxes they had been in when they were received from suppliers. The only thing store staff had to do was to rip off or tear a hole in the front of the box so shoppers had access to the products.

Even more important than SRP, though, is the packaging that the products themselves are wrapped in, and there's an entire industry designing and producing product packages. Of course, as with most other areas that we've covered there are very good examples of packaging and others that are poor at meeting our needs.

A significant percentage of shoppers need to wear glasses, and we don't often take our glasses to the supermarket, so why is much of the information on product packaging written in such a frustratingly small font? In some cases it appears that the brand starts by writing down everything they want to say about a particular product including name, ingredients, recipe suggestion, health information, and a special promotional message and then crams it all onto the packaging.

Many leading brands have experts and strategies in place to identify how best to use product packaging, but despite this not all brands know how to create good, effective shopper oriented packaging. Most of us can probably think of some examples, whether it's the food product that has its main unique selling point (USP) hidden halfway down the back of the pack, or the box of healthy breakfast cereals that fails to communicate the salt, sugar and calorie content clearly enough.

A stroll down a few supermarket aisles reveals just how wide of the mark some products are in meeting our shopping needs and instead seem to be sticking to a generic template: The product name is the biggest, then a logo or a picture and then, slightly smaller, the variant name. The other information is then randomly sprayed over the remaining packaging space.

For almost every product we buy, we have a hierarchy of needs. Although needs vary by both the type of shopper and by category, it is possible quickly and easily to identify and adhere to some best practice guidance. In some categories, the brand manufacturer is very important (Kellogg's, Coca-Cola, Cadbury's etc.), but there are also categories where the brand is barely known to shoppers and has little influence when the purchasing decision is being made. How influential is a particular brand of salt, bread or milk? Many basic commodities are just that, commodities. Although, in recent years there have been attempts to brand some commodities; Cravendale milk in the UK is one such example.

To understand our real needs as shoppers, we need to go beyond what we say in rationalised interviews or focus groups as the area of product packaging is awash with ineffective research that doesn't grasp the unique nature of shoppers and shopping. The use of inappropriate research leads to the wrong shopper needs being identified and poor packaging finding its way to the shelves.

We're often not very good at explaining our in-store needs or shopping behaviour and this also holds true when it comes to consuming. Ask someone about their specific needs for a type of product and they'll often try to provide the 'most intelligent' response. For example, having observed shopping activity in the breakfast cereals aisle, it was interesting to note the lack of interest in a new, larger sized family box. When interviewed, shoppers gave a number of reasons why they bought smaller pack sizes instead. Interviewees cited freshness as a reason for buying two smaller boxes of cereals as the ability to leave the second box sealed increased the life of the product. Another valid reason that the new larger pack was rejected was because it wouldn't fit on the shelves in the kitchen cupboard; the product designers didn't see that one coming.

Specialised CCTV observation identified an additional key reason why the larger pack was rejected. As shoppers attempted to pick it up for physical evaluation, the top of the carton literally collapsed in their hand or the shopper's finger would puncture the box. The larger packaging had been manufactured from a card that was too thin. This poor quality packaging was perceived as containing a sub-standard product and was subsequently rejected by the shoppers.

Product packaging used in the supermarket merchandise needs to meet a number of requirements. First, unlike the larger cereal box, the packaging must be a suitable means of containing the product. Second, it needs to communicate information to us at the shelf. Finally, product packaging must help the visibility of a product among possibly 50,000 other products. The one in 500 chance of being bought by any particular shopper illustrates the importance of getting this final aspect right. Even in a category like tea, there may be up to 100 different products and most shoppers only buy a single one per visit to the aisle, so again, the odds of being picked out are somewhat long.

There are several ways products can use packaging to increase their visual appeal, a simple one is to recognise how we navigate the aisles to seek out contrast in terms of shape and colour while we search for familiarity of brand names and logos. In the confectionery aisle, Cadbury 'owns' the colour purple and shoppers know they've reached the chocolate bars when they look into an aisle and see a wall of purple. Another effective way to stand out is for a brand to recognise that products have a number of facings on the shelf; that is to say, there is a line or block of the same product on the shelf, all of which are visible to us as we approach.

Some brands have exploited this by designing their packaging so that it only works effectively when there are a number of packs next to each other. For example, the marketers of the well known UK stock cube, OXO, realised that each small pack of just a few cubes having a pack front no larger than a box of matches was visually insignificant and unable to get even the fundamental brand name to stand out on the shelf. A few years ago, they took the radical step of removing the product name from the front of each pack and replacing it with a single letter 'O' or 'X'. The result was that they managed to make their product name three times bigger than that of their competitors. As OXO is never merchandised with just a single facing in a large supermarket, the marketers knew they could safely take the risk of displaying just a single letter.

By responding to how we visually navigate by recognising contrasting colours and shapes, there are significant opportunities for retailers and brands to manipulate the visibility of specific products. The use of specialist eye tracking equipment allows every fixation a shopper makes to be captured, studied and analysed in the most minute of detail. In many eye tracking studies, a common finding is that the visibility of any particular item is partially dependent on the appearance of the items right next to it. If a category has a predominant colour, such as white for baby toiletries, then the creation of an electric pink product sitting in among the 'wall of white' will stand out.

Whether mothers of newly born infants will trust an electric pink wrapped product as being suitable for their pride and joy is another matter, but this contrasting colour based product layout has been used effectively by a number of leading brands to good effect. In trials in The Netherlands, cigarettes were blocked by colour so that a particular brand was surrounded by many others of a different main pack colour. As a result of creating this halo effect, sales share of the brand rose by more than 10%.

As shoppers, we need to look at the way products are packed and understand what it is that's being communicated. Positive and beneficial information is usually on the front, and detrimental facts are often hidden away on the back. In addition, we need to decide whether the headlines on the pack are true, such as the 'organic' label, or whether they may be less factual, such as 'younger looking skin'.

When we're in-store at the fixture, we should recognise which packs contain products that actually meet our needs. This can be a difficult task as some talented designers are creating product packaging that tells you what they want you to know and might underplay some less desirable information. For example, products that are high in sugar sometimes try to divert attention through numerous packaging design initiatives. In one case, a well known manufacturer of confectionery, in addition to displaying nutritional information to the industry standard 'per 100 grams', chose to prominently display their own calorific, sugar, fat and salt content per '4 chunks', no doubt significantly lighter that 100 grams.

Frequently, we aren't able to cope with the amount of information thrown at us in the supermarket and we need a means to make sense of the plethora of data that bombards our eyes every moment we are in-store. We need to rank information so we can filter out what is important to us individually. I hypothesise that there is an overemphasis on the importance of price, promotions and special offers, which stems in part from the nature of the trading relationships between many retails buyers and brand suppliers.

As smart shoppers, we need to look beyond price and identify which products best meet our needs and how. Before doing so, we need to be aware of some of the psychological influences used by brands and retailers around supermarket pricing. Now, we'll explore price and promotion from a shopper's perspective, what we expect, want, need and perceive in-store.

Price – Fact, fiction, reality and perception

One thing that almost all supermarkets have in common is that they are known for giving us quality goods at what are perceived to be competitive prices. A large part of their advertising budget goes on reinforcing their competitive prices, added value and copious special offers. Not surprisingly, behind the hype is a more complicated story: Yes, supermarkets offer exceptional prices, but only on some items. For example, four pints of milk from the store voted 'Britain's cheapest supermarket' for the last 13 years, actually costs over 50% more compared to the price in a well-known food retailer, that incidentally isn't one of the leading supermarkets.

The website mysupermarket.co.uk compares the prices of a number of identical products: Same brand, same quantity and the same packaging and there are some interesting results. For example, a well known breakfast cereal was exactly the same price in each of the four leading supermarkets while another cereal product ranged from £2 in one chain to £2.37 in another and £2.49 in the third and fourth chains. However, in this last store, there was also a two for £4 offer on the item, so is it any wonder that our hunter–gatherer brains find it so hard to make objective and practical decisions when we take them shopping?

The fact is that we're remarkably brand loyal to a particular supermarket and in numerous studies where price was being researched, shoppers tended to adopt a blind trust. Once they accept a certain chain as 'their' supermarket, then although they make numerous value based decisions each time they do a big shop, they are much less likely to compare value with other chains on any week to week basis.

A key role of retailers and brands is to reinforce our trust in them, and in particular, they need to reinforce our perceptions of how good their prices are. Constant advertising of special offers helps to achieve this, but when it comes to the reality of prices in the supermarkets, how do we pick out good deals from bad ones? Making the right choice has less to do with maths and finance, and more to do with perception: We tend to perceive that a big special offer sign means a big special offer and a better deal. If a one metre square poster says two for £2, then that is, in the mind of many rushed shoppers, a better deal than the 50 millimetre square shelf edge strip that says the same thing.

According to an article in *Science Daily*, we need to be more aware of the mathematical details behind the various promotions, special offers and added value deals. Simple arithmetic can show exactly what kind of deal is offered: According to Dr Joseph Ganem, a physicist at Loyola College in Baltimore, Maryland, 'A lot of the real facts are buried in the small print.' Among his examples, Dr Ganem cites a leading telecoms supplier that promised 1,000 free Internet hours for 45 days. Although the deal sounds like a good one, consider this: There are 24 hours in each day, so 45 X 24 = 1,080 hours available in which to browse the Internet. For you as a consumer to use up your entitlement, you'd have to be online almost all day, every day to get full use of the offer. In the time left, less than two hours a day, you could attend to the rest of your life and take care of sleeping, eating and shopping!

In a retail example of price perception, which of the following offers do you think sounds more appealing? 'Buy one, get one free' or 'Buy two and get 50% off'? In his book, *The Two-Headed Quarter*, Dr Ganem offers us a way to see beyond the misleading numbers and save money every time we shop. Dr Ganem states that special offers are designed to manipulate or trick us, taking advantage of the fact that many of us are uncomfortable with numbers. Ganem says that depending on how the figures are presented, a person might think he is saving money when in actual fact he is paying the same as normal, it's just been communicated differently.

Further science behind Dr Ganem's work indicates that we respond better to higher numbers than we do to lower ones. For example, a food label that says a product is '90% fat free' will be more appealing than one that states it has '10% fat'. Ganem also explains that we find exact numbers more meaningful than words and phrases; we'll tend to pick '50%' over the less specific 'half' most of the time.

There's an interesting dichotomy between the messages we receive and how we're likely to respond to them, according to Juliano Laran (University of Miami), Amy N Dalton (Hong Kong University of Science and Technology) and Eduardo B Andrade (University of California, Berkeley). In one study, researchers told participants that they would be participating in a recall task. Half of the participants were exposed to names of retailers associated with saving money: Walmart, Sears, Home Depot, Ross and Dollar General. The other participants were exposed to the corresponding slogans of the same retailers: for example, 'The Good Life at a Great Price. Guaranteed' (Sears). The task was aimed at priming the brand names or slogans without the participants' awareness.

In a second task, the same participants were asked to imagine they were shopping in a mall and indicate how much they were willing to spend during their shopping trip. The participants who had been exposed to the 'saving' brands were willing to spend on average $94 compared to the participants exposed to the 'saving' slogans who were willing to spend $184 on average. The authors wrote: 'Therefore, the brands associated with saving money led participants to save money, whereas the slogans associated with saving money led to a behavioural rebellion and more spending. Companies may be trying to attract customers with slogans associated with saving money, but in fact, this strategy may make consumers spend more money than they would if they had not been exposed to the slogans.'

Talk to almost any retailer about what's important to shoppers and price will be high up on the list. Most trading relationships between retailers and their product suppliers are price related, with the phrase 'money talks' being alive and well in the world of supermarket/supplier. Brands often have to pay just to be in the store and available for sale and if a brand fails to give a retailer an acceptable profit, it can result in it being removed from that chain of stores, a nightmare scenario for most brands. Although this threat weighs heavily on brands, there are examples of how removing a flagship or signpost brand has harmed the retailer. In one example, a leading UK retailer removed from their store the leading brand of a specific non-food category. They did so because the brand had set up an online store where shoppers could buy directly from the manufacturer. An unforeseen consequence of this removal was that shoppers started to desert the category in that store chain. Quite simply, people thought that because the category didn't contain the leading brand, then the offering wasn't perceived as credible. Later, the brand was reinstated and shoppers returned.

The subject of price is actually much higher up the agenda of the brands and retailers than it is for shoppers. If price was the most important thing to us, then why aren't the discount supermarkets such as Aldi, Netto and Lidl much bigger than the mainstream ones? That doesn't mean that price isn't a consideration, but for many of us, it isn't the only consideration and we largely rely on perception to judge price. If the store has a large promotional display, then it must be a good offer.

As we discussed in the brands section, supermarkets have introduced their own brands and pitched them at different price points. At the bottom of the scale are the value (or cheapest) variants, then serving the middle of the price range there is the mainstream supermarket brand. At the top of the scale are the 'Finest', or 'Taste The Difference' brands. Where the external, supplier brand has the main product, the supermarket can offer a much cheaper alternative (value), a slightly cheaper (mainstream) or more expensive (extra special) variants. Now shoppers are faced with even more decisions in-store. Not only do they need to recall which products they like, they need to factor in which brand they prefer and which level of pricing is acceptable, depending on their need.

There are even some shoppers who are known to buy value products and then repackage them into branded packaging once at home, for example pouring a cheap and runny tomato ketchup into a Heinz ketchup bottle. Some shoppers even avoid buying some of the cheaper 'value' brands because they don't want to be seen with them by other shoppers at the checkout; conversely, some might shop in a value store and put their goods into the carrier bag from a more upmarket chain.

Much of our shopper price sensitivity is actually related to how we want to be perceived by others, which links back to evolution and the central six fitness indicators. The price we will pay for an item is directly related to how much general intelligence, openness to experience, consciousness, extraversion, agreeableness and emotional stability we believe that others will perceive we have as a direct result. As an example: A shopper will readily pay the same amount every week for the block of mature cheddar cheese that their family regularly consumes. However, when friends and peers are coming round for dinner, more consideration and mental effort goes into buying the contents of the after dinner cheese board. Why is it that the same item purchased for a different need state can alter the psychology and physiology of a shopper so much?

Typically, the dinner party shopper will spend a number of minutes in the cheese aisle and probably at the deli counter as well, selecting the right combination of flavours of cheese, different sized pieces, and even brands of cheese; the process itself taking on some form of ritualistic importance. No longer is the shopper concerned with anything as mundane as supporting Maslow's hierarchy of needs and although esteem and self-actualisation form part of the in-aisle calculations, they aren't responsible for the outcome. That all important dinner party is in part a vehicle to feed one's own central six fitness indicators.

The inclusion of a nice, runny Camembert produced in a small village in the La Mothe Achard region of France helps to portray the general intelligence of the dinner party host, particularly if she also knows about the provenance of the cheese. Lying by the side of the Camembert is a block of Bavarian smoked cheese, which portrays openness to experience. Next on the fitness indicator cheese board comes a piece of organic, locally produced ewe's milk cheese to communicate how conscientious the shopper is. A piece of jalapeno pepper jack cheese from the US is included to show a bit of an extravert aspect. For the agreeableness, a mild cheddar is included, and finally for the emotional stability aspect, a piece of mature, Cathedral City branded cheddar. This relatively typical cheese board has more meaning to it than just being the course that follows the Black Forest gateau.

Based on all the work that has gone on in the creation of something of real significance to the host, does it really matter whether any of the cheeses actually costs £3 or £4? Probably not. Much of the cheese aisle in the supermarket is dedicated to a commodity driven repeat purchase; a wall of yellow interspersed with special offers and the occasional branded product. From an evolutionary, psychological point of view, retailers and brands could better meet the needs of the shopper by altering their marketing tone of voice. Forget the BOGOF for Cathedral City and consider more aspirational marketing: How about 'eat cool creamy Philadelphia and make a better lover' or 'eat cool creamy Philadelphia and bear more children'. These may be flippant examples, but on a serious note, they are intended to illustrate the difference between price led retailing and shopper needs based retail.

Price is the blunt tool we use to judge brands and retailers. But, what do we want if not just price? For many of us, the thing we're really seeking is value.

Value

What is value? Although it's a term used throughout the consumer world, what does it mean? Put simply, value is about getting the maximum benefit from the resources available. Decisions about value for money are a daily reality in our lives, we're constantly choosing which items or services to buy, and part of our evaluation relates to comparing quality and cost.

In essence, value is about the quality (positive or negative) that renders something desirable or valuable, or the amount (of money or goods or services) that is considered to be a fair equivalent for something else. When we're shopping, something that represents value to one person will quite possibly be very different from what represents value to someone else. For some of us, being able to obtain a pack of eight burgers for less than the cost of a toilet roll may represent good value. To others, being able to purchase Aberdeen Angus beef from a supermarket chiller that happens to sell every food item we could possibly need represents better value, albeit at a significantly higher price.

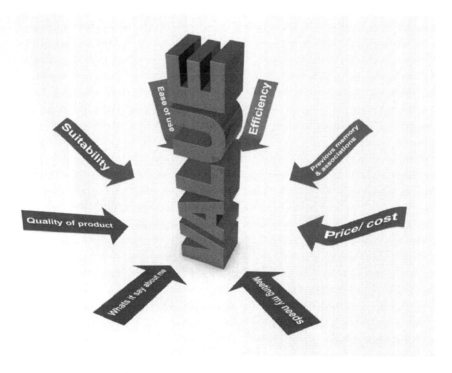

Figure 44 - Aspects that drive value

We know that most of us suffer from significant mental overload when shopping. It's not easy for us to calculate which is the best price between two brands of lager; one promoted at £1.10 per pint (570 ml) and the other at eight cans (each 440ml in size) for £7. What if we are then faced with another mentally challenging variable: We are offered the choice of a 'value' pack of lager (a two litre bottle) or the added value pack of 15 284ml bottles of a different brand of lager.

What does this sort of activity accomplish? Does it encourage or discourage our shopper loyalty or does it lead to becoming less brand loyal and more price led? The fact is, when it comes to the impact on our mind-set and decision making process, this sort of activity often does little more than confuse.

What retailers and brands should consider is how they can add value to meet our fitness indicator needs more effectively in-store. How does a particular variant of toilet cleaner help us meet our central six?

If this sounds farfetched, why do shoppers choose certain brands? They often cost more money, offer less in terms of quantity and the quality may be irrelevant too. From an objective, rational and even reasonable perspective, why would you choose a brand of toilet paper over another when the more expensive product is no softer and has fewer sheets in each pack? Despite this, many of us do choose what appears to be the less rational choice. It might be because that particular brand is advertised as a luxury or associated with a little puppy; whatever the reason, the value can't just be in price versus quantity or even quality.

Another example of where values differ considerably is when we're buying wine. There are hundreds of similar bottles with different labels, each of the bottles contain a wine from a different country or region, coming in a range of flavours and styles. However, when a selection of the wines is given a premium display or is glorified in some way on shelf, the wines are often perceived as being better. Add in a price reduction from £9 to £6.99 and that product appears to be better value. Why is this the case? Or on a more cerebral level, what should a bottle of wine cost the average supermarket shopper?

We can choose where to invest our time, money and attention and we have more choices than ever about where and how to do so. The more progressive retailers and brands will need to develop more complex and effective value related strategies if they really want to meet the needs of shoppers, now and in the future. They have to recognise how value differs from shopper to shopper and how it's influenced by what we are buying and for what purpose. For our part, we should challenge our own perceptions of value and go beyond accepting what advertisers and marketers say represents good value and develop our own, independent set of needs and values. This forms part of the final section of this book – How to become a smarter shopper.

The most important point to make is that price and value are rarely the same thing; if they were, the cheapest supermarkets would attract almost all of the shoppers, so why don't they?

Why we don't all shop at Aldi, Netto or Lidl?

As some store chains are cheaper than others, why don't all the shoppers go to those cheaper stores? What is it that attracts shoppers to Waitrose, Marks & Spencer and other 'premium' retailers? The answers to some of these questions, like so many others, come from the way that we have evolved, particularly as social beings. On the one hand, we have a hard wired desire to be with other likeminded folk and on the other, we are concerned with how we are perceived by society in general. This simple fact helps us understand why different people prefer to shop within the stores belonging to various retailers.

Originally, our hunter–gatherer ancestors were focussed on feeding their families as best they could. For the hunters, this meant taking bigger risks, associated with going after the more dangerous kills. For the gatherers, they would try to find the better quality berries to feed their families. In modern supermarket shopping, we still associate higher price with better quality; this means that we're going to the more expensive stores to get the better meat (already killed) and the higher quality berries. Whether the quality of the food for sale varies and if so by how much, is outside the scope of this book, but it's important to understand the evolutionary psychology that influences our choices.

There are a number of other reasons why we prefer to shop at one particular supermarket chain over another. One of the most important is convenience; most of us have a limited amount of time and generally take the easiest route, both physically and mentally, to a particular outcome. We tend to self-educate when it comes to shopping, beginning when we are young singles who have only recently flown the family nest. The young singles socio-demographic group tends to have the least interest in cooking, fine food or supermarket shopping and will tend to frequent their most convenient supermarket. Once a shopper has educated himself on how his local supermarket works and how to best shop it, he tends to stay loyal to that chain unless given a sufficiently strong reason to change.

Another factor that influences loyalty involves evolutionary group society. Our ancestors worked together in groups; a number of males were much more effective at trapping and killing a meal than a lone hunter. A significant part of social group culture required that members trusted each other and could actually work together, resulting in groups being made up of likeminded individuals and their families. It's no surprise that as modern shoppers, many of us prefer to shop with others we perceive to be similar to us or with whom we aspire to be associated. This could even link the very brand of the supermarket back to the central six fitness indicators.

My company has carried out many supermarket research projects and in almost every case, when shoppers are asked in which supermarket they shop, around 90% say the one they are in is their usual place to go for groceries. It's rare if more than 7% or 8% of shoppers state they ever do a big shop in any other supermarket; most don't even frequent other outlets owned by the same chain. In other words, the vast majority of us have one single supermarket that we remain loyal to when it comes to buying groceries when doing our big shops.

With this self-education and learned loyalty to a single supermarket, it's no surprise that the majority of people in the UK are loyal to the big four as there are many more of their outlets than there are of the discounters.

One final aspect that it's worth discussing is the importance of where we shopped in our childhood, i.e. when our parents took us. Strong loyalty can be created in these early years, a loyalty that retailers can target when we become adult shoppers. In research carried out in the UK and in South Africa on laundry products, the biggest deciding factor for brand choice was simply because it was used by the shopper's mother.

Another example of loyalty is to a product as omnipresent and everyday as you can imagine, soup. Soup is probably not a product we spend a great deal of time thinking about or actively desiring; it might be nice on a cold day, but rarely is it more than a quick meal solution, or a prelude to a more interesting main course. However, thinking about soup is very important to manufacturers like the Campbell Soup Company and they wanted to understand the consumers' hidden feelings about soup so they could improve their packaging.

Campbell's marketers were struck by several problems. First, neither shoppers nor consumers thought much about soup; when talking to people about soup they just didn't get that excited. Campbell's knew that people actually had a warm emotional feeling about their products; when a child was ill or cold, their mother would often feed them soup.

Research showed that this warmth faded in the supermarket soup aisle, when the shopper was confronted with a wall of nearly identical red and white Campbell's cans. So, Campbell's started testing design changes while monitoring how shoppers responded to them. As a result of the research, Campbell's distributed new packaging and displays that were specifically designed to connect better with customers' emotions. Interestingly, the subject of how much Campbell's or any other soup cost just didn't arise, nor any reason why it should be bought from either a top end or value retailer. The research was originally reported by the *Wall Street Journal* and reporter Ilan Brat who persuaded Campbell's to go on record about the story.

There are a number of reasons we don't all shop at the discounters and many are linked to our evolutionary heritage. First, we are wired to live in groups, and groups usually consist of likeminded individuals and we prefer supermarkets that are shopped by people similar to us. Second, as children, we developed loyalty to a particular supermarket that we visited many times with our parents. When we grew up, left home and became supermarket shoppers, the emotional bonds of childhood triggered by the thoughts, sights and aspects of our parents' chosen supermarket, manifest themselves as a solid brand loyalty to that same supermarket chain. The third area that significantly influences our loyalty is straightforward convenience; the supermarket is part of our lives because it's close to where we live or work. As most of us are time starved, having a particular chain nearby is convenient and so offers considerable value.

In-store communications

Even before entering the supermarket, we've already been exposed to numerous consumer, supermarket and product messages. From TV advertising and product placement to press advertising and billboards, products try to embed themselves into our mental shopping lists. It's estimated that on average, each of us is exposed to around 3,000 advertising messages per day. Assuming that we sleep for eight hours, that means we're exposed to 180 messages per waking hour or three every minute. Their omnipresent existence and spread in society demonstrates that these messages must be effective. They work in part because of the effect known as priming, which we covered earlier. To recap: Priming relates to imagery and messaging initially processed in peripheral vision and then on some occasions, is given foveal attention, looked at directly and actively mentally processed.

The three adverts per minute average is much, much lower than the number of special offers we are exposed to when in the supermarket. In December 2009, data compiled by mysupermarket.co.uk for *The Sunday Telegraph* showed that 18,553 items were on special offer across Tesco, Asda, Sainsbury's and Ocado compared to 13,804 the same time, the previous year – a 34% increase and the highest number in at least three years. One in five items in supermarkets was on special offer over the busy Christmas period. If, as data from Shopping Behaviour Xplained show, the average weekly big shop takes us around 40 minutes, and in that time, we typically pass by just half of the 50,000 products available from that store, then it follows that we have been exposed to 5,000 special offers in a 40 minute period of shopping. Incredibly, in this scenario, we would each have been exposed to a staggering 125 special offers every minute, two every second!

Whether you've been primed or not, once you arrive at the supermarket, you enter an arena crammed full of imagery, logos, words, strap lines, video and audio plus a host of other attempts to attract your attention. From an objective standpoint, you'll typically be exposed to three different types of information during a visit to the store. First, there is mandatory information such as opening hours and regulatory messages. Second, there are the informative messages such as overhead aisle contents signs and in-aisle category signage. Finally, and by far the most widely used type of information in-store is that which is awareness based.

The first type, mandatory information, tends to be quite negative in tone. For example, there are messages such as 'Thieves will be prosecuted', 'No dogs' and 'No entry' (to staff areas). This negativity is accentuated by the inclusion of many 'No' and 'Don't' related logos like 'No sale to under 18s' and 'No photography'. Although this type of messaging is necessary, it primes us with negative messages. At a time when the supermarket wants us to be positive and to think 'yes' to browsing and buying, these negative signs don't help.

One solution some retailers have used is to locate this information strategically in the places where we're least likely to look. We know that we take more notice of things below our eye level than we do of things above, so an obvious place to hide 'bad news' is up in the air, which isn't very practical or customer friendly. Another, more subtle, means of communicating those mandatory negative messages is to locate them in areas where our eyes are less efficient or where there's something much more visually impactful that will draw our attention. To further a point made earlier, if the shopper comes into the supermarket from direct sunlight, then for the first few seconds inside, they are partially 'blind'; where better to hide the negative messages?

In terms of using competing visual cues to distract attention away from negativity, there are plenty of opportunities; these might include promotional gondola ends, the more visually appealing products themselves and even other shoppers; if a store knows where queues form, they can locate messaging so that it is obscured by the line of people.

The second form of shopper facing communication is the information itself: Navigational signage, pricing and which checkout to use are all examples. This type of messaging is designed to help us shop the supermarket more effectively. The navigational signage presents us with a hierarchy of messages, intended to direct us from the middle power aisle to an actual product and provide the information we need to buy it.

At the top of the informational hierarchy would be the headline contents of the aisle, usually communicated by way of large hanging signs; 'pasta and rice' for example. As we enter the aisle, we are faced with a number of category or sub-category signs saying thing like 'rice' and 'pasta'. When arriving at the rice bays, the products are laid out (category managed) to be navigable to us shoppers; flavoured rice blocked together, next to 'boil in the bag' rice, next to speciality rice, etc. At this stage, the product packaging takes over and guides us right to the particular product we are looking for. This informational signage is there to help us, has no obvious evolutionary connection and is, for the most part, just useful – very refreshing! In the days of prehistoric man, there were no nice hanging signs directing hunters to their next kill or gatherers to the 'fruits of the forest' bays.

The final form of communication in-store is to do with awareness; brands and retailers doing all they can to raise the visibility of particular items to make us more likely to buy them. These messages can take many forms; the most widely used tool is the blunt promotional message such as BOGOF (Buy One Get One Free) or '3 for the price of 2'. Although these and other deals are effective, retailers have started to question whether they actually benefit anyone apart from the shopper. Recent evidence suggests that if a product is on offer, the shoppers already loyal to that particular brand and item will take up the offer and stock up their cupboards; there's little long term benefit in terms of other shoppers switching to the promoted brand or increasing consumption over a longer period of time.

From a shopper perspective it would appear to be a case of 'buy now, while stocks last' as the indications are that the number of added values such as '2 fors' and '3 fors' will reduce. There will still be deals for us to hunt and gather for in-store; supermarket retailing is a very fluid, global business and due to its nature, change is never far away.

In November 2008, Woolworth's, a large chain of stores in the UK, went into administration, closing its doors and ceasing to trade. This had a direct impact on several supermarket categories and ranges, especially chocolate Easter eggs, as Woolworth's was one of the largest retailers of Easter eggs in the UK. The chain's demise meant there was a serious over supply to which the supermarkets quickly reacted.

They bought the surplus eggs, and in early 2009 all of the supermarkets appeared to be offering amazing deals on Easter egg multi-buys: '2 fors', '3 fors', '4 fors' and the like were on numerous gondola ends in most supermarkets around the country. This was nothing to do with any strategic master plan by the supermarkets or the Easter egg producers but was a direct tactical reaction to a change in the market. Situations like these are constantly arising and retailers are particularly skilled in adapting, benefiting their turnover and profits and providing shoppers with apparent added value and good deals.

When communicating messages that draw attention to a particular product, we're conditioned to be more aware of certain things, good examples being red and white or red and yellow. Retailers and brands recognise this and use it to raise the visibility of specific lines and also make some things appear to be better value than they actually are. We should be mindful of offers that are hard to quantify, for example 'bulk buy' or 'When it's Gone It's Gone' (WIGIG). A large, impressive display of product supported with a big and bold message can easily alter our perceptions and result in irrational purchase decisions.

A recent example that shows how 'blindly' some of us shop, are some apparent errors in-store regarding the pricing of multibuy products where it's more expensive to multibuy if we selected a number of the products singly. In one example, a juice drink was on offer at two for £2, but in actual fact each only cost 98p (£1.96 for two). In another instance, two 250 gram packs of dried spaghetti actually cost less than the 500 gram value pack in at least one of the leading supermarkets. The point these examples make has nothing to do with the supermarkets themselves, but they highlight that we aren't able to shop for weekly groceries in a mentally efficient way. Although the example of the juice drink deal wasn't actually a better offer, shoppers bought it; lots of it. And there were plenty of sales of 500 gram value packs of dried spaghetti by all accounts. Our poor brains aren't capable of being an objective, rational and mathematically capable asset in the supermarket.

Another area where we need to be more aware is buying in bulk, which, contrary to popular belief, doesn't always save money.

According to Rachel Wait of lovemoney.com, this is the case whether the shopper is simply buying a bigger pack of product, or where they're buying a multipack rather than a single item. In addition, Wait points out: 'Buying in bulk isn't always practical either. After all, storage space is often minimal and as a result, buying large packs of cereal, washing powder and toilet roll might not always be convenient.' It should be pointed out however, that in some cases, buying in bulk does indeed offer better value for money, but, as always: buyer be aware.

Before we reach the final section, we'll discuss the subject of adjacencies, which products should be next to each other in the supermarket.

Adjacencies

For the most part, 'adjacencies' refers to retailers and brands grouping products by how, when and where they are used. For example, apple pie next to custard and cheese next to butter. However, this is an area that due to the intensely competitive nature of supermarkets and brands, often leads to many of the adjacencies we might want not being available. Retailer head offices have numerous teams, each responsible for a specific category of merchandise. They might have a team in charge of confectionery, another group responsible for beers, wines and spirits, and yet another team for ready meals. Unfortunately, there is no head office team responsible for an often requested product grouping known as 'a good night in'.

In this scenario, if the ready meals were adjacent to the bottles of wine and the confectionery for sharing, this would provide us with an entire occasion solution and increase the average weight of purchases. Unfortunately, these types of occasion oriented product adjacencies rarely happen; they are uncommon because of the dynamics of the retailer head office. The team in charge of confectionery will fight tooth and nail to retain the amount of retail floor space they have, but so too will the beers, wines and spirits team and those responsible for the performance of ready meals. Therefore, if any usage based adjacency strategy is to succeed, one of the teams will have to surrender space, but which one? The answer for the most part is none of them, so we shoppers don't always get the adjacencies we want.

Shoppers are usually on a specific mission; it might be a big shop mission, a top up shop mission, a seasonal shop (such as Christmas) or another specific purpose. It's rare for shoppers to go for a casual browse around the supermarket; such behaviour is more likely in a department store or shopping mall.

When we're in a supermarket, we want to complete our mission as efficiently as possible; remember that our brain will be struggling to manage the entire mission process itself. The short term memory will handle the repeat purchases and a combination of emotions, cognition, beliefs and feelings will assist us in the selection of our preferred brands. But what about those spur of the moment niceties in life, such as impulse items? These need to be seen, mentally processed and decided upon by a brain that is working flat out just to remember to get a loaf of bread – wholemeal, square cut, fresh and with a far off sell by date.

To help us with our missions, retailers could do more to group products in shopper oriented and less category specific ways. For example, a leading American supermarket chain hit upon a winning formula (subsequently copied in the UK), when they merchandised cans of lager adjacent to disposable nappies. The thought processes of the retailer were founded on solid, research based facts: Observers had identified that it was often men who would be in-store buying nappies. The mother of the baby would stay at home caring for the child and dispatch the male to buy nappies if she ran out. When arriving at the nappy section, he would also see a nice stack of lager. Feeling suitably justified, he would pick up a number of cans and buy them along with the distress purchase of nappies. The end result was that the retailer sold an extra item, the man was happy because he had beer and the mother of the baby was content because the man had bought nappies. Truly a win, win, win situation.

There are many other opportunities for such 'creative' adjacency strategies that would both sell products and please shoppers. However, there remains an inbuilt resistance in the form of the inter-category competitiveness within retail head office teams. For example, as the opportunity to mate is one of the hard wired reasons why many men are keen to buy Valentine's Day cards, why not market them alongside condoms? Or, on a more mundane topic, why not merchandise jams, butters and spreads adjacent to the bread section?

In most stores, layouts for product adjacencies are anything but shopper friendly. Certain aspects are understandable, such as putting frozen goods at the far end of the store to stop us leaving as soon as we've put frozen food in our trolley, which we seem to prefer to do. The evidence suggests that a more sophisticated and 'cross category' adjacency strategy would be beneficial to the retailers, the brands and shoppers. Retailers could expect to increase what we buy and the value of our purchases.

A good example of an effective adjacency strategy is in the relatively new category of 'Food To Go': sandwiches, pies, crisps, confectionery and cold drinks. This category is usually located near the entrance of the supermarket and is designed to meet the needs of shoppers who just wish to buy food for their own immediate consumption.

Our own Food To Go research, carried out in petrol forecourts, uncovered an interesting and potentially profitable shopper insight. Shoppers buying several products from the category would buy the items in the order they were to be consumed. For example, they would buy a savoury item before selecting any confectionery, even if the latter was earlier along the typical route through the category. This resulted in shoppers having to retrace their steps after buying their savoury Food To Go. We recommended that sweeter products be relocated after savoury ones as this would better meet the needs of the shoppers and it was expected that more would impulsively add a confectionery item to their main savoury meal solution.

However, before the true potential of the adjacencies can be met, there will need to be a change in the way in-store category managers defend the space they have.

Targeting the shopper, conclusion and summary

In this section of the book, we discovered how the human race has evolved based on a need for survival, from hunting and gathering to the modern supermarket shopper. In evolutionary terms, the supermarket is a very recent invention indeed, having been in existence for less than 100 years. But even over this short time, supermarkets have come a long way, from 5,000 square foot stores to 100,000 square foot hypermarkets. With the current diversity of supermarket types, came a need to categorise them, which has led to more in each town or city. Nowadays, there are the largest out of town stores, smaller town centre stores and the smallest convenience or neighbourhood outlets.

With the creation of the supermarkets came shopper choice – shoppers could actively choose between different products and help themselves to what they preferred. This led to the development of the brand, a means of differentiating apparently similar commodities to make them appear more appealing to shoppers. In addition, branding allows the brand owner to charge a premium for their product. Typically, brands are created by developing emotional associations between a particular product and us as shoppers or consumers. Although the majority of new product launches fail, evidence demonstrates how financially valuable a brand is and why the new product launch gamble is worthwhile.

We then examined the store environment and discovered what happens to our mind and brain in a modern supermarket. There are differences in our own shopper perceptions, behaviours and purchasing activities depending on whether we are in our own local, familiar store, or some strange outlet far, far away. Regardless of the type of shopper we are, a plethora of messaging bombards us before we even reach the store; each message has a media value that can be used to generate attention, and prime us for shopping.

From a retailer perspective, every square foot of retail floor space costs money, so they want to get us shopping as much of it as possible, as quickly as possible. Therefore, supermarkets employ areas known as deceleration zones: Reception areas of stores near the entrances that are designed to get us into a mind-set of actively shopping.

We behave differently whether we are in a busy store or alone in the aisle. According to the evidence, it is possible to introduce a mild form of mass hysteria in a supermarket and even on an everyday level, it is hypothesised that the numerous special offers on all of the gondola ends along the main central 'power aisle' do cause some of us to behave in an exaggerated manner.

We also explored the subject of category management and in particular, the fact that all too often, the needs of shoppers themselves aren't sufficiently taken into consideration. The actual process of category management is a retailing process where all the similar products from a retailer's entire product range are grouped together in things called categories. Examples of traditional categories within supermarkets are condiments, ready meals, beers, wines and spirits and hot beverages. There are numerous missed opportunities for added sales and increased shopper satisfaction by introducing a more shopper centric category management strategy.

Shoppers are often less concerned about some of the retailer and brand led sub-categorisation and simply want categories laid out in a suitable way so they can be shopped to meet our needs, central six aspirations and missions.

A major issue relating to creating shopper oriented category management is the problem of understanding what shopper needs really are, as we're not able to state what we want, for reasons documented in the first section. Most category management is based around the structures within brand and retail head offices and the ensuing trading relationships, rather than meeting our needs as shoppers.

We then looked briefly at packaging, beginning with the latest developments in shelf ready packaging. Next, packaging communication was discussed from a perspective of a hierarchy of importance and needs to shoppers. Packaging can help or hinder our experiences in-store with a key point being that we are suffering from severe information overload, both in-store and elsewhere.

Price is a topic that any book about retailing, particularly supermarket retailing, has to address. In this chapter, the whole issue of price perception and its importance were qualified. Retailers and brands seem convinced that price is the mainstay of their relationship with each other; however, from the shopper perspective it's a somewhat different story. No doubt price is important for some shoppers buying certain items, but the evidence suggests that it isn't the only thing on our minds in-store.

A subject often confused with price is value; we started with a definition of value for money and discussed value propositions. Combining value and price should lead to the reason why we choose a particular store over another; however, there are a number of other reasons why we like to frequent a certain chain of supermarket. These include evolutionary, social group reasons, where we shopped as children and the convenience and location of the store.

We then explored the types of in-store information: mandatory, informational and attention seeking and which type of information was most and least beneficial to retailers, brands and shoppers.

Finally, the subject of adjacencies was examined: What products are next to each other and why? As is the case with category management, shopper needs could be better met by the retailers and brands.

Where Section One of the book discussed how and why we function as we do, this section concentrated more on how the store and brands meet (or don't meet) the needs of shoppers. It identified a number of differences between what shoppers want and what is available.

In the final section, you will be able to understand yourself as a shopper; namely how you shop mentally and physically and then develop a strategy for supermarket shopping. Not only will you be able to work around some of the issues we've already identified, but you will also be able to understand what causes the various brain overloads we all suffer from in-store. When you've developed your shopping strategy, you'll be able to enter the supermarket with a new found confidence and authority.

The aim is simple: To reduce the amount of 'why did I buy that?' buyer's remorse and to help you learn to be a smarter shopper. There's a serious gap between the average shopper's need to make sensible, objective and rational decisions in the supermarket and their brain's ability to do so. For what I believe is the first time, I combine the findings and research from a number of specialist schools of psychological and physiological expertise specifically to help all of us who want to shop better.

The next and final section will provide you with a structure and plan to help rewire your brain to cope with modern shopping. No tricks or gimmicks, just a set of responses to the latest, ground breaking psychological and physiological findings regarding how shoppers think, behave and purchase. If you want to understand how you and other shoppers operate, read on. Whether your desire stems from a professional standpoint of wanting to sell more as a retailer or brand, or whether you're a shopper, who wants to make wiser choices when in the supermarket, please commit to undertaking the strategy in Section Three of this book.

Int

How to become a smarter shopper

roduction

In this part of the book, we'll bring everything together and show you how to apply this knowledge so that you can shop more effectively, save money and become a smarter shopper.

We'll begin by looking at the five different 'modes' of shopping that each of us adopts depending on what we're purchasing and understanding them, which provides a good foundation for shopping in a more informed way.

We'll then look at developing a shopping strategy that works for you, examine how you can build your motivation, explore the core principles of smarter shopping and detail a number of practical techniques that you can use in the supermarket.

We'll finish with a summary of the key points and some final thoughts.

The five modes of shopping

We all shop for different things, some items we buy frequently, such as everyday groceries, confectionery, newspapers or cigarettes, while other items are purchased much less frequently, including Christmas cards, new cars and electrical goods. As shoppers, we adopt one of five different purchasing modes at any one time, depending on what we are planning to buy.

The modes are: inexperienced shopping, experiential shopping, considered shopping, grab & go shopping and impulse shopping. Numerous aspects can influence the mode we'll adopt, including the type of store, reason for the purchase (for example distressed purchase of something that has been run out of) and the type of the store we're in, such as corner shop or hypermarket. The five different modes are distinctly different from each other and each one is identifiable purely by observation. That is to say, this is not a segmentation based on demographics, lifestyles, consumer needs or preferences, but more that it splits shoppers by their actual physical behaviour in-store. As such, it is undeniable, irrefutable and incontrovertible.

Each mode is identifiable through observation of behaviour, and also through its own set of merchandising, display and shopper communications requirements. Next, we'll explore these five modes of shopping and illustrate how the retailers and brands can best serve us as shoppers, depending on the mode we are in at the time. Before detailing the individual behaviour aspects of each mode, we should note that as shoppers we'll switch between modes while on a shopping trip for any number of reasons including needs, familiarity with the store, the amount of time we have available and more. We will also switch between modes depending on what is on the shelves in front of us, for example we may well buy canned vegetables in a grab & go mode, but then switch to impulse mode to take advantage of the 'buy one get one free' offer on tinned tomatoes.

The modes tend to be constant across categories and product groups by specific store type (supermarkets, convenience stores, etc.). For example, buying a pint of milk each day from the local 7-eleven store will almost always be grab & go; conversely, when we are choosing what bottle of wine to take to the in-laws after accepting an invitation to Sunday lunch, we'll often involve a degree of considered shopping. The point is that shopping modes, although exhibited by the shoppers, actually belong with the category. To illustrate this point further, you may call at the local convenience store for a loaf of bread (grab & go), but while there, decide to treat yourself to a bar of chocolate (impulse). If you are a woman who spends time testing and trying on various cosmetics (experiential) you may notice and then decide that you need an exfoliating body wash scrub with an added ingredient that you've never heard of (inexperienced).

The subject of the five modes of shopping is based on the fact that shoppers aren't all the same; we don't want the same from all stores or even all categories. If retailers and brands can segment and meet the requirements of the various shopping modes, they will grow share and sell more by better managing the needs and emotions of their most valued asset: the customers.

Shopping modes offer both retailers and brands a powerful means to scientifically and effectively target their in-store communications. It allows them to refine their messages and messaging style to help their content be more likely to be seen, processed and responded to by as many shoppers as possible.

Over the next few chapters we'll discuss each of the five modes of shopping, along with how retailers and brands can best meet our needs and how we can identify our own shopping mode.

Inexperienced shopping

The first of the five shopping modes is inexperienced shopping; as the name suggests, this mode of shopping occurs when you are unfamiliar with the product you are attempting to buy. In essence, inexperienced shopping is the search for education and information in-store. When in this mode, you'll tend to travel quite slowly between products and absorb any available information from displays, leaflets and packaging.

As an inexperienced shopper, we require time, space and detail. A typical example of inexperienced shopping is when we are trying to buy a certain type of product for the first time. Typically, you'll approach the products relatively slowly and stand back from the products to understand what the range in front of you is all about. After a short time, you are likely to approach the products and start your self-education. Either you'll have a predetermined set of needs that you'll try to confirm the products on the shelf will meet, or you may just read and absorb all the available information and decide which one to buy.

Categories where inexperienced shopping is common include health foods, computers, electronic goods, DIY and a number of household chemicals, such as oven cleaners.

From the retailer and brand perspectives, it is important to recognise not only what shoppers in an inexperienced mode want, but also the effect they have on other shoppers. For example, inexperienced shopping tends to be the slowest and most time consuming of all five modes. This creates a potential problem as the shopper who takes time seeking information at a fixture acts as a physical barrier to others trying to access products from the same place. Imagine you're an inexperienced shopper standing in front of a typical one metre wide, self-select cosmetics display. As you explore and learn about the latest anti-wrinkle, pentapeptide laden, youth preserving serum, no other shopper can get to the other products on that fixture. Unfortunately, retailers and brands often forget about our needs as shoppers, and focus more on operational issues such as how efficiently they can cram hundreds of lip glosses, nail varnishes, eye liners and the like into a one metre wide shop display.

When we conducted tests across Europe and then incorporated the needs of the shoppers into the designs of self-select cosmetics fixtures, there was a 15% increase in share of sales for the brand that took this 'revolutionary' step. They reported that such a dramatic increase in their share of sales helped them to recoup the cost of the shopper needs research in just 104 trading hours.

When meeting the needs of inexperienced shopping, retailers and brands need to understand the hierarchy of shopper needs and then communicate how the products meet these needs in a format that is logical, comprehensible and efficient. For example, take the everyday commodity of spectacle lens cleaners: Small bottles of liquid that we can use to clean our glasses. If you are the shopper and consumer, then it's very likely your primary need will be related to being able to clean your spectacles; you need to know what types of glass, Perspex, coated or uncoated lenses the product can be used on. Initially, this seems to be a product category where it's easy to educate shoppers; they just want cleaner glasses, quickly. Why? To be able to see more clearly.

Why is it then that some of the leading brands of glasses cleaning fluids include this sort of information in text smaller than that on this page? According to Harrisinteractive.com, 78% of adults wear some form of vision correction with 67% wearing glasses or spectacles and 16% wearing contact lenses. For the eagle eyed mathematicians, around 5% wear both glasses and contact lenses. When we conduct in-store research, one of the metrics we capture is how many of the shoppers wear glasses in-store while they shop. Depending on the category being studied and the age profile of the shoppers, glasses wearing typically ranges between 20% and 40%; whatever the precise number, the fact is that a significant percentage of shoppers who normally wear glasses don't wear them in the supermarket. As a consequence, some simply can't read while in-store, and retailers and brands compound this by presenting key information simply printed too small to be legible.

Another issue that needs to be addressed when designing the optimum in-store offering for inexperienced shopping is how to identify the actual relative importance of our needs in-store. Apart from the short term memory issues discussed earlier in this book, we often won't admit to researchers that we don't fully understand a category; this is especially true of male shoppers. Rather we will tell them what sounds like a sensible and rational answer and often, the researchers then fail to validate our factual responses from other fictional, rationalised guesses. This leads to the wrong conclusions and hierarchy of needs being reported as fact and in turn, the resultant display of products in the store doesn't meet our needs.

A final retailer and brand consideration regarding inexperienced shopping is the fact that different demographics of shoppers don't like to mix with each other and often don't want to stand next to one another in-store. A good example is at the hair styling fixture, where there are typically experienced, older shoppers who want more of their preferred brands of product. Also at the fixture are younger shoppers who might be shopping for putty, gel and wax, etc. in an inexperienced mode. As the young and old typically don't mix well in supermarkets, the category should be designed to accommodate both of these 'factions' of shopper. In this example, the solution was to merchandise the products bought by older shoppers beside, instead of below, those shopped by the younger ones. Incidentally, as a result of making these changes, sales from the category increased by 6%.

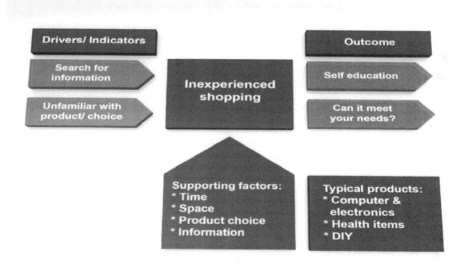

Figure 55 - Inexperienced shopping

When accommodating those of us shopping in an inexperienced mode, retailers and brands should remember that it is the shoppers who are driving the profits of the company and paying the wages of the store staff; without paying shoppers, there is no store. With no store, there is no need for store staff. As a shopper, never be hesitant or reluctant to ask for help in-store. We have a wider choice of stores, retail channels, brands and products than ever before, in other words we have more purchasing options. Not only that, but as you become a smarter shopper you recognise that you can actively choose where to invest your time, energy and hard earned money; a fact that's too often overlooked by the retailers.

Inexperienced shopping then is a time consuming and information hungry process. It is not the most inefficient form of shopping for the retailers or the brands, but it is the first step to product trial and then, hopefully, loyalty. Before a particular product can become a regularly purchased item for a particular shopper, at some stage it has to be bought for the first time. If brands and retailers want to get their products firmly established as part of our purchasing repertoires, they should invest in understanding what we as an inexperienced shopper wants and then meet our needs in-store as effectively as possible.

Experiential shopping

The next of our shopping modes is experiential shopping; the differentiating factor while shopping in this mode is that you will use cues from senses other than your sight to make your purchasing decisions. In this mode, you literally want to experience the product before buying it. You might want to smell the latest tea tree and mint shower gel, and in a recent study, 23% of shoppers buying shower gel opened the product and proceeded to smell the contents before purchasing. Another example of experiential shopping occurs when observing shoppers buying things like breakfast cereals, dog biscuits and boxes of teabags; a significant percentage of us actively shake the boxes prior to purchasing, conducting a subconscious 'is it full?' and/or 'is it fresh?' check.

As with inexperienced shopping, experiential shopping takes time and requires space. A key difference though is that when shopping experientially, you don't just want information, it's more that you require the actual product to experience in some way.

When shopping experientially, you will typically begin by seeking permission to interact with the products. In some countries, particularly in the UK, shoppers remain conservative and will be reluctant to cross invisible barriers in-store in case they are entering what they perceive to be 'staff only' areas. This permission may come from the layout of the area, where it's clear which parts shoppers can frequent, such as the aisles of the supermarket. Alternatively, permission may come from a learnt set of behaviours such as knowing that the store permits the in-store trying out of televisions and audio systems, but not washing machines or dishwashers. Sometimes retailers and brands actively invite us to experience products; cosmetics and perfumes have testers, clothing stores have changing rooms and mirrors.

Once you've gained permission to shop a category experientially, you'll begin to explore products physically. When experiential shopping you'll typically have a hierarchy of needs, but in this mode, the hierarchy is based more on your sensory needs. For example, when buying shampoo in an experiential manner, female shoppers will often touch their own hair, and by doing so, sub-consciously communicate that they want to know how a certain product will make their hair feel. They also want to know how their hair will smell and will open a product to smell it. The sensory hierarchy for female shampoo shoppers is typically touch, followed by smell.

Categories in which experiential shopping is common include beauty products, household furniture and electricals, clothing, perfumes and toiletries, boxes of chocolates and other gift related items.

For the retailers and brands, recognising and responding to our needs when we are shopping in an experiential mode can reap rich rewards by converting more of us from being browsers to becoming actual purchasers. Allowing us the opportunity to interact physically with products offers us the chance to take ownership, and a product in the hand is halfway towards being a product in the basket.

However, there are also a number of possible pitfalls to avoid. Offering an experiential shopping environment helps to increase the emotional connections between shoppers, the store and the products. Taking away opportunities to touch, smell, etc. turns the category into something of a commodity. For example, French supermarkets tend to blister pack cosmetics, meaning they are sealed so that shoppers can't access the products. This prevents mess and wastage, but turns the category into a bland and emotionless commodity, which presents shoppers with something that is emotionally at odds with what they want to shop for.

Retailers also need to be mindful of how seemingly innocuous aspects of the store environment can have a significant impact of the experience perceived by the experiential shopper. Some years ago, a European department store commissioned our researchers to study the impact of a newly installed 'fast track'; a wide aisle with a hard floor covering that had no products on it. The aim of the walkway was to help shoppers travel between different departments more quickly. However, because it was free of products and because it communicated a cold and impersonal underfoot sensation, shoppers simply avoided the walkway all together, preferring instead to hide themselves away among products, while standing on nice soft carpeting.

During this study, the researchers observed a somewhat incongruous set of behaviours in the lingerie section. The products were on open display, and although there were plenty of visitors to the department, hardly anyone bought anything. Further behavioural analysis of the shoppers discovered that women were making subtle facial expressions of disgust and contempt as they browsed the department, with some even rubbing their noses to indicate that something didn't smell good.

The researchers headed to the lingerie area and immediately identified an odour like a mixture of rubber and spice that was emanating from a promotional display of rubber backed bath mats nearby. At an unconscious level, the shoppers were seeing lingerie, but smelling something quite incongruent with new, hygienic, clean underwear and were walking away empty handed. Once the offending mats and aroma were removed from the area, sales of lingerie returned to normal. This illustrates the importance of offering shoppers a congruent multi-sensory shopping experience.

In another example, the perceived quality of torches displayed without batteries inserted was significantly lower as they weighed much less in the hand, which led shoppers to perceive that they were of poorer quality. The same weight and quality associations are sometimes made by shoppers evaluating camcorders, cameras and telephones; however, focus groups rarely criticize products for not being heavy enough.

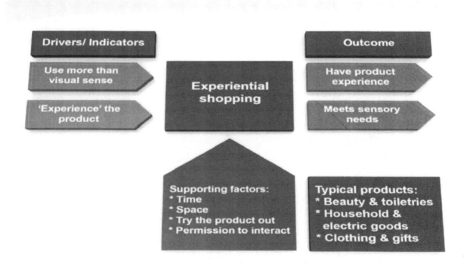

Figure 66 - Experiential shopping

Highly trained observers are needed to pick up the subtle behaviours of actual shoppers in-store, where most purchasing decisions are made. As a final example, a Bang & Olufsen remote control unit typically contains a lump of metal for no reason other than to convey a perception to potential customers that they are holding something solid, robust and weighty enough to warrant being of a good quality and so a high price.

When you are shopping experientially, you should be aware of your own sensory acuity: Try to understand what senses are acting as triggers to purchasing (baking bread smell in the supermarket) and which are acting as barriers to sales (spicy rubber in the lingerie department). You should also be attentive to which senses you use to evaluate various types of products, as this will help you take better control of your own purchasing activity.

Experiential shopping, then, is a relatively time consuming product evaluation process that involves using more than just visual cues with which to arrive at our buy or reject decisions. Often, we aren't even consciously aware of the sensory information we are receiving, processing and responding to. Retailers need to ensure that the stores, categories and displays look good, and that they smell, feel and sound good too. This will open up previously untapped methods of effective communication with us as we shop experientially.

Considered shopping

As the name suggests, considered shopping means that we spend time actively considering between choices, whether between different products in a single store or by travelling to a number of outlets. We need the time and space to consider different items in a retail environment, and most importantly, a choice of actual products to consider. To the untrained eye, considered shopping can look similar to inexperienced shopping as in both cases the shoppers appear to spend time absorbing information and actively make decisions at fixture. To the trained observer though, considered shopping can be recognised by a number of differentiating factors. Shoppers will tend to travel around in-store, with a more extravert manner, walking faster, looking around and not being intimidated in any way. The considered shopper will often compare a finite number of options, whereas the inexperienced person will adopt a much more random style of information gathering.

A simple example of a considered shopping scenario is the woman buying coffee to serve at her dinner party. She knows she wants coffee, and she knows that her favoured premium brand is Carte Noire, but what she's considering is whether to buy regular, espresso or their deeply aromatic decaffeinated blend of instant freeze-dried coffee. Alternatively, she could try the ground coffee for filters and cafetières, again as either regular, decaffeinated, espresso or even as whole bean. Why would she be considering these various options when she knows what she likes? The answer lies in the six fitness indicators discussed earlier: general intelligence, openness to experience, consciousness, extraversion, agreeableness and emotional stability. These core fitness indicators lie behind much considered purchasing and the coffee shopper is mindful of what her dinner guests will think of her, due in part to the coffee she serves to them.

Another example of considered shopping can be seen when watching shoppers buying gifts for other people, as there is often a lot of reverse psychology at play. Like the woman buying the coffee, the shopper buying the gift (the giver) is considering how the recipient will perceive them as a result of receiving the gift. Equally, and in some instances more importantly, is how the giving of the gift makes us feel about ourselves, directly resulting from our perception of how it makes the recipient feel about us.

Categories where considered shopping is predominant include many big ticket items, greetings cards, gifts, ready meals and even what meal to select in the store, restaurant or snack bar.

For the retailers and brands, considered shopping probably represents the most difficult set of shopper needs. To begin with, considerations vary wildly from category to category, and by retail channel and the needs of the shopper. When we're actively considering, we're fully mentally engaged and able to, in the majority of occasions, come to a more reasoned decision. Considered shopping can include active considerations and comparisons between prices and special offers and also factors in a wider range of other aspects, such as organic food and fair trade purchases. So from a brand and retailer perspective, either every category has to be looked at separately and the hierarchy of considerations arrived at, or retailers and brands can pool their knowledge and expertise.

It often turns out to be more beneficial and practical for the retailer to provide us with what we need to be able to consider items. If the proposed purchase is going to be a considered purchase, we will prefer to select from a store or stores that make such behaviour possible. In other words, it isn't very easy to consider different plasma TV sets from either a catalogue retailer or from a branded store such as The Sony Centre, unless it has already been determined that Sony is the only brand to select from. Even if the considered purchase is something straightforward like what to have for dinner that evening, it's still worth selecting from a store with a good range; we wouldn't arrive at the local 24 hour independently owned petrol station expecting an entire aisle full of gourmet ready meals.

To accommodate considered shopping effectively, retailers need to provide space, a good product range and time. For shoppers to make the most considered choice, we should seek out stores that actively allow us to consider products. In the UK, Boots the Chemists, a national chain of health and beauty stores, has around 15 to 20 brands of cosmetics that shoppers can openly consider, compared to a typical supermarket that might have just two or three. In France and now in some UK supermarkets, manufacturers blister pack these products, making it impossible to consider them in any meaningful way.

In addition to having the time, space and a product range to consider, we also need to be able to carry out the consideration itself. For example, we researched the effectiveness of free-standing supermarket display units; secondary sites that offered products in locations away from the main category location. We identified a number of considered shopping related issues. The research compared numerous promotions for alcoholic beverages in the run up to Christmas, which is by far the busiest time of year for the beers, wines and spirits category. There were promotional fixtures in store reception areas, along back walls, on numerous gondolas and in the main beers, wines and spirits aisles themselves. The research discovered that although shoppers saw and interacted with the promotional fixtures, they wanted to compare and consider the various added value offerings together and the only place to do this was in the main aisle itself, and 90% of sales came from this location; this is despite the fact that only a minority of the drinks on offer were available in the main drinks aisle. Essentially, the numerous off-fixture displays were no more than prompts and signposts to the main beer and wine aisles, especially during the peak trading season.

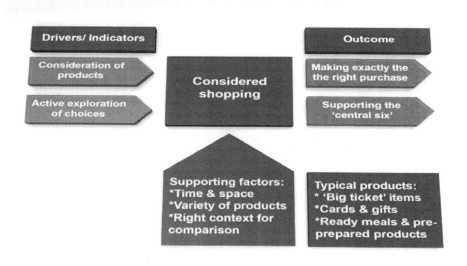

Figure 77 - Considered shopping

We want the process of comparing products to be as practical and easy as possible. Looking back at our example of buying coffee, if we know that we want to buy Carte Noire but want to consider between freeze-dried coffee, ground coffee or whole beans, it would make sense to merchandise them adjacent to each other. However, and because most stores stock a number of brands, they tend to display brands next to each other by type; all the roast and ground coffee together, all the instant coffee together etc. This is presumably because shoppers have told researchers they want the hot beverages category laid out, by type and then by brand within type.

This indicates how important it is to understand what shoppers really want as opposed to what they say is important to them. Often, shoppers will say one thing in an interview and behave differently when actually buying a product. This is why segmenting by shopping behaviour can be such an effective and shopper oriented part of retail merchandising strategy. Additionally, it allows retailers and brands to better forecast the likely return on investment (ROI) from any particular piece of in-store communication. They can compare how best to create the message and factor in such things as whom the message is for and what mode of shopping will they be using when they see the message.

Considered shopping is the hardest for retailers and brands to align with the needs of shoppers and tends to be the most calculated, and some would say 'intelligent' shopping mode. However, brands in particular have to stand up and be counted and considered. If too many considerations result in rejection, then it's time to research the situation and find out the main consideration for a particular product group or category; whether that's added value, health, ingredients, pack size, format or a host of other variables.

Remember, too, that we have the right to consider alternatives; after all, it's our hard earned money that the retailers and brands are vying for.

Grab & go sh

The fourth of the five shopping modes is termed grab & go shopping and accounts for the majority of regularly made repeat purchases for things like staple groceries, the daily bag of crisps, a newspaper or packet of cigarettes. Grab & go shopping requires minimal mental effort and is often managed by either the short term memory of the shopper or as a learnt single scripted behaviour. A simple technique for identifying this mode of shopping it to watch shoppers in supermarkets as they travel up and down aisles making selections; often they won't even come to a halt at the fixture but will walk along and appear to 'sweep' items off the shelves as they pass.

As another example, a shopper will call into the same store every morning for a packet of cigarettes or newspaper and leave with what they want, with little recollection of the transaction; they won't consciously engage with the process in any way.

Supermarket categories in which grab & go shopping is common include staple food items such as bread and milk, frequent purchases including the daily newspaper and many things bought every week from the same store (coffee, washing powder and the like).

When you are grab & go shopping, your need is simple: you want a fast and straightforward means of obtaining more of the same thing you've bought many times before. It could be argued that grab & go shopping isn't shopping at all but more of a replenishment process; no choosing or comparing, just collecting. The more often you make the grab & go purchase from the same store, the more embedded and hard wired the single scripted behaviour becomes. Another striking aspect of grab & go shopping is that when it is over, i.e. when we walk out of the newsagent with our newspaper, we are unable to recall the mechanics of conducting the purchase. It's as though we were on autopilot or in some form of trance.

For the retailers and brands, grab & go shopping offers both advantages and disadvantages in-store. First and foremost, from a loyalty perspective, this mode of shopper automatically buys more of the same, time after time. Providing the item is in-stock and on display, it will be cleanly swept from the shelves over and over again. Second, these types of shopper can be accommodated in the largest number compared with the other modes: They travel fast, spend only minimal time at fixtures and then they leave with their product. The grab & go shopper pays little or no attention to price or value for the most part.

This mode of shopping does present challenges to both retailers and brands. A serious issue is that because we make purchases automatically when in grab & go mode, without mental engagement at the fixture, it is hard to communicate things like new flavours, variants or pack sizes. Additionally, if a brand isn't the subject of lots of grab & go purchasing, it's harder to switch us from another product.

Fortunately, grab & go shopping behaviour can be influenced and changed. An example that's loathed by shoppers but often carried out by retailers is to change the layout on the fixture. As a direct result, we're forced to re-engage with the category at a more conscious level. We have to study the products just to find out where our regular repeat purchase item is now. During this time we're more likely to take notice of other things in the aisle, including other brands, private label alternatives, special offers and different pack formats.

During recent years, there has been a dramatic reduction in the amount of brand funded point of sale display materials in supermarkets. These are typically tools used by brands to help differentiate their products from those of their competitors. Items can be differentiated by price, offer or simply brand values, associations and emotional connections.

This reduction in the amount of brand messaging in UK supermarkets has resulted in more and more of the categories changing from enjoyable shopping experiences into price led commodities. As a direct result, shoppers have less of an experience in-store and fewer choices between commodities; we are left with little to compare on other than price. Recessionary times in the UK have no doubt contributed to the rapid growth in share of supermarket branded, own label products and there's also the hypothesis that the mass commoditisation of the 21st century supermarket is a contributory factor to the rise in Internet based food selling.

Retailers have stripped away many of the very things that distracted grab & go repeat purchasers and which made them consider other items, both in terms of alternative purchases or as additionally bought items. Although this functional retailing is efficient, it's highly questionable whether it's what shoppers want.

From our standpoint, yes, there are categories in-store from which we just want to grab & go, but there's also overwhelming evidence that we want more enjoyable oases in the supermarkets' 'deserts of commodities'. Examples of an oasis might include the beers of the world section of the main beer aisle, indulgence bays in the chilled yoghurt section and the self-serve salad bars found in a number of supermarkets. I suspect there is additional evidence that we want more of a retail 'experience' from the supermarket as shown in the increased popularity of traditional produce markets and farm shops.

When we conducted shopper research of the cooked meats category, we found that a premium section wasn't shopped much and contained a large number of underperforming products. Our client requested that we remove the area as part of a trial and as a direct result, there was strong criticism from shoppers who said the aisle had become dull and hardly worth visiting. The original hypothesis was shoppers wanted a simplified range with a small number of core items so that they could much more efficiently grab & go, however neither the retailer nor the brand that commissioned the research realised exactly how the premium cooked meats bay influenced shopper perceptions of the entire aisle.

Figure 88 - Grab & go shopping

This single example suggests where supermarket retail should consider heading: Structured and efficient food selling, interspersed with positive emotional triggers and a number of clearly differentiated, inspirational and enjoyable-to-shop product areas.

Grab & go shopping, then is a fast and automatic repeat purchase process that retailers and brands can only interrupt by blunt methods, such as moving the products around or not stocking them at all. For shoppers, grab & go is what we often say we want, but in practice too much of it only serves to commoditise the store and the shopping experience. This results in less motivation to actually shop, and simply fulfils a need to replenish.

Impulse shopping

The last of the five modes of shopping is termed impulse shopping, and refers to purchasing something on the spur of the moment. If you observe an impulse shopper in a food category like sweets and chocolate, you'll see them typically walking slightly past the product and then taking a small step back as the brain determines the chocolate bar is simply too good to miss. Shoppers appear to make a sort of 'double take' movement as an impulse product catches their eye and then causes them either to buy or resist it.

Impulse shopping offers brands and retailers the opportunity to generate that all important add-on sale. For example, we see this when the shopper visits the 'food to go' section for a sandwich and while they're there are unable to resist that 'naughty' bar of chocolate. Another example of impulse purchasing well known to the retail industry relates to merchandising sweets, drinks, magazines and the like to the queue of people at a main check out, kiosk or petrol forecourt shop. The queue consists of a captive audience that has little to occupy their minds and is therefore more likely to look around their surroundings. Offering them a self-reward or tempting treat is a great way to generate additional sales.

Categories in which impulse shopping is common include confectionery at the petrol station or from the checkout in the supermarket, indulgent items such as cream cakes and puddings and pretty much anything else that we can ingest but that is bad for us.

Back in 2005, we conducted a research study into petrol forecourt shops and discovered that 26% of shoppers who visited petrol forecourts with grocery stores bought only fuel during their visit. More recently in 2010 another study of similar outlets identified an average of 21% of visitors bought only fuel. In other words, more shoppers had increased their weight of purchase. Whether this is due to an active strategy to drive impulse purchasing isn't known, but we do know that a number of large brands have teams dedicated to impulse purchasing.

In the supermarket, there are many locations that generate impulse purchasing and trials have been conducted into grouping products by occasion: For example the 'girls' night in', consisting of a DVD, some confectionery and a bottle of wine. Although these provide shoppers with positive emotional experiences and reportedly generate more sales, they are notoriously difficult to arrange as each category in-store is managed by a different group of people at head office and generally, no-one likes giving up valuable shelf space.

Figure 99 - Impulse shopping

Impulse purchases aren't confined to small items. For example, research in electrical departments identified an increase in sales of camcorders by up to 15% by presenting them more as impulse purchase opportunities. Researchers identified that shoppers were less concerned about the technical specifications of the units, and were more interested in simply capturing memories. They wanted to film the family growing up, record their holidays for posterity, etc. Once the camcorder displays were enhanced with images of the family having fun, children playing and other emotionally laden images, interest in the category grew, as did sales.

There are several other interesting impulse related aspects of shoppers that researchers have uncovered. Shopping Behaviour Xplained Ltd compared the likelihood of shoppers to impulse purchase at different locations within a number of supermarkets.

The research discovered that the more time shoppers spend in-store, the more impulsive they became, but only up to a point; after this they tend to reach a temptation saturation point and mentally switch off, ignoring most offers, promotions and possible impulse purchases. Another interesting finding was that at the beginning of a big weekly shop, people were more likely to impulse purchase for others rather than themselves, but the more they travelled the store, the more 'selfish' they tended to become. Mentally, they perceived that as they had worked so hard doing the shopping, they were justified in rewarding themselves with a bar of chocolate or cream cake.

Looking at things from a different perspective, there has been plenty of publicity on retailers and brands using tactics to tempt children with certain products in-store. This activity is known as pester power, which encourages the child to 'nag' the adult into letting them have a particular product. This activity doesn't occur as much in supermarkets now, at least overtly, but children do still see products and pester their parents for them; however this may be more to do with the nature of children than the retailers themselves.

Fascinatingly, men are more likely to impulse purchase than women. The exact reasons why aren't known, but it can lead to a heated discussion when the items are placed in full view on the checkout conveyer belt!

As shoppers, we often criticise retailers and brands for encouraging us to impulse purchase, but for the most part, we actually feel better as a result. We get to reward ourselves or others, which is emotionally positive. However, we may suffer a feeling of buyer's remorse as well; this is the regret we sometimes feel when we get a product home and we realise the purchase was unwarranted, unneeded or a waste of money.

Impulse shopping refers to us making spur of the moment decisions to buy something we hadn't previously considered. The activity offers retailers and brands the opportunities to drive additional sales. As a result, a number of them invest in specialist teams of 'impulse' experts and a significant proportion of promotional spend in-store goes to increasing our likelihood of making an impulse purchase.

Understanding your own mode of shopping

This brings us to the end of the modes of shopping, but as you develop your strategies and techniques for shopping more effectively, it's useful to bear these in mind, especially as you may use the techniques slightly differently depending on which mode you are using.

Next time you're in a shop, stop and think about the type of shopping that you are engaging in, and with practice, understanding your shopping mode will become second nature.

We'll now look at the benefits and techniques you can use to transform yourself into a smarter shopper.

Becoming a smarter shopper, developing your strategy and using the techniques

Learning to shop more effectively is a step by step process that will need some thought and planning from you. To achieve your goals, you'll need to think about what you want to get out of shopping, develop a strategy for doing so using the techniques in this section, apply them in the supermarket and review your shopping trips so that you can identify what worked and where you might want to focus in future.

We'll start by developing a shopping strategy, which is fundamental to being a smarter shopper.

Creating a strategy to shop more effectively

Developing your shopping strategy is comprised of several main areas:

1. Understanding the benefits and working out what you want to get out of being a smarter shopper and finding the emotional impetus to put your strategy into practice

2. Understanding the core principles of shopping more effectively and reviewing the techniques within each one

3. Choosing several techniques to use when you are next in the supermarket

4. Applying them in the supermarket

5. Reviewing what worked and what didn't and refining/expanding your techniques for the next time you shop

We'll examine each of these in turn.

Understanding the benefits and working out what you want to get out of being a smarter shopper

The first thing we need to do is to establish what you want to get out of shopping more effectively; is it financial gain, freedom from the influence of the supermarkets, self-improvement or something else?

Whatever it is, it's important that you identify what's most important to you, as keeping these reasons in mind will encourage you to follow through on your strategy.

Because finding the reasons for being a smarter shopper is so important to your success, we've provided two separate and distinct techniques that you can use to identify your motivation. The first of these is starting with your outcomes and benefits and understanding the underlying reasons and the second is called 'Leverage and Anchoring'. Have a read through of each technique to decide which you want to use, or simply mix them together to create what works best for you.

Technique One – Focussing on Outcomes and Benefits

Write a list of outcomes and benefits

The first thing to do is brainstorm a list of what you want to achieve. Simply think about the benefits and what you want and jot them down on a piece of paper. Don't try to edit your thoughts too much, at the moment it's important to ensure you capture what's most relevant to you.

There could be many reasons and we've listed a few below to get you started:

- Be more aware of your decisions in-store

- Take greater control of your purchasing habits

- Reduce both the external and internal influences on the way that you shop

- Save money

- Work towards a long term goal

- Shop in a more informed way

- Make better choices about what you buy

- Ensure that you only buy what you need

Once you've jotted everything down, go through and select the two or three most important reasons, as these are the ones we'll be focussing on.

Understand why your outcomes and benefits are important

The two or three outcomes and benefits that you've chosen are what we're going to explore further to identify your reasons. We do this using a technique called 'The Five Whys' which is designed to see what the causes of your thoughts and beliefs are.

Simply, it involves taking each of your key points in turn and asking 'why?' a few times (although the technique is called 'The Five Whys', sometimes you might only need three or as many as six or seven).

It's easiest to illustrate this with an example: Say you've written down 'Saving Money' as one of your key reasons, your Five Whys might go like this (although this example only uses four):

1. I want to save money – Why?

2. Because I don't have enough to do the things that I want to do – Why?

3. Because I want to spend money on a nice family holiday – Why?

4. Because I want to treat the people I love to something they deserve

Generally, once you reach the 'nugget' of the point, you can stop. How do you identify that point? It's often something emotional (as in the example above) or it might simply be that asking the question again results in a circular argument (i.e. it answers itself).

Here's another example:

1. I tend to throw a lot of food away at the end of each week – Why?

2. Because I always buy too much in the supermarket – Why?

3. Because I am often very rushed and don't see exactly what I need, so I over-buy – Why?

4. Because I don't plan ahead and have to do a whole week's shop with very little preparation – Why?

5. Because I'm not preparing to shop properly – Why?

6. Because before now, I didn't think planning was important

If possible, it's good to make the last point a positive one, as it's easier to focus on positive emotions and thoughts, so in the example above your last point might be 'I know it's important to plan ahead'.

Describe and imagine how achieving these benefits will make you feel

Once you have your core two or three outcomes or benefits and the reasons you've discovered through the Five Whys, write them down on a separate piece of paper, so it might be something like this:

- I want to save money shopping so I can treat the people I love to a nice family holiday

- I'll reduce the amount of food I throw away by making sure I plan properly for my shopping trips

Once you've done this, it's important to make these reasons more real to you as they'll be part of your motivation for changing your behaviours.

You can do this by thinking about each point in turn and imagining how that would make you feel. Remember that we're creatures of emotion, so understanding the benefits on an emotional level for the things you're working towards will help to reinforce them in your mind.

In the example above you could think about how good a family holiday would feel and what that would mean to you emotionally, or the satisfaction of having an empty fridge and an emptier dustbin (thus avoiding that feeling of guilt) at the end of the week.

If you can then tie the thought into a specific image or word, that can really help as well. For example, you might have a particular place in mind for the holiday, so you could write 'Malta' or 'Barbados' or wherever you fancy down next to your examples. The more concrete and real you can make them, and the more positive emotions you have as a result, the easier putting your strategy into practice will be.

Technique Two – Leverage and Anchoring

If you want to take a more pragmatic approach to working out your motivations, we've provided another technique here called 'Leverage and Anchoring' that will help you do just that.

When we're talking about smart shopping, leverage means creating sufficient mental desire, urge and need to follow through on the recommendations you'll find throughout the rest of the book.

If you want to save money and use that to leverage your desire to become a smarter shopper, please take some time to quantify how much you spend per year in the supermarket. Check bank statements or till receipts if you have them and be as thorough as you can; your annual spend will be a key part of the leverage you will need to commit to the plan, then imagine if you could save 10% of that and what you could do with the money.

There could be numerous additional reasons, and whatever yours is, it is vital that you apply real and powerful leverage so that you can commit fully to the process. You need to have a genuine desire and need to succeed, and for the most part, this form of commitment has to be emotional.

I'm reminded of an example that the master of motivational psychology, Anthony Robbins told me. In his earlier career, Robbins became relatively well known, among other things, for his ability to help people kick habits. Anthony was waiting in a hotel meeting room for a particular client to arrive so that the client could be helped to give up smoking. This client had been given the emotional leverage to give up by his young daughter and as a result had sought out one of the world's leading authorities on how to get results from rewiring the brain and mind.

Robbins found the somewhat nervous client outside the hotel, having just one last cigarette; such was his belief that Anthony would indeed stop him smoking.

So what had driven this client to go to such lengths to give up smoking? Not just to give up some day, but to kick a deeply ingrained habit? It was a single sentence, said to the man by his daughter. One evening the client was working in his study and as a relatively heavy smoker, was consuming a number of cigarettes. Having been a smoker for all of his adult life, it wasn't a habit he was too keen to give up. However, with a few words his daughter dramatically changed his outlook and generated the emotional leverage needed for the man to commit to giving up smoking.

How did this man's daughter create such a strong leverage in a single sentence? As he sat in his study working, the daughter entered the room and asked what he was doing: 'Working', was the response. Next the daughter asked why daddy was smoking and why he smoked so much. Unable to give a good answer, the man continued to work studiously. At this point, the daughter began to shed a tear, first gently weeping and then after a few seconds, sobbing uncontrollably. Somewhat alarmed, her father looked up from his work and asked why she was crying. Her response gave him the leverage to take action, she said: 'But daddy, I don't want you to die, I want you to be there at my wedding when I grow up.' Now that, is emotional leverage.

As a result of a single meeting with Anthony Robbins, combined with this leverage, the man did indeed quit smoking

When it comes to committing to do something, there has to be a good, emotional reason to do so. Otherwise our over-burdened brains will come up with a reason to take the easier option; spend more in the supermarket, accept a little waste, or continue with our bad habits.

Before embarking on these changes, ask yourself what your genuine reason is for wanting to take the first step. Only once you have that real need to succeed, will you fully commit to the changes we're going to discuss. To help you find the leverage you need, I'd like you to write down five reasons why you might not commit to becoming a better, smarter shopper; you could even call them your five excuses. Please put down this book and spend some time thinking about and identifying the top five reasons why you may not commit 100% to becoming a smarter supermarket shopper.

Examples of excuses might include: 'I don't have the time', 'well, it's not all that important', 'we can afford it anyway', and 'we've paid for it so it doesn't matter if we waste some of it'. To get to the real reasons, you will have to look beyond your initial answers. For example, if you write down that a lack of time is one of the reasons you won't fully commit to being a smarter shopper, then you'll need to do a further exercise to identify why you have no time. Where is your time being taken up? If the answer is, for example, at work, then compare how much you earn per hour in your job compared to how much you could save a week by being a smarter supermarket shopper. Once you commit to and become a smarter shopper, it hardly takes any extra time to maintain your new-found skills.

Once you've written down your five reasons for not wanting to be a better supermarket shopper, I want you to take a long, hard look at them and then do something that may seem a little unnerving: replace each of the 'excuses' you have written with positive alternatives. These will be your 'five to drive', the five self-empowering reasons why you simply must become a smarter shopper

At the end of the process, you will have five new beliefs about shopping. Once you've identified your limiting beliefs and replaced them with positive alternatives, you're nearly ready to begin becoming a better, smarter supermarket shopper. The next part of the process is to embed your beliefs into your long term memory, something that can be achieved by using 'anchoring'.

There are a number of different techniques for anchoring beliefs and my recommendation is to start with the following: Write your 'five to drive' on a small piece of paper, put it in your purse or wallet and take it everywhere you go. This small step helps tell your brain that a new process is on its way and it begins to associate your five to drive with the one thing most of us use in a supermarket: our wallet or purse. Next in embedding your new, shopper related positive beliefs, you need to learn them and one of the best ways to do this is to say them (out loud if socially acceptable) on a daily basis, over and over again. As we've discovered, tagging information with emotion is a good way of cementing it into long term memory, so when you say each one, don't be afraid to be emotional. You might say them in an excited tone of voice or mentally attach each one to something you appreciate or cherish in your life (a different thing for each of the five to drive). To help this process, you may want to write your five to drive on to a sticky note and attach it next to your alarm clock so that they are the first and last things you see every day.

The final step of anchoring your five empowering beliefs is to attach a trigger to each anchor so that you can fire them (bring them to the front of mind) at a moment's notice. An example would be to say your five to drive when you first start pushing the trolley each time you go to the supermarket. This builds the habit of your brain reminding you of your five to drive beliefs every time you start to push a supermarket trolley. Over time, you'll discover that you no longer have to recite your beliefs. Once they are emotionally embedded and each has a distinct anchor to trigger it, the brain takes over and does things automatically. To put things another way, what this process does is to prime your brain in a way that is beneficial to you personally as opposed to being for the good of the retailer or brands.

If the subject of leverage sounds somewhat strange, please don't be alarmed; like everything in this book it's based on proven teachings from some of the world's leading psychologists. I'll finish the subject of leverage, beliefs and anchoring by offering an example from my own life. As a child, I would tell anyone who would listen that one day I would own a Mercedes Benz. Many years ago, while working as an account manager for a retail display company, and at the time driving the typical company rep car, I still yearned for a Mercedes Benz.

To me, it enhanced my perception of how intelligent (via financial success and resultant Mercedes Benz car) the world would think I was. Putting my own fitness indicator preferences to one side for a moment, I actively decided to anchor a Mercedes Benz car with my success in selling retail displays. I did this by attaching a picture of the latest C Class Mercedes inside my briefcase. Therefore, whenever I turned up at a client or prospects office, the first thing I'd do would be to open my briefcase to retrieve my note pad. Each time I did so, I saw an image of my dream car; my route to general intelligence in the eyes of the world.

A year later, I had changed jobs and was now merchandising development manager for a leading UK retailer. During a house move, I cleared out the loft, and in it was my old briefcase; when I opened it, the image of the C Class Mercedes was still attached inside. I excitedly came down from the loft and showed this picture to my wife and then immediately opened the front door so that we could see my own C Class Mercedes parked on the drive. Although I thought I had forgotten about my dream car, my brain had the desire wired in and kept going until it got what I wanted.

Once you're able to commit to your five to drive, you're ready to start on your smarter shopping strategy. There are four basic parts to this. First, you'll be taken through a summary of your evolutionary makeup. Second, we'll examine what we can do about how the shopping brain works. The third section of the smarter shopper plan addresses the influences of emotion and feelings, and we'll finish by summarising the physiological influences on shopping.

In each of the sections, there are three basic building blocks: What is going on, what to do about it and how to go about making the change. At the end of the process, you will be empowered to go out there and to be a smarter shopper and have the tools and skill set to take better control of your own mind, brain and body. When you next find yourself in a supermarket, you'll be better equipped to deal with shopping and take a more effective course of action.

Understanding the core principles of shopping more effectively and reviewing the techniques in each one

Now that you have your reasons to be a better shopper, it's time to review the various principles and techniques through the rest of the book to decide which ones you want to use. There are quite a few techniques (Around 40 in total) and using all of them every time you go shopping would be overwhelming! I recommend you pick a handful that you're happy with and apply them until they're second nature, and then expand on this with more techniques the next time you shop.

We've divided the techniques so that they support one of the core eight principles of being a smarter shopper which are:

- **Prepare yourself properly for shopping** – Methods to use before you even get to the supermarket to put you in the right frame of mind

- **Understand that you will be swayed** – Information on how you can be influenced in the shop and what you can do about it

- **Be aware of your surroundings in the supermarket** – Techniques to improve your perception and ability to consider all your options when shopping

- **Create more reasoned motives for your shopping behaviour** – Things you can do to ensure that you're making choices for the right reasons

- **Make conscious decisions about the way that you shop** – Methods to allow you to properly evaluate all of your decision making when considering and purchasing products

- **Add structure to your shopping experience** – Practical suggestions to make the process of shopping more organised and less open to influence

- **Shop differently to change your perspective** – Different ways of approaching the shopping experience to help you engage better with the ideas of being a smarter shopper

- **Review purchases to make better decisions in future** – Techniques you can use when you're back at home to make your next shopping trip more of a success

Choosing several techniques to use when you are next in the supermarket

Now it's time for you to read through each of the key principles and jot down the ones that make the most sense and would be easiest for you to consciously apply the next time you shop. How many techniques you choose are up to you, and of course some you will carry out before you even get to the shop. However I would recommend that you don't pick more than three or four to try at a time as keeping track of more and remembering to use them can be tricky.

To make it easier to select the techniques you might want to use early on, I've prefixed the ones that will have the most immediate beneficial effects with the words 'Key Point'. The first time you pick your techniques, you might want to restrict your selection to just these ones as they'll give you the best value for time invested in applying them, at least initially.

Once you've decided on your techniques, it's time to bring everything together, prior to your shopping trip. You should write down at the top of a small piece of paper your key reasons / motivators and then the three or four techniques that you plan to use and importantly how you will put them into practice. It could look something like this:

Why do I want to be a smarter shopper?

1. I want to save money shopping so I can treat the people I love to a nice family holiday in Malta

2. I'll reduce the amount of food I throw away by making sure I plan properly for my shopping trips

   - I know that sounds in the shop can influence me so I'll use my MP3 player to block out external influences

- I'll make every third purchase today a different brand to what I would normally buy

- I will shop the store backwards

- I will pay by cash

Then, take your piece of paper with you when you shop and stick it in the trolley or put it on your shopping list and refer to it a couple of times as you're going round to remind yourself.

Applying your techniques in the supermarket

Once you get to the store, it's important to stay mindful and focussed on what you want to achieve as a smarter shopper. Having your piece of paper to hand will be very useful in helping you do this. As you're shopping, be sure to 'consciously shop' and consider what you are doing and how you're behaving.

Don't rush around the supermarket but take a calm and measured approach to your shopping, leave yourself good time so that you're not anxious about finishing as quickly as possible. It can also help to re-imagine the positive emotions that you associate with being a smarter shopper as this will help your brain and mind to fully concentrate on the task at hand.

Conversely, if you do forget one or two techniques, or you don't apply them to every single purchase, don't give yourself a hard time about it. It's more important to see the value of getting things right most of the time and have a sense of satisfaction than it is trying to get things right all of the time and being frustrated if you forget once or twice.

Reviewing what worked and what didn't and refining/expanding your techniques for the next time you shop

Once you've returned from your shopping trip, it's useful to consider what worked for you and what didn't. There are some specific techniques in the 'Review purchases to make better decisions in future' section, but overall, it's also useful to:

- Think about how using the techniques made you feel

- Consider what worked well and what could be improved

- Making a note of how you could enhance your use of the technique for your next visit

- Re-read sections of this book to help you focus your mind and discover new techniques to use

- Add or change techniques to refine what's already working

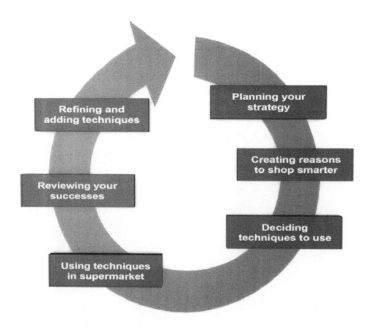

Figure 20 – The Smarter Shopper Lifecycle

There are several ways that you could go about this. You might take your piece of paper and briefly list the pros and cons of each technique, or you might already be satisfied that you did a good job. Regardless of how you approach this review time, it's important to be objective so that you can refine how you shop to enhance your continued success at being a smarter shopper.

Remember that this is an ongoing process – Planning your strategy, carrying it out and reviewing what worked can be seen as the lifecycle of the smarter shopper.

Now that we've discussed how to put your strategy together, it's time to look in detail at the techniques that you can use. Remember that you should pick and choose from here the ones that make the most sense to you and which you'll find easiest to use. In particular, please review any of those marked 'Key Point' as these are the ones that are likely to have the most benefit to you as a smarter shopper.

Prepare yourself properly for shopping

Once you've started to think about your individual shopping strategy, the next thing to realise is that preparation starts before you set foot in the supermarket. You can find several simple techniques below that you can think about before you even start shopping.

That way, when you're in the supermarket, you will have already properly prepared yourself for your shopping trip.

The techniques we can use are:

- **(Key Point)** Don't shop if you are hungry, thirsty or tired

- Adopt a positive physiological state when you are shopping

- **(Key Point)** Prime yourself to shop in the right way by focussing on longer term goals

- **(Key Point)** Make a shopping list based on your needs

- Be mindful of the subtle techniques used to influence you

Don't shop if you are hungry, thirsty or tired

When shopping, each of your senses is being bombarded with stimuli, leading to choice and temptation. You need to reduce the impact of those tempting pictures of food and drink on product packs and in-store advertising, with a golden rule: Never, never, visit the supermarket when you are hungry.

This way, those expensively crafted images won't cause you to salivate autonomically because your blood sugar will be balanced and your brain will be receiving internal dialogue that you are full. This also applies if you are thirsty or tired, as your autonomic reactions to things will cause you to react in powerful ways to these stimuli. Ensuring you are fed, watered and rested means you can better focus on being a more effective shopper, rather than being distracted by your physical needs.

Adopt a positive physiological state when you are shopping

Your emotions, feelings, moods and states of mind come from the combined efforts of your brain and your body. To have a certain feeling, you need to alter psychologically and physiologically. If you smile broadly and sit up in the chair while reading this and then try to feel miserable without changing your facial expression or posture you will probably find it extremely difficult.

Recognise that supermarkets can influence both your state of mind, and your physiology. We'll speed up when walking down narrow aisles and slow down when we see our reflection; the style and tempo of in-store music can influence mental processing and physical behaviour.

When you're supermarket shopping, try to filter out as many distractions as possible and, to paraphrase Johnny Cash, 'Walk tall and look the world right in the eye' – adopt a positive physiological state as you shop for groceries; you'll find that your mind and brain start to adopt the same positive and beneficial outlook.

Prime yourself to shop in the right way by focussing on longer term goals

Because of the way that supermarkets work, it's likely that you are primed as a shopper before you arrive at a particular product category. The technique of priming is about the ability of a store or brand to alter how you feel before you reach a particular aisle or category and influence your behaviour and purchase decision.

There are many ways to prime consumers, for example, the larger than life promotional displays in the reception areas of stores prime us to start associating that store with better deals, prices and financial value. Another example is the fresh produce section of the store, typically near to the entrance and a brightly coloured, fresh and healthy onslaught on a number of our senses. This helps prime us on all the good things relating to food – that it's healthy, fresh and natural.

The smell of freshly baked bread primes us to consider if we're hungry, and can actually make us feel hungrier. Many stores have giant graphic friezes showing larger than life food stuffs which also work as priming devices, manipulating us into a positive susceptible mental state when we happen to be buying groceries.

You have a real battle on your hands if you want to combat priming. The problem is that it happens everywhere. Our brains are constantly assessing the current situation to adjust behaviour for the most appropriate fight, flight or fornicate related course of action.

There are steps you can take to improve the situation. First, you can partake in a little self-priming by focussing on what you want as a result of saving money and shopping more effectively. You could get hold of a picture of something you'd dearly like to buy but can never really save enough money for: That new dress, a luxury holiday or even a Mercedes Benz car.

Simply attach the image to the handle of your shopping trolley so that you are constantly looking at it as you shop. This will remind your brain of the bigger goal that you are working towards, and spending more wisely in the supermarket is part of that process.

Make a shopping list based on your needs

It's easy to be distracted in the supermarket and be tempted to buy more than you want or need. Before setting out, put some time into developing a comprehensive shopping list that contains the items you need, and when you're in the supermarket, stick to it as much as you can.

Then, if you're tempted to put an item in the trolley that you don't really need, you can ask yourself if you really need the item; if not, leave it on the shelf. We'll cover shopping lists in more detail later on.

Be mindful of the subtle techniques used to influence you

It's impossible to turn off a particular sense in the supermarket so we need to prepare our senses for the trip and remind ourselves of the importance of not believing everything we see, hear, smell, touch or taste.

Be aware of different types of lighting used to make certain products look more appealing; be mindful of in-store tastings as a morsel of something can be very tempting but may have a different result compared with consuming an entire portion. Pay attention to the background music or smells and how they are influencing you. We will cover various aspects of how you can be influenced in the next section, so you know what to look out for.

Understand that you will be swayed

Being influenced is inevitable, whether it's by our surroundings, the actions of others, our own internal drives and instincts or the clever marketing of the brands and retailers. Although there isn't much we can do to not be influenced, being aware of how we can be affected means we can develop better methods of dealing with these stimuli, feelings and behaviours and ensure that we're acting in our own best interests.

The techniques we can use are:

- Realise and accept that you will have an instinctive reaction to every situation

- Be aware that you may be influenced differently depending on your gender

- **(Key Point)** Accept that only some aspects of your shopping behaviour can be quickly and easily improved

- **(Key Point)** Learn to recognise your conditioned behaviours

- Realise that emotions always drive your purchasing decisions

- **(Key Point)** Understand the power of pride, shame and guilt over your shopping behaviour

- Rise above the crowd mentality of other shoppers

Realise and accept that you will have an instinctive reaction to every situation

The initial reaction to any incoming physiological stimuli is from the limbic system, a part of the brain solely concerned with fight, flight or fornication. Initially, we will adopt a physiological state that prepares us for one of those three courses of action. A fourth physiological reaction is also possible, and that is freeze: Standing absolutely motionless while the situation changes or our brain uses the added time to come up with a course of action.

Readiness to fight, flee, fornicate or freeze can all be witnessed in the aisles of the supermarket. Taking each one in turn, readiness to fight can be seen at the deli counter, when shoppers take a number and wait for it to appear; just watch the outraged reactions of patiently queuing shoppers when they think somebody has jumped the queue, a behaviour that is a sanitised version of how we behaved thousands of years ago.

In terms of fleeing, we're only prepared to invest a certain amount of time and effort in buying a product. We can sometimes be seen diligently trying to make a purchase, comparing products, reading packs and perusing on-shelf literature. All of a sudden, often caused by other shoppers approaching, we will put the products down and stride swiftly out of the aisle empty handed: We literally give up and run away.

The final 'f' refers to freezing, and while observing shoppers for professional reasons, I have seen it on a number of occasions. When a shopper drops a jar or bottle in an aisle, on most occasions, they will stand absolutely motionless for a moment or two.

Responses to each of the four 'f' situations are initially purely reactive. Don't worry that your brain is directing your body to do things without your cognitive permission but recognise how and when retailers and brands use techniques specifically to cause your limbic systems to trigger a physiological reaction. Then you can use your higher brain to take control, influence the result and create a more beneficial outcome.

Be aware that you may be influenced differently depending on your gender

Men and women can be swayed purely according to our evolutionary gender roles, and it's useful to bear these in mind. Modern women can still behave like matriarchal gatherers when travelling down the aisles, collecting seeds, vegetables and berries for their family groups. In the context of shopping, this means that women have developed a wider peripheral vision and tend to see many more temptations than their male counterparts.

A particular problem for female shoppers is that they are wired to see more things, useful when gathering nuts and berries while keeping an eye on the children. But faced with so many temptations in the supermarket, it's a much harder feat to resist all of them.

When it comes to being smarter shoppers, women in particular need to understand that they will be tempted and will need to think twice. 'Do I really need that box of Krispy Kreme doughnuts?' In your early forays into smarter shopping, you may find the process somewhat exhaustive and tedious, but rest assured it quickly becomes second nature.

On the other hand, men in the supermarket tend to behave like ancient hunters, darting around the shop purposefully, their missions clear and their goals precise. The trouble with this apparently efficient behaviour is that men tend to be just too focussed: If tasked to buy flour that's what we'll do. Whether there are different pack sizes at different prices is just distraction – hunter needs flour, hunter gets flour. Although an over simplification, this example does illustrate the male tendency to treat shopping as a goal oriented hunt and uncovers a significant shopper limitation.

Because men are so intent on reaching their goal, completing a task and killing their mammoth, they often overlook important details. The man may return to the family home with the freshly slain bag of flour, but was it the best value and is it the right size for the needs of the family? When it comes to smarter shopping, men need to slow down, wake up and smell the flours! In other words, for men to be smarter shoppers, you need to consider the choices in connection with your needs at that time.

Accept that only some aspects of your shopping behaviour can be quickly and easily improved

Humans are much better at developing technological solutions to problems than we are at using that technology. As a result, technological advances are happening much faster than we can evolutionarily keep up with. We have created this wonderful, technologically advanced structure called the supermarket but are actually not that well equipped to get the most out of it.

By recognising this fact we will be at a distinct advantage. Simply by accepting that there are only certain aspects of supermarket shopping activity that can be quickly and easily refined is a positive step forwards. As smarter shoppers we can recognise that we are only partially able to handle the supermarket. But, importantly, we can learn to recognise the aspects we can and can't control and understand what could lead to imprudent purchase decisions.

Learn to recognise your conditioned behaviours

The key techniques that we use to minimise the mental effort involved in shopping, single scripted behaviours and chunking are habitual behaviours and at this stage in your shopping efficiency are probably more negative than positive.

Our brains use both single scripting and chunking to save the short term working memory from overload. To explain both behaviours by way of example: When a smoker first buys 20 cigarettes, they do so consciously and have to think about each component of the behaviour. However, as the days, months and years go by, they are able to chunk various aspects of the behaviour into a single action. Opening the door of the tobacconists with the right hand leads instinctively to allowing that hand to continue to the back pocket to retrieve the money. With money in hand, they arrive at the counter and almost without any awareness, ask for 20 of their preferred brand, hand over the money, collect any change and turn to leave the store. After leaving, they typically light up and life goes on.

The point is that over time, each of the actions involved in buying 20 cigarettes first get chunked into groups of behaviours and then eventually chunked into a single action, caused by a single trigger such as seeing the tobacco store on the way to work each morning. Finally, these chunked behaviours all meld into one and this is what is known as a single scripted behaviour. The issue here is that because a group of actions become a single behaviour, as a smarter shopper you have to be alert to the fact that often you will be blissfully unaware of subtle alterations to your surroundings. In the case of buying 20 cigarettes, if it is a true single scripted behaviour, then our shopper wouldn't be aware of any in-store POS, special offers or alternative, newly launched products.

Brands and retailers will endeavour to break single scripted behaviours to communicate with you. Sometimes they do this unintentionally, for example, when a particular brand is out of stock.

Upon being told this, you have to re-engage with the store and once again become aware of your surroundings.

To develop from shopping on autopilot to smarter shopping you need to recognise your own single scripted shopping behaviours: Often, there is nothing wrong with these behaviours, providing that the purchased product is the best to meet your particular needs. If you buy certain things by way of single scripted behaviours, then every once in a while interrupt the script yourself and check that you aren't missing a better alternative. An example of how you can interrupt your own single scripts could be going to a different supermarket every now and again, just to 'weigh up the competition'. Even small alterations to your behaviour can have dramatic effects; when you enter the supermarket to do a big shop, you could walk all the way to the far end of the store with your trolley empty and begin shopping from there. This puts the entire store in a different perspective and significantly reduces instances of single scripted and chunked behaviour purchases.

Although single scripted behaviours are often efficient and beneficial, as a smarter shopper you should sense-check them once in a while.

Realise that emotions drive your purchasing decisions

Almost all products are bought primarily based on 'emotional reasons'. If I asked you the colour of the car that was directly in front of you last time you drove into the supermarket car park, you'd probably struggle to remember. However, if for some reason there was an emotional reason to remember that particular vehicle, then you would be able to do so. You may have run into it, it may have stopped suddenly and surprised you or perhaps you just remember the driver. That's the emotional link needed to consign that vehicle to your long term memory.

We are driven by emotion and there's no more powerful driving force. Luckily, as we'll discuss later, we can cognitively manage our emotions via the cerebral cortex in our higher brain. If you're truly committed to becoming a smarter shopper, you have to get emotional about the subject; that's the only way you'll be able to understand and get to grips with the emotions that constantly shape your decisions.

Recognise how brands and retailers attract your attention by triggering specific emotional responses. Only when we realise how we're being targeted can we start to defend against these messages and our automatic responses to incoming stimuli impact on pretty much every decision we make.

Understand the power of pride, shame and guilt over your shopping behaviour

We possess two different types of emotions: Universal, primary ones concerned with fight, flight or procreate, and a number of more modern, socially and culturally aligned emotions that lead to and manifest as feelings. Our universal emotions are managed by our limbic systems and their main aim is to keep us alive and ensure the continued existence of the human race. Our social emotions are more related to how we perceive we are seen by others.

When it comes to smarter shopping, the influencing power of social emotions and feelings is significantly greater than that of the universal ones. It's useful to pay attention to three particular feelings you may get while supermarket shopping: pride, shame and guilt.

We buy many products to make us feel proud; lots of gifts are bought partly because the buyer wants to feel pride when giving it to a recipient. Another equally powerful social emotion is shame. An example of shame related marketing can be seen in the skincare aisle, with numerous products promising to get rid of unwanted this and unsightly that. They are making the shopper ashamed that they need to get rid of their own this or that. The third particularly effective social emotion is guilt. This often manifests itself when people are buying for their loved ones, children or pets. The image of a sad faced dog on a premium pet food can instantly turn the strictest pet owner into a guilt ridden individual whose only road to redemption is by purchasing a better pet food for their faithful companion.

Try to cut down on how much you are swayed by emotions, particularly social feelings, when in the supermarket. One technique that can help is to identify and write on your shopping list the primary purpose of the product you're buying, which is often different from the reason for buying it. Instead of rationalising that you are buying a washing powder because it contains a new, biologically advanced formula, consider that the primary reason to buy that washing powder is because you want you and your family to be dressed in clothes that look clean and smell nice. A key shopper need if you want to wash 'whiter than white' may be that a powder contains optical brighteners that make white clothes look less yellow.

Rise above the crowd mentality of other shoppers

A key part of human physiology is concerned with us communicating our feelings non-verbally, which can lead to changes in the moods and feelings of other shoppers in the vicinity. To recap on the evolutionary background, our ancestors were social creatures who preferred to exist in groups. They discovered that their chances of survival were greater if they all looked out for each other. However, it wasn't easy to look out for danger coming from any direction, so we developed a way of recognising and responding to the facial expressions of others. This way we could look out for danger in one direction and be mindful of the facial expressions of those looking in other directions by using peripheral vision.

We've retained that same innate ability; the sight and sound of unruly children in an aisle can cause shoppers nearby to express disgust and anger using their faces. This can also spread to other shoppers. Just observe how a queue of shoppers start a chain reaction of facial expressions when someone at the front of the line forgets their PIN or isn't ready to pay for their goods.

When it comes to functioning as a smarter shopper, it's a case of knowing your mind, using your brain and rising above the crowd mentality of many other shoppers. If you catch yourself becoming frustrated, just check what the cause is: If it's a response to the anger of others, rise above it and smile. Once you get proficient at recognising facial expressions and subsequent emotions and feelings, you will be able to express the emotions that you want, which in turn can positively influence others. This can help you to stay focussed and prevent you falling into a trance which leads to less beneficial purchase decisions being made.

We can also be influenced by other people's facial expressions. Our brains are hard wired to exist in social groups and as a result we are constantly weighing up others in our vicinity and checking the dynamics and harmony of the group. As a form of long distance communications and a means of spotting potential threats and mates, we are able to recognise and respond to facial expressions more than any language based communications, such as in-store messaging or promotional information. Long before we were able to read, write or even talk, we communicated by way of facial expressions and this still holds true today.

We need to understand that the presence of other shoppers can influence our own in-store perceptions and behaviours. A store full of happy shoppers makes you feel happy. Conversely, lots of angry shoppers in the same checkout queue can have an adverse impact on your mental state. Being surrounded by hoards of supermarket shoppers who are behaving irrationally and making impulsive and rash purchasing decisions can cause you to behave in the same way and in an exaggerated manner. To combat this lemming like mentality, you need to stay focussed and mission oriented. Don't get caught up in any mass behaviour that means you deviate from your goal.

To summarise the brain related characteristic of behaving differently in a crowd, remember you are an individual, not a number. Behave as you do when you're away from the grocery store, stay in touch and in control of your mental state as much as possible.

Be aware of your surroundings in the supermarket

Paying attention to your surroundings is a crucial part of shopping more effectively. Only by considering all of your options can you make the best choice, so ensuring you're aware of what's around you in the supermarket is a very useful skill to develop. The techniques in this section are designed to enhance your perception and help you use all of your senses to support your shopping experience.

The techniques discussed here are:

- Pay attention to your environment so that you can see all the options

- Recognise marketing for what it is; don't just be attracted to the boldest and brightest products

- **(Key Point)** Realise that images aren't everything they seem and put them in context where possible

- **(Key Point)** Be aware of the sounds in your environment and try blocking out external influences

- Understand that what you physically touch can also affect you emotionally

- Realise that scent can be a powerful motivator

- Don't let your taste buds be tricked, distance yourself from the thought of consuming the product

Pay attention to your environment so that you can see all the options

A key part of shopping effectively is to be more aware of what's around you. Don't just be drawn to products between eye and waist height; there are typically three shelves outside this range, be aware of them and start considering what's on them. Remember that some products are promoted at such low prices that the retailers actually lose money when they sell them. These items, known as loss leaders, can be heavily advertised, but harder to find in-store because they are outside our eye lines; the aim being to give shoppers every opportunity to 'give up the hunt' and purchase a higher margin item instead.

Because humankind is hard wired to look down, recognise this and look over the whole range of shelves when in the supermarket.

Recognise marketing for what it is; don't just be attracted to the boldest and brightest products

Brands and retailers leverage emotional connections in-store for their own benefits and they do this via shopper marketing. Consumer marketing has existed for decades, but now it is recognised that shopping and consuming are very different things and shopper marketing is developing in its own right. It's now reaching the point that traditional advertising agencies are jumping on the bandwagon and proclaiming themselves as instant shopper and shopping experts.

Shopper marketing is about understanding how target consumers behave as shoppers, in different channels and formats, and using this intelligence for everyone's benefit; for retailers, brands, shoppers and consumers. Price led promotions, in-store tastings and in-store brand activation strategies all qualify as forms of shopper marketing.

As a smarter shopper, you have to try and recognise marketing for what it is: An attempt to make you buy one product either instead of or in addition to another. This means actively considering whether you really want the product that's visually jumping off the shelves for some reason or other. By all means investigate those eye catching deals and partake in the free tastings, but when you do, consider your options without all the paraphernalia and associated marketing hype.

Realise that images aren't everything they seem and put them in context where possible

Visual images have been processed by human brains and their evolutionary predecessors for 10,000 times as long as language and words have been around. This means that we are naturally wired to recognise and respond quickly and more emotionally to pictures than words.

We are initially attracted by images on posters and product packaging and only after that do we start to notice and factor in any words. A picture really does say a thousand words and another benefit of image based communication is that it lets us add our own meaning to it, by allowing it to trigger individual, specific memories and associations.

In the supermarket environment, around 70% of the stimuli we receive are via our sense of vision. It's no surprise that brands and retailers invest so much in crafting just the right images for us to see. Pictures are carefully tweaked and airbrushed so that we see the perfect cooked meal or other product. This isn't a new practice, before

Photoshop, images would be manually enhanced to optimise their appeal to shoppers and consumers.

Something else to be mindful of, particularly in relation to shopping for food items, is that as our brains were wired long before photographs and product packaging had been invented, we are naturally attracted to images that show the real food products, more than mood based imagery.

You need to place in-store visual images in a context whenever possible: The image of a mouth-watering plate of muffins on a dried muffin mix pack means you still have to create the muffins, which will take time and some degree of culinary skill. Be aware of all those pictorial 'serving suggestions' as many of them are simply to tempt you to buy that product and may contain a number of other items you would need to purchase to create that 'suggestion'.

Your brain has evolved to be initially attracted to pictures; in a sense, the image gets the emotional attention, and then cognition uses words to arrive at a subsequent decision.

Be aware of the sounds in your environment and try blocking out external influences

We are constantly processing and analysing the sounds arriving in our brains from our ears. As with the visual sense, auditory cues prime us in readiness for situations we have yet to encounter and deal with. The brain is very advanced in the way it analyses sounds and can decode sound – where it comes from, how far away it is and the speed at which whatever is making the noise is travelling.

In a retail environment, the influence of sounds can be remarkably powerful. Several research studies have illustrated how much we respond subconsciously to music playing in-store. The tempo of the music can change our walking speed; the faster and more upbeat the music, the quicker we stride along, almost as if we are subconsciously walking in time to the music.

The genre of the music playing can also alter our perceptions of the prices and value of the products available. Evidence shows that simply changing from pop to classical music in a store can significantly increase how much the average shopper pays for their wine.

You either need to be aware of the sounds influencing how you shop or actively prime yourself in such a way to manage your own auditory input. For example, listening to your MP3 player while in the supermarket will offset any external musical influences, but please be mindful of the tunes and genres of music you choose. Songs like 'Money, Money, Money', 'Hey Big Spender' and 'We're In the Money' might not be the best tunes to play!

Of course, music isn't the only type of sound that can influence your behaviour; laughter can be infectious and the sound of someone crying can upset other people. Even the effectiveness of Tannoy messages read by shop staff can vary depending on the regional accent and where the store is.

Understand that what you physically touch can also affect you emotionally

The tactile nature of products, store fixtures and fittings can and will alter your perception of product quality. We have touch sensors over every part of our body, so it isn't just our hands that touch and sense things. Our feet subconsciously respond to underfoot sensations, and we've all felt the heat of the sun when it shines directly onto our faces.

We are constantly receiving kinaesthetically (touch) related stimuli. Our brain actively makes judgements about these stimuli depending on how they physically feel. When you shake hands with someone, you can't stop your brain making a judgement about the other person, just from the way they shook hands.

The weight of many portable electronic devices is often associated with quality; too light and the gadget must be poorer quality, and yet they are designed to be portable, aren't they? A favourite example relates to shoppers associating the quality of products in a catalogue, in part by how the catalogue feels. Shopper perceptions of a leading European retailer improved and became more positive after they increased the thickness of the cover on their Christmas catalogues.

It's important to be aware both of what you are touching, and what is touching you. For example, if you suddenly find yourself walking on a softer, carpeted floor, expect to pay more in that part of the store. Conversely, if you catch yourself turning your nose up at the poor tactile quality of that box of chocolates, consider who you are buying them for; if they are a gift for a valued friend, then you are right to turn your nose up (as they probably will, subconsciously, when they receive them). But if they are for you, remember you will probably eat the chocolates without paying any more attention to the box.

What you touch physically can very often touch you emotionally. We all find it difficult to avoid making judgements about things by the way they feel. When smart shopping, use your sense of touch, but use it cognitively as well as subconsciously.

Realise that scent can be a powerful motivator

The human sense of smell is processed by the brain in a different way to the other four senses; it doesn't pass through any form of mental filter and so can slip 'under the radar'. Research strongly suggests that the presence of chemicals in the air can cause changes in subconscious behaviour, for example, the scents that females produce that attract males, such as copulins, or chemicals that affect the menstrual cycle. It is generally accepted that what we smell influences how we react, perceive and behave. It is no surprise that retail and brand marketers often target us by way of our sense of smell.

The most well-known is probably that of circulating the smell of freshly baked bread around the supermarket; the purpose being to make us hungry in a place that sells food. But there are also other, more subtle, smell related influences in stores. Often, the retailers aren't even aware of them and don't actively utilise them. For example, there is a definite smell in the laundry detergent aisle that can cause us to become subconsciously nostalgic, thinking of our childhood and the smell of freshly laundered clothes.

It's better to accept olfactory influence and to react to the consequences of it, rather than walk around the supermarket with a peg on your nose.

Don't let your taste buds be tricked, distance yourself from the thought of consuming the product

Our taste buds can be 'tickled' without any morsel of food passing our lips. In other words, the thought of food can create internal chemical changes as we shop and alter our behaviour in-store at fixture.

If I were to describe a large chocolate cake, covered with chocolate icing and stuffed with fresh cream, you may start to fancy a slice. What if I went on to describe how you carried the cake across a room and got some chocolate icing and freshly whipped cream on your fingers, which you then had to lick off? I suspect that you are salivating right now. I've managed to alter the chemical management of your body using a few words. Imagine if I were to drop you into a large warehouse full of 50,000 different products, mostly edible and many mouth-wateringly irresistible. How much could you be influenced then?

What if I were able to present you with images of how the most basic of ingredients could be turned into everything mouth-watering, and that I could surround you with giant images of all those things you love to eat. How much do you think the chemical processes in your body could be influenced then? Of course the scenario I have illustrated is that of the typical supermarket and yes, your taste buds are tickled every time you go there. You don't have to eat anything, the images and smells just set your body off. To be a really good smarter shopper, you need to distance yourself from the end uses of a product; those promises made by the pictures on the pack, and remain focussed on shopping for commodities. This helps to limit the amount of gustatory influence on your decision making.

Create more reasoned motives for your shopping behaviour

Because we are creatures of emotion, we need to align our motives and behaviours with what we're hoping to accomplish in being a smarter shopper. This involves breaking our conditioning and feelings towards preconceived ideas and understanding what the value of something is to us.

The techniques that can help with this are:

- Understand you are uncontrollably drawn to things and sense check the purchases you make

- **(Key Point)** Think twice and actively question the 'value' of the product you are buying

- **(Key Point)** Always compare prices in context to ensure you're not just being influenced because something is declared as 'cheap'

- Break your emotional conditioning and memory of certain products and items

- Buy supermarket only brands

- Ask yourself how your purchasing relates back to the central six fitness indicators

Understand you are uncontrollably drawn to things and sense check the purchases you make

For 98% of the time we've been evolving, we have only been concerned with fight or flight, eat or be eaten, and opportunities to procreate and reproduce. What does this mean when it comes to browsing the aisles of the supermarket? First, we are always looking for danger signals (that is one of the reasons why red and white messages stand out so much). Second, our brains are programmed to find a mate, which means we're susceptible to buy things if we believe that it'll help us find Mr or Ms Right, or keep Mr or Ms Right now.

As a smarter shopper, you'll learn to recognise that you are uncontrollably drawn to things that may not be an advantage to your ability to shop for groceries effectively. To counteract this, begin to develop a mental strategy of questioning each of the purchases you make. This needn't be time consuming, just a simple sense check as to 'why am I really buying this, what is my real motive?' If you're happy with your answer, go ahead and make the purchase, otherwise you might want to leave the item on the shelf. Remember that due to your five to drive leverage, part of your brain is already working towards your new best interests.

Think twice and actively question the 'value' of the product you are buying

The fifth of our limitations has to do with the limbic system, the part of the brain that reacts faster than the more 'intelligent' cerebral cortex. The limbic system operates below your level of consciousness, so you will have little idea what this part of your brain is up to.

However, although the limbic system can cause you to stop in your tracks, gasp with surprise or cause your pulse to race, there is an upside. After the initial reaction by the limbic system, the higher brain, particularly the pre-frontal cortex, gets the opportunity to sense-check the situation. This is the moment when you need to take control. If you find yourself inexplicably standing in front of a wonderful display of '3 for £2' cans of cat food, then once again, just think twice. Whatever has caused your limbic system to react initially may not be to your benefit. Start by briefly questioning the value of the product you are looking at and ask yourself things like 'is this offer really worth buying?' or even 'do I have a cat?'

Always compare prices in context to ensure you're not just being influenced because something is declared as 'cheap'

The brain can often only compare things if it has a context in which to do so. For example, prices will be evaluated in the context of the prices of similar, nearby items. When it comes to value, we'll often consider much more than the price, but we still need to evaluate value in some context.

Beginning with the subject of price context, telling a shopper that 'Eight cans of beer are just £7' doesn't mean as much as saying that 'Eight cans of beer are just £7, reduced from £12', now there is context. When you are shopping smarter, look at prices and especially promotional prices in context, and if there is no context, proceed with caution. Even if there is a context, such as reduced from £9.99 to £6.99, be mindful of whether the original price was too high to be believable, which means that the offer is misrepresentative. For example, a special offer for beer in the main beer aisle allows you to compare the price against many other offers and deals there. Alternatively, a standalone bulk stack in the store reception area doesn't allow for any checking as it is out of context with the products in the immediate area.

Moving on to the subject of value, brands and retailers are always talking about the added value of this and the extra value of that; more often than not, the value they refer to is financial in some way, such as a bigger pack for the same money. However, for us, value can mean many things: Value can indeed be financial, but can also be associated with other factors such as saving time, convenience or ease of use. You need to understand what represents value to you and if the value offered by the brand or retailer isn't in your own personal value hierarchy, then don't be taken in.

Break your emotional conditioning and memory of certain products and items

We buy a large number of products primarily because of what we remember about the item and memory needs emotion to function. Once you accept that all three types of long term memory, procedural, declarative and episodic, are intrinsically linked to emotions, you'll begin to recognise that your memories of an event can be quite different from what really happened. Our memories are significantly influenced by our perception and this is why we can make some strange in-store purchasing decisions.

Your role as a smarter shopper is to reduce your dependence on emotional decision making and create more reasoned motives for buying and rejecting specific products. Instead of buying that brand of washing up liquid because your mum used it years ago, try to find the product that best washes dishes. A good starting point is to understand the differences between certain products and your reasons for purchasing them to counter historic perception with more rational cognitive reason.

Buy supermarket only brands

One of the more radical things you can do to reduce your emotional ties to a particular brand is to buy only supermarket brands for part or all of your shopping trip. You might restrict this to certain product categories or, if you're feeling brave, ensure every item in your trolley comes from a non-branded alternative to what you would normally buy.

If you do decide to do this, you'll discover the very strong emotional attachments that you do already have to some brands, which is another indication of how strongly we can be influenced.

Ask yourself how your purchasing relates back to the central six fitness indicators

The central six fitness indicators (general intelligence, openness to experience, consciousness, extraversion, agreeableness and emotional stability) are an excellent way to link the evolutionary needs of the human species, survival and sociability, with modern day supermarket shopping.

Many more products than we would like to admit are bought to meet one of these fitness indicators and a great number of brands are positioned to affirm our perceptions of how others view us, our fitness to mate or to raise a good family.

We covered the central six in detail in the first section of the book, but from a smarter shopping perspective, remember that a lot of the things you buy, you do so to enhance one or more of your six fitness indicators. Using Lynx deodorant may help you to have a higher perception of your own sex appeal than is actually the case, but as a result, your self-confidence would be boosted and so the 'Lynx effect' is working.

A simple step to manage your own fitness indicator related purchases is to ask yourself: how exactly does it indicate your fitness? You can also ask the same question regarding the brand: How wise is the purchase if there isn't any indication which brand it is? Then sense-check yourself to see if there may be another option.

Shopping for the central six fitness indicators is what most of us do much of the time, but there are many occasions when, during post purchase rationalisation, we realise that the item we bought doesn't actually help support our perceptions. Now that you are progressing with smarter shopping, if you're buying more expensive, branded items in the supermarket, ask yourself why. Don't accept the first answer your brain provides but dig a little deeper and try to uncover the real fitness indicator reason for the purchase.

The central six fitness indicators are at the very heart of many product choices you make. Be prepared to challenge yourself as to which fitness indicator perception you are meeting and whether what you intend to buy is really the best solution. If it is, then all well and good, if not, then consider your purchasing options.

Make conscious decisions about the way that you shop

Central to the techniques you will be using are those at the 'moment of truth', the key decisions that you make about what to put in your shopping basket. Ultimately, all of the preparation and good intentions that you have are most tested when making the decision to buy or not to buy a product. These techniques can help:

- Ensure that you understand the range of products on offer so you can objectively make an informed choice

- **(Key Point)** Think twice, sense check and carefully consider your instinctive purchasing decisions

- **(Key Point)** Interrupt your habitual purchases to stop you making the wrong decisions

- Understand why you make a decision to purchase a particular brand

- Try to save 10p on the cost of every item

- Try making every one in two or one in three purchases a different product to something you might habitually buy

Ensure that you understand the range of products on offer so you can objectively make an informed choice

We have an enormous number of options in the supermarket and a vastly wider array of items we can consume now compared with our ancestors. Faced with the choice of up to 50,000 different products during your trip to the supermarket (the only real restriction being a trolley to put them all in), you need to develop a strategy or strategies for making the right purchasing choices.

We can begin with a very simple form of best practice. When in-store, comparing 23 variants of plain potato crisps, or 17 versions of plain digestive biscuits, which is the best product to meet your needs, and more importantly why? If you can come up with a reason that your newly empowered brain is happy with, then good, go ahead and buy. But if you are hesitant, think twice, compare other product solutions and do so as objectively as you possibly can.

Continuing with the potato crisps example, what would be important to you? If you like Gary Lineker, then you may demand Walkers. Conversely, if you recognise that ready salted crisps are all 'much of a muchness', then let price be the determinant factor. But as a discerning shopper, if you want the best sea salt and crisps made from the finest Maris Piper potatoes, then perhaps you've been a victim of... marketing!

Think twice, sense check and carefully consider your instinctive purchasing decisions

Because our brains aren't yet sufficiently evolved to modern shopping, they are forced to operate well out of any comfort zone, relying on instincts and triggers that were wired in a long, long time ago.

Like some of my previous advice, the approach here is simply to think twice. Whatever your first thought, instinct or evolutionary based trigger, you as a modern and 'advanced shopper' have the opportunity to develop the cognitive part of your brain's decision making. In other words, be prepared to let instincts and triggers autonomically do their worst then take more control using the cognitive 'reasoning' part of the decision making process.

Evolution has been hard at work on the human brain for millions and millions of years, so creating change is a bit like turning a fully laden oil tanker in the middle of the ocean: It takes time first to slow it and then more to alter its course. As we're dealing with a brain that's yet to evolve into something good at shopping, we can combat that by training ourselves to carefully sense-check and consider our instinctive purchase decisions. If you find yourself putting an item on the checkout conveyor that you suddenly have doubts about needing, use your new found confidence to leave the product behind.

As a smarter shopper, use the more cognitive, higher section of your brain to take your decision making to a more beneficial level. Shoppers are emotional and we all experience these emotions, but now that we recognise that fact, we can begin to make purchasing decisions rationally and objectively. Over time, you'll find that it becomes both easier and more natural to shop this way.

Interrupt your habitual purchases to stop you making the wrong decisions

Although our brains have numerous departments to handle different aspects of life, they aren't very efficient when it comes to doing the big supermarket shop; they have to rely on short cuts and are far from ideal. For example, if your brain receives visual stimuli confirming that your regular, preferred brand of coffee is right in front of you, then into the basket it goes. Your brain may miss out actively considering anything at the fixture, which means it may not absorb information like price per 100 grams and the amount in a pack.

As smarter shoppers we need to create our own, more shopper oriented shortcuts: For example, when you catch yourself making one of those instinctive repeat purchases, just pause and ask yourself why that brand and pack size is the ideal option? Start to interrupt those grab & go purchases and consider whether there is a better alternative.

This is probably one of the most important changes to make as a smarter shopper. Not only should your higher brain actively help you come to the best decision regarding which products to buy, it must also be constantly on guard to prevent the wrong purchase decisions being made without its input. For example, letting your brain get away with buying a 5 kilogram bag of ready washed potatoes, and paying more mainly because they are washed and already in a bag. Don't let your brain take shortcuts and get away with being lazy.

Understand why you make a decision to purchase a particular brand

In tight economic times, we trade down from the well-known brand names to the lower cost supermarket own label alternatives. One chain of UK supermarkets witnessed a leading branded breakfast cereal dropping its share by more than 10% with the own label product seeing a similar increase at the time. Once we trade out of the big brands onto supermarket own label, how do the brand owners get us back? The own label items may be made with slightly different ingredients, but once the brand values have been removed, all we are left to choose between is a more expensive product with a brand name on it and a cheaper one with the supermarket's name on it. With little apparent difference between the items, it's not surprising that we are turning to the product that costs less, more and more often.

In defence of the brands, they're often important in helping us with our central six fitness indicators. For example, having that branded bottle of champagne feeds one or more of your fitness indicators much more effectively than offering supermarket own label sparkly to your potential in-laws when they come over to dinner to 'vet' you for the first time.

My advice regarding brands is simply this: If you consider that a brand serves a purpose that warrants you buying it over any other alternatives, go ahead and buy it. Conversely, if you always buy own label coffee, seeing that Carte Noire is on offer isn't really a sufficient reason to switch to it, unless it is cheaper than the own label alternative. Learn to be more selective and actively consider which brands are of actual or perceived benefit to you.

Try to save 10p on the cost of every item

A very simple technique to use is simply to save 10p on the cost of an item that you might normally buy, by looking for a slightly cheaper alternative. This will sometimes mean purchasing the supermarket own brand item, or even their 'regular' range if you normally go for 'premium'. Whatever you decide to do, the savings can quickly add up, as over 100 items that would be £10 saved on the trip.

Try making every one in two or one in three purchases a different product to something you might habitually buy

An alternative to substituting every brand with a supermarket own one, or identifying savings on every single item is to make every second or third item a different brand from what you might normally purchase. Of course, it might be the same price, but what we're looking for here is again a breaking of the conditioning that ties you to buying a particular, specific brand.

Add structure to your shopping experience (shopping lists etc.)

In addition to planning before you shop, it's also very useful to put more structure around the shopping experience itself. This will help you focus your mind on the act of shopping itself and can encourage wiser and more considered choices.

Techniques you can use include:

- **(Key Point)** Create detailed, specific shopping lists that tell you exactly what you need to buy in store

- Use your last till receipt for reference when creating a shopping list

- **(Key Point)** Restrict what you buy to only what is on your shopping list

- Adapt your behaviour to the type of shopping you are doing

Create detailed, specific shopping lists that tell you exactly what you need to buy in store

Once you are in a store, you are not forced to buy the only food available – you have more choice than at any time in human civilisation. Too much choice can be a problem for the human brain; it gets overloaded choosing between 23 variants of plain crisps or 17 different digestive biscuits I mentioned earlier. It has to choose between price points, brands, sizes of packs and the like. Your job is to create the shortcuts that your brain can follow that are beneficial to your shopping needs. Instead of responding to your instincts and single scripted behaviours, turn things around and develop mental short cuts before you get to the store.

One of the most effective shortcuts is the simple shopping list; always try to use one but don't allow shortcuts to creep into your shopping list either, otherwise that lets your brain make some of the instinctive decisions before you can stop it. When writing your list, put down exactly what you want, not just a word like 'biscuits'. For the items you know you will need, be specific and write down exactly what you want: 'Twin pack of McVitie's wholemeal digestive biscuits'. What this does is reduce the odds of any part of the brain making the final purchase decision behind your back.

Use your last till receipt for reference when creating a shopping list

Another way to find out what to write on your list is to use your last till receipt for reference: It not only gives details of the item you want, but also shows what you paid last time, which you may want to write down as well.

Creating and using a shopping list works on a number of levels; as the brain is dedicated to helping you, the very act of writing down the exact thing you want helps that item get more solidly wired in your head.

Restrict what you buy to only what is on your shopping list

Much of our evolutionary make-up drives us to hunt and gather everything possible to avoid starvation and the possibility of extinction in the immediate future. Despite this, you may have noticed there aren't that many reports of supermarket shoppers starving to death because they couldn't find any food.

As a smarter shopper, to address this limitation you simply need to restrict the number of things you buy. Although this sounds obvious and straightforward, it rarely happens. How many times do you treat yourself or have a pack of something 'just to try it'?

Adapt your behaviour to the type of shopping you are doing

We almost always adopt one of five physiological modes when shopping; each serves a different purpose and has its own set of in-store needs.

Inexperienced shopping requires lots of information, as shoppers want to educate themselves about a product or category while experiential shopping involves us using more than visual cues to make purchase decisions; we may want to smell products, shake packs or even taste items. When shopping in this mode, we don't want anything other than the genuine sensory article. If we're partaking in considered shopping, we want the time, space and choice to make the right decision.

When we're grab & go shopping, we simply want an efficient means of getting hold of the products. Grab & go shopping is not so much shopping, but replenishment and product collection. You wouldn't go to extraordinary lengths just to buy a pint of milk. Finally, there is impulse shopping which supports those spur of the moment decisions to snap up an extra item. When in this mode, we want and need to be able to purchase without thinking twice.

When smarter shopping in any of the modes, make sure your physiology matches the mind-set you need to be in to make the best purchases. For example, reduce the number of inexperienced purchases you make by learning more about products or replace some of those 'blind' grab & go purchases with more intelligent, considered shopping selections; the same goes for impulse purchasing. Finally, if you are prone to shop experientially, make sure you are making your purchasing decisions based on solid logic. For example, don't think a torch is better quality because it is heavier because it already has batteries in it.

Shop differently to change your perspective

Part of being a smarter shopper is doing things in a different way. This can range from subtle changes to your behaviour to actually approaching the whole idea of shopping from a different angle. The techniques in this section can help you do this, and they are:

- Make your preferred supermarket less familiar to keep you on your toes

- Shop the store 'back to front'

- Always pay cash to stay more focussed and objective

Make your preferred supermarket less familiar to keep you on your toes

We will behave and respond differently depending on whether we are frequent or infrequent visitors to a particular supermarket. Specifically, when we are in our familiar supermarket surroundings, we're able to 'drop our guard' and filter out more of the environment. We know the types of information that are there and don't really need the majority of it. We also tend to be with people who are socially similar to us and can relax in this more familiar group situation.

Conversely, if we find ourselves in an unfamiliar supermarket, we are less familiar with our surroundings. Because of this, our brains, being wired for fight or flight, have to remain more alert and on the lookout for threats, meals or mates. From a smarter shopping perspective, this added alertness is actually a positive, but all too often we would rather shop in the sanctuary of our preferred supermarket where we then drop our guard and shop on autopilot.

If you're in your preferred supermarket, make it less familiar by shopping it in a different way. By doing this, you keep your brain on its toes and more focussed on the task in hand, making the best possible purchasing decisions when buying groceries.

Alternatively, try shopping different stores; they don't have to be of different chains, just not your preferred store. Although this can be more difficult, it will take you out of your comfort zone and help you to become a smarter shopper.

Shop the store 'back to front'

Another technique to help reduce the amount of subconscious shopping activity is to shop more consciously; an effective method that we've already recommended is to shop the store backwards. You can walk to the end of the store, start there and work your way back towards the store entrance.

Always pay cash to stay more focussed and objective

One technique that will help counter in-store priming is to always pay cash in the supermarket; don't even take cheques and credit cards with you as they can create temptation. If you have a finite amount of money with you, then you have to be aware of how much you've spent. This reduces the amount of priming going on in the brain and helps you stay more focussed and objective.

Review purchasing to make better decisions in future

Of course, not every technique you will use will be in planning for your trip or on the shopping trip itself, some are designed to be used when you're back home, to better prepare you for your next visit. The techniques in this section are useful for objectively evaluating your shopping experiences and getting you in the right frame of mind to continually improve. Some of the things you can do are:

- **(Key Point)** Review what you actually purchased when you get home

- Examine the types of products that you throw away because you don't use them

- Reflect on why you prefer a particular brand over another brand or unbranded product

- **(Key Point)** Note down and examine how much you spend over time to identify savings

Review what you actually purchased when you get home

As you know, you should always shop with a specific list, and you should also be prepared to do a bit of self-analysis when you get home. Tick off all the things you bought that were on the list and then study any other products you've purchased: Is there any sort of pattern to the types of things you succumb to in the temptation of the supermarket environment? I suggest you keep a list of the add-on items that you bought so that you can identify patterns over a longer period of time if none are obvious the first time you try it.

Examine the types and cost of products that you throw away because you don't use them

Wasting food because we buy too much is an endemic problem for much of society. The easiest way to avoid this is to understand the quantity and cost of what we're putting out in the rubbish.

Next time you empty out the fridge or cupboard, make a quick note of the items that have gone past their use by dates, and then look up the prices on your receipt or one of the online shopping sites. You can then multiply this by how often you throw items away and once you start to add up the cost of what you're throwing away over the year, you'll find a strong motivation to only buy what you will actually be able to use.

Reflect on why you prefer a particular brand over another brand or unbranded product

Now that you're committed to becoming a smarter shopper, there are steps you can take to help both parts of your memory improve your supermarket shopping expertise. In-store and back at home, when reviewing your purchases, simply ask yourself why you prefer a particular brand, and don't be put off by a superficial response from your long term memory. Keep pushing until you either do or don't get a good objective reason why you accept (or subsequently reject) that particular brand. To help the short term memory, once again use a shopping list and don't be afraid to use a calculator or pencil and paper.

Because the long term memory is responsible for a lot of your brand loyalties, make sure they are appropriate. Because the short term memory struggles with all the options available, don't forget to lend it a hand whenever you can.

Keep your receipts, note down and examine how much you spend over time to identify savings

A strong motivator for continuing to enhance the way you shop is in seeing how much money you have saved. Collecting your receipts over a period of time and then comparing them to see where you've made savings can be a very powerful way to support your perspective as a smarter shopper.

Examine this book before you shop next to help develop your strategy

Remember, before your next shopping trip, have another look through the techniques and review what you can do to ensure you keep your motivation high and develop your approaches to shopping. Only through your continued commitment can you make smarter shopping a powerful habit that will save you time and money in the short and long term.

A summary of key points

Because we've covered a lot in Section Three, here's a brief summary of the key things that you need to do to develop as a smarter shopper.

Creating a strategy to shop more effectively by:

1. Understanding the benefits and working out what you want to get out of being a smarter shopper and finding the emotional impetus to put your strategy into practice

2. Understanding the core principles of shopping more effectively and reviewing the techniques in each one

3. Choosing several techniques to use when you are next in the supermarket

4. Applying them in the supermarket

5. Reviewing what worked and what didn't and refining/expanding your techniques for the next time you shop

Select a handful of the following techniques to use each time you shop, with an initial focus on those marked 'key points'.

Prepare yourself properly for shopping

- **(Key Point)** Don't shop if you are hungry, thirsty or tired

- Adopt a positive physiological state when you are shopping

- **(Key Point)** Prime yourself to shop in the right way by focussing on longer term goals

- **(Key Point)** Make a shopping list based on your needs

- Be mindful of the subtle techniques used to influence you

Understand that you will be swayed

- Realise and accept that you will have an instinctive reaction to every situation

- Be aware that you may be influenced differently depending on your gender

- **(Key Point)** Accept that only some aspects of your shopping behaviour can be quickly and easily improved

- **(Key Point)** Learn to recognise your conditioned behaviours

- Realise that emotions often drive your purchasing decisions

- **(Key Point)** Understand the power of pride, shame and guilt over your shopping behaviour

- Rise above the crowd mentality of other shoppers

Be aware of your surroundings in the supermarket

- Pay attention to your environment so that you can see all the options

- Recognise marketing for what it is; don't just be attracted to the boldest and brightest products

- **(Key Point)** Realise that images aren't everything they seem and put them in context where possible

- **(Key Point)** Be aware of the sounds in your environment and try blocking out external influences

- Understand that what you physically touch can also affect you emotionally

- Realise that scent can be a powerful motivator

- Don't let your taste buds be tricked, distance yourself from the thought of consuming the product

Create more reasoned motives for your shopping behaviour

- Understand you are uncontrollably drawn to things and sense check the purchases you make

- **(Key Point)** Think twice and actively question the 'value' of the product you are buying

- **(Key Point)** Always compare prices in context to ensure you're not just being influenced because something is declared as 'cheap'

- Break your emotional conditioning and memory of certain products and items

- Buy supermarket only brands

- Ask yourself how your purchasing relates back to the central six fitness indicators

Make conscious decisions about the way that you shop

- Ensure that you understand the range of products on offer so you can objectively make an informed choice

- **(Key Point)** Think twice, sense check and carefully consider your instinctive purchasing decisions

- **(Key Point)** Interrupt your habitual purchases to stop you making the wrong decisions

- Understand why you make a decision to purchase a particular brand

- Try to save 10p on the cost of every item

- Try making every one in two or one in three purchases a different product to something you might habitually buy

Add structure to your shopping experience (shopping lists etc.)

- **(Key Point)** Create detailed, specific shopping lists that tell you exactly what you need to buy in-store

- Use your last till receipt for reference when creating a shopping list

- **(Key Point)** Restrict what you buy to only what is on your shopping list

- Adapt your behaviour to the type of shopping you are doing

Shop differently to change your perspective

- Make your preferred supermarket less familiar to keep you on your toes

- Shop the store 'back to front'

- Always pay cash to stay more focussed and objective

Review purchasing to make better decisions in future

- **(Key Point)** Review what you actually purchased when you get home

- Examine the types of products that you throw away because you don't use them

- Reflect on why you prefer a particular brand over another brand or unbranded product

- **(Key Point)** Note down and examine how much you spend over time to identify savings

Examine this book before you shop next to help develop your strategy

Final thoughts

So there you have it, the results of 600,000,000 years of evolution condensed into a single, hopefully enlightening, book. I sincerely hope that you have learnt more about how your own brain, mind and body function and that you got as much enjoyment from reading these pages as I did from writing them. It allowed me to adapt what I have learnt in my professional career as an analyser of people, into a type of owner's handbook for the 21st century supermarket shopper.

In the first section of the book, we took a journey around the human brain – how it works and the substantial influence evolution has on the way we function and shop today. We covered detailed aspects relating to modern supermarket shopping including the different types of human memory, instincts, emotions, cognition and feelings. There was information on the importance of the central six fitness indicators and the role of the human body in terms of modern day supermarket shopping.

In the second section of the book, we explored the subject of supermarket shopping from the perspective of the brands and retailers themselves. We looked at some of the things commonly found in supermarkets and by comparing them with how humans think and behave, were able to identify how and why we are influenced in supermarkets. Topics covered included category management, pricing, value, shopper facing communication in-store, category management and product layout.

The third and final section of the book presented some core principles and a number of techniques that you can use to improve the efficiency of your own supermarket shopping activity. I can confidently predict that if you follow these techniques you can save a considerable amount off the price you spend in the supermarket.

Even if you aren't driven by price, there are still significant rewards as you become better at shopping: You'll be able to recognise quality in the context of the type of quality you want. You might be able to better understand what you want others to perceive when they see or consume the things you buy. The same goes for value: When you recognise what you want from value, at both conscious and emotional levels, you'll be better equipped to understand how to find it and to purchase the most suitable options from the supermarket.

By adopting some or all of the recommendations, you are responding to how your own brain, mind and body have developed and will be able to teach them to shop better in the supermarket.

What if, after reading this book, you don't have the drive, courage, commitment or even interest to become a smarter supermarket shopper? Well here's the thing, which I purposely avoided saying throughout this book so that you didn't view its contents as yet another self-help publication. I hope I have explained and evidenced how a human being functions, how we think, react, respond and behave. If I have achieved this goal, then the last 20 years of reading and absorbing hundreds of academic papers and books on all things human psychology and physiology related have been more than worthwhile.

Potentially your greatest payoff from investing in this book could be if what it has taught you about yourself and others and the way we all think and operate isn't just of benefit in the supermarket. Armed with this wealth of new information, you have the capability to transform any number of aspects of your life. You can understand and better interpret the behaviour of your bosses and co-workers to advance your career, recognise how and why others behave as they do and be able to positively influence other's thoughts, emotions, feelings and behaviour.

Finally, let me leave you with an absolutely truthful account of a single example from my own life. As I was travelling along my journey of discovery regarding my own brain and mind, I came across the writings of someone I now consider to be one of the most insightful men ever, Mr Anthony Robbins. After reading a couple of his books and attending a four day seminar, I was able to make that elusive link between understanding how and why I function as I do, and what to do about it: I now refer to it as the 'so what' factor.

As a direct result of making this link, I recognised what drove me, the hierarchy of my own central six fitness indicators. What I discovered was that I had an almost pathological fear of debt and it was this that was holding me back. I decided to take decisive action and to take control of my own brain. In this specific example, I set about tackling my fear head on. I went out and bought the biggest house the bank would lend me the money to purchase. It was a property with many bedrooms and that had magnificent views and an eight square mile ancient woodland as part of the back garden. In essence, I exposed myself to as much debt as possible through this single purchase. At this point in time, I had a 20-plus year debt that was, from my own mental perspective, nothing less than terrifying.

Having such a large and threatening debt hanging over me gave me the leverage I needed to take action and I created and implemented my own mental strategy almost without any conscious awareness. I let my brain learn about itself and explored how it could be used in a more commercial context.

I quickly realised that I was altering my lifestyle in ways that felt so natural, but that I couldn't explain. For example, I found that my company, Shopping Behaviour Xplained Ltd, was costing more to run and had more staff. Initially, this alarmed me, but as the accounts showed, we were spending more, but also selling more. So by taking on more debt, the company could reduce that debt more quickly. If anyone had asked me about investing to grow the company at a time when I owed more than I had ever owed before, I can't believe that my response would have been all that favourable. As I said earlier, these sorts of things just happened.

In another example, like many people, I am not a confident public speaker, but I began to find myself in situations where I was in front of more and more people who expected me to talk. I started by making presentations to entire company departments, and then advanced to public and trade conferences and even appeared on radio and TV. The really strange thing was that once I began speaking, my brain seemed to take over and seeing the speeches played back, was almost like looking at another person giving the same talk. But it wasn't, it was me.

To the results: less than three years later, I'd paid off the mortgage in full. My brain had helped me completely remove this debt that was, at the time, so front of mind you simply wouldn't believe. So all I can say to myself is 'Well done, brain!' And I say to you all 'Your brains are remarkable in every way, so train them and use them to turn your dreams into reality'.

Anything you want to achieve, you can achieve – You just need the belief to do so.

Thanks for reading.

Glossary

A brief glossary of some of the terms used in this book.

Autonomous nervous system	Part of the peripheral nervous system that acts as a control system functioning largely below the level of consciousness
Brand	A brand is the identity of a specific product, service, or business
Catarrhini	Catarrhini is one of the two subdivisions of the higher primates
Categories	A range of products sold by a retailer, broken down into discrete groups of similar or related products
Cerebral cortex	The cerebral cortex is the outermost part of the brain. It plays a key role in memory, attention, perceptual awareness, thought, language, and consciousness
Chunking	A strategy for making more efficient use of short-term memory by recoding information
Cognitive Load Theory	The load related to the executive control of working memory

Electroencephalography (EEG)	The recording of electrical activity along the scalp produced by the firing of neurons within the brain
Fixation	The maintaining of the visual gaze on a single location
Fixture	Any display in a store that is used to display and merchandise products
Foveal vision	The foveal vision adds detailed information to the peripheral first impression
Functional magnetic resonance imaging (fMRI)	A type of specialized MRI scan. It measures the change in blood flow related to neural activity in the brain
Fusiform gyrus	Part of the brain used for processing of colour information, face and body recognition, word and number recognition
Gondola	A particular display in a supermarket usually made of steel or wooden racking and with adjustable shelf heights
Limbic system	Manages a variety of functions including emotion, behaviour, long term memory, and olfaction
Long term memory	Memory that can last as little as a few days or as long as decades

Macro facial expressions	Facial expressions that last from ½ second to 4 seconds; we see them in our daily interactions with other people all of the time
Marketer	Someone who performs various forms of market research, selling products and/or promotional services of products
Micro facial expressions	Facial expressions that occur when a person is just starting to feel an emotion. These last less than ½ second
Moment of truth	In-store when the shopper decides to pick up and buy a product
Neural pathway	Connects one part of the nervous system with another and usually consists of bundles of neurons
Neurons	An electrically excitable cell in the brain that processes and transmits information by electrical and chemical signalling
Parafoveal vision	Peripheral vision – less focussed or intense than foveal vision
Physiology	The science of the function of living systems
Point of sale	The place at which a retail transaction takes place; either when the item is selected or paid for

Product groups

Otherwise known as categories: Ranges of products sold by a retailer broken down into discrete groups of similar or related products

Retail channels

Different formats of retail such as convenience, supermarket, out of town and online

Retail ready packaging

The containers and packaging for retail goods which are ready to be displayed instantly

Retailer

A person or organisation offering goods for sale to members of the public from within a bricks and mortar store

Saccade

Quick, simultaneous movements of both eyes in the same direction

Senses

The physiological capacities within organisms that provide inputs for perception

Sense of auditory or hearing

The sense of sound perception

Sense of gustation or taste

One of the two main 'chemical' senses. There are at least four types of tastes that 'buds' (receptors) on the tongue detect

Sense of kinaesthetic or touch

A perception resulting from activation of neural receptors, generally in the skin, including hair follicles

Sense of olfaction	The sense of smell
Sense of vision	The ability of the eye(s) to focus and detect images of visible light on the retina in each eye
Shelf ready packaging	Otherwise known as retail ready packaging: The containers and packaging for retail goods which are ready to be displayed instantly
Shopper's weight of purchase	Amount of items a shopper buys – number or value
Shoppers	People who accept products in return for handing over money. Typically in bricks and mortar stores
Shopping Behaviour Xplained Ltd	A specialist market research company that analyses all aspects of shoppers and shopping
Short term memory	The capacity for holding a small amount of information in mind in an active, readily available state for a short period of time
Single scripted behaviours	A group of sub-behaviours carried out collectively without conscious involvement, such as shaking hands
Statolith	A balance organ present in some aquatic invertebrates

Stimulus	Something external that influences an activity
Supermarkets	A form of grocery store, a self-service store offering a wide variety of food and household merchandise, organized into departments
Synapses	A junction in the brain that permits a neuron to pass an electrical or chemical signal to another cell (neural or otherwise)
Unique selling point (USP)	Any aspect of an object that differentiates it from similar objects
Utricles	Organs located in the vertebrate inner ear

Selected reading list

If you'd like to find out more about the subjects covered in this book, I'd recommend the books listed here as a good starting point.

Evolution

The Expressions of the Emotions in Man and Animals, Charles Darwin, Harper Perennial, 2009 [1872]

Life Ascending: The Ten Great Inventions of Evolution, Nick Lane, Profile Books, 2010

The Emerging Mind, Vilayanur Ramachandran, Profile Books Ltd, 2003

On the Origins of Human Emotions: A Sociological Inquiry into the Evolution of Human Affect, Jonathan H Turner, Stanford University Press, 2000

Emotion

Emotions, Advertising and Consumer Choice, Flemming Hansen, Copenhagen Business School Press, 2007

Emotion, James W Kalat and Michelle N Shiota, Thompson Wadsworth, 2007

The Emotional Brain: The Mysterious Underpinnings of Emotional Life, Joseph LeDoux, Weidenfield and Nicholson, 1998

Emotions and Life: Perspectives from Psychology, Biology and Evolution, Robert Plutchik, American Psychological Association, 2002

The human brain

A Rough Guide to the Brain, Barry J Gibb, Rough Guides Ltd, 2007

The Private Life of The Brain, Susan Greenfield, Penguin Science Books, 2000

Biological Psychology, James W Kalat, Thompson Wadsworth, 2007

A User's Guide to the Brain, John J Ratey, Pantheon Books, 2001

The human mind

Efficiency in Learning: Evidence-Based Guidelines to Manage Cognitive Load, Ruth C. Clark, Frank Nguyen and John Sweller, Pfeiffer, 2006

Descartes' Error: Emotion, Reason and the Human Brain, Antonio Damasio, Vintage Books, 2005

Gimme! The Human Nature of Successful Marketing, John Hallward, John Wiley & Sons, 2007

Kluge: The Haphazard Evolution of the Human Mind, Gary Marcus, Mariner Books, 2007

How the Mind Works, Steven Pinker, Penguin Books, 1998

The Human Mind and How to Make the Most of It, Robert Winston, Chartered Institute of Personnel and Development, 2006

Popular psychology

Predictably Irrational: The Hidden Forces that Shape Our Decisions, Dan Ariel, HarperCollins, 2008

The Tyranny of Numbers: Why Counting Can't Make Us Happy, David Boyle, Flamingo, 2001

Influence: The Psychology of Persuasion, Robert B Cialdini, Harper Business, 2007 (Revised edition)

Cognitive Illusions: A Handbook on Fallacies and Biases in Thinking, Judgement and Memory, Rüdiger F Pohl (Ed.), Psychology Press, 2005

59 Seconds: Think a Little, Change a Lot, Richard Wiseman, Macmillan, 2009

Quirkology: The Curious Science of Everyday Lives, Richard Wiseman, Macmillan, 2007

Understanding others

Observational Research Handbook: Understanding How Consumers Live with Your Product, Bill Abrams, McGraw-Hill, 2000

The Book of Tells, Peter Collett, Bantam Books, 2004

Unmasking the Face: A Guide to Recognizing Emotions from Facial Expressions, Paul Eckman and Wallace V. Freisen, Malor Books, 2003

Blink: The Power of Thinking without Thinking, Malcolm Gladwell, Penguin, 2005

Consumerology: The Market Research Myth, the Truth about Consumer Behaviour and the Psychology of Shopping, Philip Graves, Nicholas Brealey Publishers, 2010

Nonverbal Communication, Albert Mehrabian, Walter De Gruyter Inc, 1972

What Every Body Is Saying: An Ex-FBI Agent's Guide to Speed-reading People, Joe Navarro, HarperCollins Publishers, 2008

Shopping

Carried Away: The Invention of Modern Shopping, Rachel Bowlby, Faber and Faber Ltd, 2000

The Shopping Experience, Pasi Falk and Colin B Campbell, Sage Publications, 1997

Why We Shop: Emotional Rewards and Retail Strategies, Jim Pooler, Praeger Publishers, 2003

The Call of the Mall, Paco Underhill, Profile Business, 2004

Why We Buy: The Science of Shopping, Paco Underhill, Orion Business Books, 2000

Consumerism

The Soul of the New Consumer: Authenticity – What We Buy and Why in the New Economy, David Lewis and Darren Bridger, Nicholas Brealey Publishing, 2001

Buyology: How Everything We Believe About Why We Buy is Wrong, Martin Lindstrom, Doubleday, 2008

What Customers Really Want: Bridging the Gap Between What Your Company Offers and What your Clients Crave, Scott McKain, Nelson Business, 2005

Must-Have: The Hidden Instincts Behind Everything We Buy, Geoffrey Miller, Vintage Books, 2009

How Customers Think: Essential Insights into the Mind of the Market, Gerald Zaltman, Harvard Business School Press, 2003

Your own mind

Frogs into Princes: Introduction to Neurolinguistic Programming, Richard Bandler and John Grinder, Real People Press, 1989

Get the Life You Want: The Secrets to Quick & Lasting Life Change, Richard Bandler, Harper Element, 2009

Unlimited Power: The New Science of Personal Achievement, Anthony Robbins, Simon and Schuster, 1989

About the author

Phillip Adcock is a leading authority on shopping and consumer behaviour. With more than 30 years of human behavioural research, he has developed a unique ability to identify what it is that makes people tick, both psychologically and physiologically. He works in an advantageous position of not being constrained within any particular brain science field. Moreover, Phillip has developed his skills by combining the teachings of experts on numerous aspects of neuroscience, psychology and emotion within his professional role of helping leading brands and retailers better understand their customers – you, the shoppers.

Phillip has a passion for watching others and trying to understand why human beings do what they do. Even at school, he would observe and then analyse the interpersonal behaviour of others and himself. Phillip realised that understanding the human brain, but not being confined to any specialist viewpoint offers rewarding career opportunities.

Phillip recognised that there weren't any relevant college or university courses that would ready him for a professional life in commercial psychology. There were numerous opportunities to study a particular discipline, neuroscience, which was traditionally the study of the nervous system, but which has now become an interdisciplinary science involving other disciplines such as psychology, computer science, mathematics, physics, philosophy and medicine. He could have taken a more classical route and studied one of traditional aspects of human psychology: The science and knowledge of the human brain from a point of view of relieving dysfunction and distress. Alternatively, he could have majored in business or motivational psychology; the subject of helping individuals reach their full potential by way of re-programming their brain for success.

With a real passion for understanding what makes people tick, Philip began a thirty year course of self-teaching, which has culminated in the writing of this book. In the early years Phillip worked as a retail display consultant, frustrated that many shop fixtures and fittings were designed and manufactured based on cost. Phillip identified that by understanding how the shopper behaved in-store and aligning that with their needs and desires, it was possible to deliver point of purchase (POP) display solutions that dramatically increased sales and market share for an ever-increasing list of leading retailers and brands.

As merchandising development manager for a leading chain of stores in the UK, he again studied shoppers and shopping. This entailed employing research agencies to analyse, quantify and qualify how shoppers behaved in the hundreds of store estates. In addition, he was very interested in knowing more about the attitudes, needs and opinions of shoppers. Armed with the knowledge of how shoppers behave, and combining that with the emotional aspects, he was able to develop in-store initiatives that better aligned shoppers with the ranges of products available.

In 1999, Phillip founded one of only a few specialist shopper research agencies, Shopping Behaviour Xplained Ltd (SBXL). It is now one of the leading shopping behaviour and emotions specialists, which combines a range of state-of-the-art technology and techniques with academic studies and on-going research. This approach enables it to provide retailers and brands with tangible and useable data to help them make changes that will enhance sales. The SBXL team uses techniques such as in-store filming to capture detailed behaviour, Xtraviews for the study of facial expressions and non-verbal communication, unaccompanied shops to identify the decision making process, and eye-tracking to uncover what shoppers respond to in-store.

Having spent so many years understanding what makes shoppers and consumers tick, and armed with a powerful combination of unique academic knowledge and comprehensive practical experience, Phillip Adcock has committed his expertise to print. It is hoped that while this book provides retailers and brands with a wealth of new shopper understanding that they can incorporate into their strategic and tactical business decisions, the book will also provide supermarket shoppers with an informative guide that will help them get more out of shopping, both in terms of efficiency and value for money.